INDIVISIBLE

INDIVISIBLE

GLOBAL LEADERS ON
SHARED SECURITY

EDITED BY RU FREEMAN
AND KERRI KENNEDY

OLIVE
BRANCH
PRESS

An imprint of Interlink Publishing Group, Inc.
www.interlinkbooks.com

First published 2019 by

OLIVE BRANCH PRESS
An imprint of Interlink Publishing Group, Inc.
46 Crosby Street, Northampton, MA 01060
www.interlinkbooks.com

Text copyright © American Friends Service Committee, 2019

Library of Congress Cataloging-in-Publication data available
ISBN-13: 978-1-62371-972-2

Printed and bound in the United States of America

*To those who continue to work toward
an inclusive peace & security for all*

Contents

Preface

Ru Freeman is a Sri Lankan and American writer and activist. She is the author of the widely translated novels A Disobedient Girl *and* On Sal Mal Lane, *the latter of which is a* New York Times *Editor's Choice Book and winner of the J. H. Kafka Prize for fiction by an American woman. She is also the editor of* Extraordinary Rendition: American Writers on Palestine *and her writing appears internationally in the* UK Guardian, *the* Boston Globe, *and the* New York Times. *She teaches writing at Columbia University and blogs for the Huffington Post on literature and politics.*

A few weeks ago, upon hearing news that the United States Supreme Court had upheld the travel ban that turns into law the prejudicial treatment of people from certain countries, my seventeen-year-old middle daughter, a young activist in her own right, burst into tears. What is the point of this country, she asked, what is the point of all this power and wealth if you can't be good? It was a simple and all-encompassing question.

My daughters are of a generation that has grown up with the world in their sights. Their connections are trans-continental even as the forces of profit and greed arrayed against them are similarly global. Their minds and their hearts move unfettered past borders even as borders are being drawn and fortified by an older generation accustomed to, and reliant on, the creation and sustenance of fear. This new generation does not wait for permission to act, for the right kinds of support structures to be erected, in order to ask for change and seek solutions to the things that ail us. The teenagers from the Parkland massacre who brought 800,000 people to DC to advocate for the de-weaponization of civic life in America, take their place among the youth leaders in this book, Victor Ochen, Kessy Martine Ekomo-Soignet, Hussein Murtaja, Malual Bol Kiir, Thevuni Kotigala, Saba Ismail, Hajer Sharief, and Jayathma Wickramanayake. Collectively, they have overcome bullet wounds, lived as refugees, built reconciliation efforts around empathetic dialogue, advocated for young girls and women, and risen to prominence in their communities and on the world stage. They are powerful reminders that youth embody the promise and hope of all our survival in a manner unparalleled in human history, and are very much a part of a globally connected, culturally sensitive, and innovative solution.

It is a way of thinking that is echoed by their elders in this collection, from Archbishop Desmond Tutu, and former President Jimmy Carter, to international peace activists Dr. Maria J. Stephan and Khaled Mansour. Each of them reminds us of the foundational principles of peace-building: open, difficult conversations, underlined by the presumption of goodwill and the commitment to enduring relationships. Twenty-five years ago, Jimmy Carter negotiated a meeting that could have ended the stalemate between the two Koreas, only to be circumnavigated by a White House beholden to the arms industry. Still, he persisted, going on to address issues of climate control and public and societal health around the world, for which he was recognized with the Nobel Peace Prize. These efforts are reflected in the quiet diplomacy of the American Friends Service Committee (AFSC), which has worked in the Korean peninsula since 1953, and specifically in North Korea since 1980. As the group's general secretary, Joyce Ajlouny, puts it, the AFSC is the first American public affairs organization to send a delegation to Pyongyang and, since 1996, to partner with farmers on issues of food security. Others, like the parents of Rachel Corrie, who was slain by the Israeli army while standing before a Palestinian home about to be demolished, have dedicated their life to working internationally as courageous ambassadors of the cause to bring an end to the occupation of Palestine.

This common thread that unites a generation in their eighties and nineties with those in their twenties is a heartening reminder that the solution to what ails us has always been present, if only we could unite our efforts across the globe.

In reading these essays, we are able to recognize that the effects and outcomes of internecine war in South Sudan, as articulated by Malual Bol Kiir, have an underlying resonance with national and regional policies pursued in Jamaica, as described by Terri-Ann Gilbert-Roberts, who is guided by the Jamaica national pledge which opens this way: "Before God and all [humankind], I pledge the love and loyalty of my heart, the wisdom and courage of my mind, the strength and vigor of my body, in the service of my fellow citizens." The freedoms sought through the diligent efforts of young Rakhine civil society activist Khine Thurein and Burmese Muslim community organizer Aye Sandar Chit are possible in the inclusive nationalism described by Oxford-based economist, Dr. Maya Tudor. Khury Petersen-Smith and Lucy Roberts, hailing from separate generations, both tie the domestic policies of the countries of their citizenship, American and British respectively, to the way people of a certain hue, or nation of origin, are considered lesser human beings, undeserving of the right to lives of dignity where they may reach their full human potential and, instead, are brutalized. The baton that is being passed from the "capable and vigilant hands" of young Kessy Ekomo-Soignet in the Central African Republic to generations she may never see, was once passed to those of her generation by much older peace activists like John Paul Lederach, whose essay closes this collection with a reminder of the characteristics that have united change-makers across the world: the ability to see with the eyes of a grandmother, a child, an artist, and like a voyager willing to set forth into the unknown with dogged optimism.

Like the people of the fictional, morally bankrupt town of Omelas in the Ursula K. Le Guin short-story, "The Ones Who Walk Away from Omelas," whose joyful conduct of life is predicated on the brutal imprisonment and sacrifice of a child, the peace workers in this anthology recognize that a status quo that disfranchises people, impoverishes others, and subjects still more to unimaginable cruelty, cannot be allowed to go unchallenged. Their work is of critical importance today as civil society organizations, no matter their size or reach or ethnic composition or funding or cultural relevance, face growing restrictions on their efforts to create or foster equitable communities. Restrictions of associations such as have occurred in Turkey, China, Egypt, Jordan, Brazil, Bahrain, the US, and France, are mirrored in smaller countries, villages, and towns around the world under the guise of protecting a national "security," which seems directly proportional to the levels of wealth and power of those feeling the need to secure themselves from others. At the macro level, the old dominance predicated on ideological arguments has been replaced by the creation and nurturing of fear which "necessitates" protection of the seemingly innocent from the angry hordes at our imaginary gates, a case amply demonstrated by Jason Tower as he discusses the fate of the Myistone Dam project in Southeast Asia.

Resistance to attacks on the efforts of like-minded people to create a habitable, viable, inclusive global culture requires its own innovation. As I read through these essays, I was struck by the fact that we begin with, and are ruled by, our definitions, including our ability to clearly define the problems we face in the same way that those who walked away from Omelas understood that acquiescing would mean validating unconscionable injustice. Reclaiming the right to define the rules of engagement, the refugees spoken of and for with moving passion by John Freeman and Diana Francis are further elevated by Libyan activist Hajer Sharief, Ugandan community leader Victor Ochen, and Sri Lankan internationalist Jayathma Wickramanayake, as people affected by conflict rather than causing it. Indeed, this entire collection is a way of restating what we mean when we seek security. For the local activists, national leaders, and international figures in this collection, security does not come at the cost of losing their own humanity. It comes from ensuring that the good they seek belongs to everyone.

Taken together, we come to realize that though their efforts take place in venues far removed from each other, and seem to address different realities, their responses speak similarly to social dislocations and a state of insecurity caused, often deliberately, by identical ideologies of exclusion and stunted notions of power. Likewise, each of them sets out to address their respective set of circumstances, culturally or nationally proscribed, with the same intention to create a world where resources are shared, and no one human being's worth is elevated above any other's. It is exhilarating to contemplate what profound change can happen when people like them come together in recognition of that goal. This anthology is a step in that direction.

Many years ago, I opened my undergraduate thesis on the inequalities that are written into the prerequisites for receiving aid from politically motivated funding agencies such as USAID and the

IMF, with a quote from my father, Gamini Seneviratne, a poet and civil servant who has dedicated his life to the wellbeing and self-sufficiency of my island-country of Sri Lanka: *the sky does not become less private because other people share it.* Parallel to that world view was my late mother's underlying words of wisdom: a teacher and guide to hundreds of young people who grew up to achieve much thanks to her mentorship, her courage, and her example, she reminded us that each human being was some mother's child. If we witnessed someone wasting their lives away in the grip of addiction or dedicating themselves to violence, she would say, *their mother did not intend that for them.* That way of seeing the world and its resources, on the part of my father, and being gentle and generous in our dealings with each person we met, on the part of my mother, bookended our upbringing, my brothers' and mine, leading us all to dedicate our lives to issues of social justice. We recognized at a very young age that we were rich in the ways that mattered, and that the wealth of our various capabilities should be given in the service of uplifting the lives of others less fortunate. It was easy therefore to join Kerri in this endeavor to collect under one roof, as it were, those who do their work often in states of exhaustion, with dwindling resources, and ever more confined public spaces, but who still believe in the better nature of their fellow human beings, and themselves.

I was raised predominantly Buddhist in a country with a strong ecumenical tradition where public and private schools are required to teach children the religion of their upbringing. As such, I grew up learning both the Buddhist prayers of my own faith and, in whole or part, the prayers of the Christians, Hindus, and Muslims around me. One of those prayers, often attributed to Saint Francis of Assisi, has since been traced back to a French priest, Father Esther Bouquerel, under the title *Belle priere a faire pendant la messe*, which translated into "A Beautiful Prayer to Say During the Mass." That prayer comes to mind as I consider the work of all the people who contributed their words to this anthology, as well as the lessons that were imparted by my parents:

> Lord, make me an instrument of thy peace
> Where there is hatred, let me sow love,

Where there is injury, pardon,
Where there is doubt, faith,
Where there is darkness, light,
And where there is sadness, joy.

The essays in this anthology open by framing the cause of sharing our resources and making our freedoms universal, and close with a clear articulation of what defines civil society and how we might make our global society more civil. Throughout, these writers share their peace-building work in the countries of South Sudan, Myanmar, North and South Korea, Palestine, Uganda, Zimbabwe, Northern Ireland, China, Sri Lanka, Colombia, Guatemala, the Central African Republic, Jamaica, Algeria, the United States, France, the United Kingdom, and Japan, among others. With a remarkable and passionate unity of purpose, they tell us stories of overcoming deep adversity and loss and the power of holding on to faith in human good. They call to each other from remote parts of the world, and they call to us to learn from their example. As Colum McCann puts it in the essay that opens this collection, speaking of the death of Algerian poet and journalist Tahar Dajout, "We have no way of knowing what else the Algerian would have said, or how he might have helped shape a different future. But the fact of the matter is that Dajout was interested in expanding the lungs of the world. That form of breath was, in essence, a form of security. Not a simple security. Not a security couched in ease. But a security of voice. A security of language. A security of access."

I hope the words of these many voices move you, each in their turn, to sow love, to pardon, to light the way of your fellow human beings, and to keep faith in the instruments of peace.

Ru Freeman
July 4, 2018
Lisbon, Portugal

 *Kerri Kennedy is a global peace-builder, activist, and strategist with twenty years of experience leading international peace and justice organizations. Currently the International Associate General Secretary for American Friends Service Committee, she has an M.S. from American University and has worked in more than 50 countries, including in war zones, post-conflict countries, and in the United States. She has spent her career working to reduce conflict and structural violence globally and to ensure that all have a voice in policy and politics. After her time supporting women politicians in Afghanistan, she created Represent PAC to support progressive women candidates in Pennsylvania and beyond.*

Sometimes your life changes in a moment of inspiration. I had such a moment in 2009. I had spent weeks in Liberia crisscrossing the country during the rainy season with a team of gender advisors and representatives from the Ministry of Gender. We were traveling from town to village documenting the experiences of women during the long civil war to help establish a gender unit for the Truth and Reconciliation Commission. We spoke with thousands of women—all with heartbreaking tales of violence, separation, and brutality. The commission and documentation was important and critical to national healing. Yet, I left the country feeling that I was on the wrong side of conflict. Too much in the after and not enough prevention.

Born to an active middle-class family in New Jersey, the only daughter with five brothers, I developed a sense of wanderlust and justice early on and learned to use my voice, to advocate and mediate conflict in our busy household. I joined the Peace Corps right after college and spent the next two years living on the beautiful, tiny, remote island Niuatoputapu, Tonga, in the South Pacific. I continued to work for international and community developments projects for the next several years.

On September 11, 2001, I was on my way to enter Riker's Island to work with youth in detention centers when the building was locked down. The World Trade Center had been hit by an airplane. My twin brother was on the eighty-fifth floor of World Trade Center 1 (the North Tower). I rushed back and arrived in Manhattan as the building collapsed. My brother made it out seconds before. It served as an epiphany. I returned to graduate school to study conflict, international affairs, and post-conflict reconciliation, focused on what motivates violence and how communities rebuild and trust again after violence occurs.

I spent the next ten years working in conflict zones and post-conflict countries on elections, democratic processes, and women in politics. It was inspiring work and brought me to Afghanistan, Ethiopia, East Timor, Liberia, and many other countries. In Afghanistan, I trained women who were running for elected office. Many were running at great personal risk, and after the 2009 election, they had more women in Parliament in Afghanistan than we do in Congress in the United States. It led me to think about why more women were not running in my home county. I came home and co-founded a political action committee to support progressive female candidates and to address the dismal representation of women in politics in the United States.

Today, I am the Associate General Secretary of International Programs for the American Friends Service Committee, a 101-year-old Quaker peace and social justice organization. I joined AFSC six years ago. Shortly after, our DC office with the Friends Committee for National Legislation (FCNL) developed a provocative fifty-year vision for a just US foreign policy called "shared security." It was a compelling worldview and I spent the next few years working on a global vision and organizational structure for policy, practice, and narrative change to challenge militarism, reduce violence and systems of oppression, and promote lasting peace in the United States and the countries in which AFSC works.

What do we mean by shared security? It is simply a paradigm for promoting the safety and well-being of people throughout the world, based on our human understanding that shared problems require shared solutions, and that our interests are best served when we foster peaceful and just relationships together.

It is essentially the idea that "my peace is your peace." The understanding that peace and security are, by their very nature, indivisible; a threat to coexistence in one corner of the world is a threat to our communal safety everywhere. Nations remain stuck in a perspective that emphasizes the idea that we are playing a zero-sum game, where there will be winners and losers.

Yet, never before have the fates of individual communities and nations been so intertwined. And never before has our safety and well-being depended so much on the safety and well-being of others. Today's problems—from acts of violence and extremism, to growing inequality and climate disruption, to restricted civic space for all—cannot be solved by any one nation, or through outdated and ineffective securitized approaches based on us-versus-them analysis.

A new approach is required; an approach where we, together, from a place of love, commit to our mutual well-being, equitable access to resources and justice, and a strong resolve to peacefully address the difficulties that arise from the complexity of our separate origins and cultures. We must push our leaders to invest in global shared security that rejects policies based on narratives of fear and military domination. We need to seek solutions that recognize that in our interconnected world, security depends on ensuring that all of us are safe, not just a privileged few. We must create conditions where people can enjoy their human rights and meet their basic needs, where we promote nonviolent responses to the conflicts that will inevitably arise in our human world.

A shared security approach invests seriously in peace-building instead of war building. It imagines a world where leaders are mobilized not to build walls, separate families, and bomb targets, but where they work together to support people-powered movements and invest in early interventions that address root causes of conflict long before violence and discrimination festers and erupts, and before institutions of cooperation and democracy further disintegrate.

What if we redefined the way in which we describe safety and sanctuary in terms of shared security? What if we collectively reject the present global status quo in which security is seen as stemming from walls, x-ray machines, armed security forces, and other militarized means of separating one population or group from another? Shared security stands in stark contrast, refusing to accept an "us vs. them" mentality, and disavowing the tendency to identify particular groups or demographics as threats to other groups.

While we can articulate this vision of shared security, even yearn for it, it is, as of yet, a work in progress. This is the vision that Ru and I had for this book. To continue to yearn for this vision and highlight the work of the many who are moving us closer to global shared security and peace every day. World leaders, community activists, and ordinary people around the world have subscribed to this idea of an inclusive, egalitarian way of conducting themselves, refusing on a daily basis to abdicate their responsibility toward protecting the lives and livelihoods of their fellow human beings, as well as their right to be shaped and defined by their own cultures, faiths, and nations of origin.

They have done this work by redefining their relationships toward one another as partners in a common pursuit: that of harmonious and sustainable coexistence. Some have taken on the role of demilitarizing their communities, as well as their language of discourse, and deconstructing systems of oppression. Others have engaged in quiet diplomacy as a means to unify those who might, without their influence, tend toward disagreement; still others have committed them-selves to building safe spaces where people may come together as allies, thereby taking down the artificial barriers that separate them.

Organizations like AFSC and their partners have chosen to focus on several distinct areas such as restricted spaces where unjust societal structures lead to widespread repression; human rights actors, activists, and peace-builders are criminalized; business practices that knowingly or unknowingly drive conflict; violence around political processes; as well as armed conflicts and unjust economies that trigger mass migration. In efforts such as these, we focus on nonviolent solutions that are universally beneficial.

Today, we see a growing need for such solutions. We are witnessing a serious global increase in restricted spaces—restrictions on individual civil liberties, on civil society, and on peace-building efforts. Civil space is shrinking. US policies on terrorism, sanctions on humanitarian assistance overseas, and bank de-risking have also increased difficulties for peace-builders and humanitarian staff and have an effect of criminalizing this critical work. In the United States and globally, politically motivated attacks on the press and growing nationalist and authoritarian rhetoric threaten our democracies and decrease our collective safety. The exclusion of minorities and vulnerable groups has increased, resulting in growing levels of social violence, and the breakdown of institutional checks and balances.

And yet we have hope. Every day, individuals, groups, and organizations dedicate themselves to the work of building a just world, one where no one human being or group or population is considered to be of less worth than any other. We must recognize that our efforts should become the norm, not the exception. A world with peace and shared security. A world where we are united, indivisible against the tyranny of oppression and violence. A world where we organize, strategize, mobilize, and energize one another. A world where we celebrate each other's work and engage in activism, politics, diplomacy, and dialogue. A world with hope, engagement, and shared security.

Every day, this happens. As civil society space shrinks, we are seeing an inverse growth in activism. Every day, courageous peace-builders and activists, religious, political, and community leaders, organizers, artists, and thinkers work in communities around the world, often at great risk to themselves, promote nonviolence, speak out against oppression and violence, mediate with those committing violence, and articulate a vision for a world with just and lasting peace. This gives hope. This is shared security.

This anthology brings together a range of voices from around the world who, together, are able to articulate a comprehensive, persuasive, and powerful argument in favor of a new way of looking at a world where we reframe security as a shared goal. We hope the leaders, thinkers, and organizers featured in the book inspire you to action, and that these essays shine light on the peace-builders, movement-builders, and artists who help us move from yearning to creating change. This compilation of divergent ideas is testament to the fact that we *can* come together, no matter how far-flung we are, how solitary our endeavors, to shape our common future and a better world.

Kerri Kennedy
July 1, 2018
Philadelphia, USA

Framing the Cause

Colum McCann is the author of six novels and three collections of stories. Born and raised in Dublin, Ireland, he has been the recipient of many international honors, including the National Book Award, the International Dublin Impac Prize, a Chevalier des Arts et Lettres from the French government, election to the Irish Arts Academy, several European awards, the 2010 Best Foreign Novel Award in China, and an Oscar nomination. In 2017, he was elected to the American Academy of Arts. His work has been published in over 40 languages. He is the co-founder of the non-profit global story exchange organization, Narrative 4, and teaches in the MFA program at Hunter College.

Our Stories, Our Lives
Colum McCann

"If you keep quiet you die. If you speak, you die. So, speak and die." Shortly after the Algerian poet and journalist Tahar Dajout wrote these words in the summer of 1993, he was gunned down in the streets of Algiers. Dajout spoke in favor of progress, secularism, decency, a shared world without narrowness. But the bullets did their work: after a week in a coma, Dajout died. His killers, a fundamentalist group, later admitted that they feared him because he wielded the mighty weapon of language.

The tragedy of it all was that Dajout's voice was shortened and amplified at the same time. We have no way of knowing what else the Algerian poet would have said, or how he might have helped shape a different future. But the fact of the matter is that Dajout was interested in expanding the lungs of the world. That form of breath was, in essence, a form of security. Not a simple security, not a security couched in ease. But a security of voice. A security of language. A security of access.

Having written, Dajout spoke. Having spoken, he endured. Having endured, he now survives.

The hope—and perhaps the enduring belief—of literature is that it can, by widening our world, help us be at least a little more secure than we were before.

What Dajout believed was that a lot of things can be taken away from us—even our lives—but not our stories about those lives. Others might repress our stories and our language, torture them, burn them, chain them, mangle them, but the proper country of language cannot be outright annihilated.

Archbishop Emeritus Desmond Mpilo Tutu, a Nobel Peace Laureate, is one of the greatest living moral icons of our time and a key player in the fight against apartheid in South Africa. He was also the first black South African Archbishop of Cape Town, South Africa, and primate of the Anglican Church of South Africa. In 1995 President Nelson Mandela appointed the Archbishop Chairman of the Truth and Reconciliation Commission, to probe gross human rights violations that occurred under apartheid. In recent years, Tutu has toured the world to raise awareness of HIV/AIDS and the tragic loss of life and human suffering it causes. He is regarded as an elder world statesman with a major role to play in reconciliation, a leading moral voice, and an icon of hope far beyond the Church and South Africa.

4

Archbishop Emeritus Desmond Tutu
Hermanus, South Africa, February 2018

There was once a notoriously dangerous stretch of road frequented by vagabonds and brigands. It could be anywhere, in Afghanistan, Sudan, the United States ... though these events actually occurred at a particular time and place.

People needing to travel from Place A to Place B had no option but to take their chances on the road; at the time there were no high-speed trains or air-conditioned coaches, just the winding dirt road they called the Way of Blood, twisting and turning its way across a dry rugged plain, over the mountain.

Adding spice to the danger was a particular cultural dynamic: The peoples of Places A and B practiced different religions. They shared an unfortunate history of violence and desecration; they really didn't much like each other at all.

There was nothing extraordinary about the traveler from Place A picking his way along the road on the day in question; one could argue he just found himself in the wrong place at the wrong time. Beset by robbers, he was beaten, stripped of all his possessions right down to his clothes, and left for dead.

Fortunately, there were other travelers on the road that day. A fellow believer, a compatriot from Place A, heaved into sight—but failed to stop. Did he not hear the plaintive groans? Why did he not help?

Then, more footsteps along the road; this time a priest. Salvation was at hand, but the man of God walked on past.

Many have speculated over the years why these men left the

traveler to suffer. Some say the priest may have believed the traveler was dead, and didn't wish to defile himself.

On the day before his assassination, the Rev. Martin Luther King—in his, *I've Been to the Mountaintop* speech—recounted this story. He had recently visited the scene of the action, and clearly given the attitudes of the two passers-by some thought. "It's possible that the priest and the Levite looked over that man on the ground and wondered if the robbers were still around. Or it's possible that they felt that the man on the ground was merely faking, and he was acting like he had been robbed and hurt in order to seize them over there, lure them there for quick and easy seizure. And so the first question that the priest asked, the first question that the Levite asked was, 'If I stop to help this man, what will happen to me?'"

Eventually, our stricken traveler received help from a most unexpected quarter, a Samaritan. The Samaritan would have had a pretty good excuse not to stop. Did not the Jews despise Samaritans; had they not destroyed the temple on Mount Gerizim?

But the Samaritan couldn't help himself; he was a compassionate human being. He did not just provide rudimentary assistance, either. He opened his heart and his pockets. He set the injured man upon his donkey and delivered him to the nearest inn, clothed him, and saw to it that he was nursed and fed.

In the Gospel of Luke, Jesus tells this parable in reply to a question: Who is my neighbor that I should love as myself?

At the end of the story, Jesus asked his Jewish audience: "Now which of these three do you think seemed to be a neighbor to him who fell among the robbers?"

"He who showed mercy on him," was the reply.

I have always been enchanted by the story of the Good Samaritan because it is an antidote to discrimination and insecurity. It tells us that the essence of our humanity is more powerful than prejudice, that love is more powerful than hatred … and it speaks to our inescapable responsibilities as God carriers, as sisters and brothers of one family, the human family, God's family.

When we invest in loving our neighbors, in listening and upholding their dignity, we are investing in God and in a secure coexistence for us all.

I am an old man now, and if there is anything more important than loving and respecting your neighbors—including those who don't look like you, speak the same language, or practice the same religion—I have yet to learn it.

Scilla Elworthy is a peace-builder, and the founder of the Oxford Research Group, a non-governmental organization she set up in 1982 to develop effective dialogue between nuclear weapons policy-makers worldwide and their critics, for which she was nominated three times for the Nobel Peace Prize. She served as the executive director from 1982 until 2003, when she left to set up Peace Direct, a charity supporting local peace-builders in conflict areas.

Peace Is Not Boring
Dr. Scilla Elworthy

For many people peace can seem boring; too well behaved, too quiet. These are usually the people who have never been in a war, never witnessed the terror of children watching their parents tortured, never seen a human skull exploding, never heard the screams of a grandfather trapped under concrete beams, never looked into the eyes of a woman who has been multiply raped.

I come from a military family. My father fought in the artillery in the First World War, my eldest brother was a paratrooper, my third brother was in the Royal Navy and was killed when I was ten years old. I learned to shoot a gun at eleven, to fly airplanes at twenty-six, and to parachute at forty. In Bosnia I sat at the bedside of a man whose eyes had been destroyed by a sniper's bullet. In the Congo I quailed before the crazed terror of armed and drunken soldiers out of control. In Japan I watched the faces of those who saw firsthand the untold horrors of the atomic explosion in Hiroshima.

The wounds of war take three generations to heal—at a minimum. Some are not healed even after seven centuries. Even a "minimal" action taken in war, for example, one sniper squeezing a trigger, a decision of a millisecond, can kill an innocent baker and send an entire family into destitution on the streets.

What is Shared Security

As a peace-builder and supporter of other peace-builders, to me shared security means above all taking responsibility for the forces that drive armed violence, because that action is essential if those drivers are to be curbed. Then it means recognizing what is already working to build peace effectively at both local and international levels, and scaling up such initiatives worldwide.

The work I do has involved me with people who seem to have a lot of power—physicists who design nuclear warheads, military officers in charge of nuclear weapons, manufacturers who produce and sell missiles and machine guns, strategists who design defense policies, as well as those who sign the checks—not just in Britain, France, China, the United States, and Russia, but also in Israel, India, and Pakistan.

This work involved bringing these key policy makers to meet each other and their informed critics, and beginning to work out agreements to cut nuclear weapons production. It was undertaken by the Oxford Research Group that I set up in 1982.[1]

After twenty-one years I handed on that work to others because I observed a phenomenon happening at the other end of the spectrum of violence, namely the growth of locally led peace initiatives. These are run by people who risk their lives to stop other people being killed, trying their best to build peaceful societies.

For this reason, I set up Peace Direct (www.peacedirect.org) to support their work in areas of hot armed conflict in many parts of the world. I spend a lot of time listening to such people, because they are the new heroes, the *unarmed* heroes.

The change necessary

At this point in history, I am strongly aware that humanity has built up looming threats to our security that weaponry cannot even begin to deal with—climate change, the rich-poor divide, migration, over-population, and terrorism. Therefore, it is time to take a hard look at both the military-industrial complex that drives war, and others for whom war means wealth. It is time to divert their skills and our skills to making what humanity now needs. It is time to access a better kind of intelligence, to demonstrate how conflicts can be prevented and resolved without armed violence. It is time to build a *Business Plan for Peace* and to make peace profitable.

The dream that gives me strength for this work is the capacity of feminine intelligence to come into balance with the masculine. For thousands of years major human decisions have been made by men, and the results are now proving disastrous. I see the possibility that humanity can evolve by recognizing and employing the wisdom of the feminine, available of course to men as it is to women. That wisdom and intelligence includes compassion, inclusivity, caring for the planet that sustains us, outlawing armed violence, and replacing the use of force with mediation.

What keeps me going with this work is two-fold. Daily, I am amazed and humbled by those facing terror, who nevertheless *walk toward what they fear*. Gulalai Ismael is one of them. She lives in northwest Pakistan, one of the most dangerous places in the world to be a woman. At age 15 she started an organization called Aware Girls to enable women to go to school; Malala Yousefzai was shot in the head for doing just this. Gulalai, undeterred, has now trained twenty teams of young men and women in Pakistan and Afghanistan to prevent other young people joining extremist groups. Using the tools of listening and dialogue, they have reached and dissuaded more than 500 teenagers "at risk" of becoming extremist.

Secondly, what sustains me is ultimately the ground. When I come home tired and dispirited, I go out to the garden and get my hands in the earth and think about nothing but helping vegetables to grow. I come back muddy and happy and peaceful.

Those who walk beside me are my family and a large, powerful, highly conscious contingent of friends and colleagues. What has recently inspired me was realizing that we can now, for the first time ever, estimate the costs of preventing war worldwide.[2]

This means that we can also demonstrate the impact that ordinary people can have to prevent and resolve conflict and help make a peaceful world possible. There are skills that we can all develop that enable us to prevent conflict in the workplace, in the community, and in the family too. In *The Business Plan for Peace* I wanted to include these skills as well as the human side of things—the mistakes I've made, what a crisis felt like at the time, the incredible warmth and courage of the people I've been lucky enough to work with, and the times when it has been nourishing and inspiring and even a lot of fun.

What I have seen of war, and the building of peace, convinces me that human beings are well able to find better ways to resolve conflict than by killing each other. It's not easy, but we now know how to do it. This short book is a first attempt to answer some of the tough questions involved. It is by no means complete or comprehensive, and your improvements and ideas will be welcome.

The response to *The Business Plan for Peace* has been remarkable. The book has been welcomed by His Holiness the Dalai Lama, praised by Oxford professors, and supported by the founder of the Institute for Economics and Peace. In addition, individuals and companies have come forward offering skills, assistance, and partnership, with particular reference to nine of the twenty-five strategies. That's what I'm working on now.

Doing this work, the key thing I have learned is that power *over* others is the problem. *Power over* is attractive to human beings convinced by the seductive idea that ultimate power brings ultimate security. That route leads to Armageddon.

Einstein warned us that we cannot solve a problem using the consciousness that created it. So, humanity now has the chance to evolve our consciousness, and develop a different understanding of power, namely *power with* others. That means rebalancing feminine intelligence with masculine. It means upgrading the value we ascribe to qualities like compassion, inclusivity, caring for the planet, and wisdom. It means insisting that women sit at all decision-making tables, at all levels, equally with men.

It means sharing power, and valuing the brilliance, courage, and capacity of (extra)ordinary people to prevent suffering. It means trusting people to resolve problems, by understanding that local people know best what needs to be done in their own areas. Tomorrow I shall get up, S-T-R-E-T-C-H (very important as I turn 75), and go out into my small garden. There I shall sit on a bench and encourage the vegetables as they grow, and listen to the bees as they work. Then I'll be ready to work. Tomorrow that work will be part of our strategies to prevent war; in this case to enable Women to Break the Cycle of Violence,[3] by training, connecting, and mobilizing networks of women worldwide, using their power to defuse bigotry, racism, and armed violence.

Notes

1. Oxford Research Group is a London-based think tank working on peace, security, and justice issues. For more information, visit www.oxfordresearchgroup.org.

2. Scilla Elworthy, *The Business Plan for Peace: Building a World Without War* (London: Peace Direct, 2017), 94.

3. One of the initiatives of *The Business Plan for Peace.*

 *Andrei Gómez-Suárez is a widely published researcher. He is the Director of Rodeemos el Diálogo (ReD) Foundation, associate researcher at the University of Oxford, and consultant on peace processes and transitional justice. His publications include* Genocide Geopolitics and Transnational Networks *(Routledge, 2015) and* El Triunfo del No *(Icono, 2016). His research on the UP genocide and the Santos-FARC peace talks has appeared in the* Journal of Genocide Research, Third World Quarterly, Genocidio, Estudios Políticos, *and elsewhere. Andrei lectures internationally on Colombian Politics, International Security, Peace Processes, Post-Conflict Reconstruction, and Transitional Justice.*

Shared Security the Tao Way
Andrei Gómez-Suárez
Bogotá, June 12, 2018

Shared security is a state of mind. A way of doing things from the perspective that our contribution to living in our global community does not depend on our rational effort to control the world, but rather in the unfolding of the entropic world we are part of. At the core of my belief system is the teaching of the Tao, the ancient philosophy whose key principle is *wu wei* or "doing by not doing." It is from the humble perspective that we cannot change the world, but rather that we change with the changing world, that we can help shape relationships between human beings, allowing them to flourish, thereby finding an unpretentious way to live our lives on this planet.

From this perspective, I do not get the strength I need to do the work I do by daydreaming. I get it from my daily interaction with nature—including, of course, other human beings. In becoming with nature, creativity unfolds, which allows me to take advantage of the multiples possibilities of affecting others and being affected by others that constantly arise. I work because I become through connecting with others, because it is in the practice of *doing* that we truly *are.* I work hard to deconstruct the fiction of a self that is afraid of changing, that, based on natural processes such as neuronal circuits, creates prejudices that could hamper the opportunity to grow with other beings who think and feel differently.

Since we are imperfect and fleeting, we must simply make the most of this opportunity to enjoy becoming with others. Thus, fear and envy disappear, and solidarity emerges. There is no need to protect what cannot be protected. There is no need to desire what we do not have. We do not need to be afraid when every second of existence shared with others is all we have to transcend. Nurturing courage is part of the determination to go beyond the bubble created around individualism; courage only grows bigger and bigger when I recognize in the other a new way of doing and becoming in the world. Courage is the character of a clear mind. It is mainly the product of empathy, not of reasoning.

Since the day I was taught to walk, I never walk alone. I walk with others who have taught me the value of respect for those who are different, of having the generosity to offer the best of ourselves to others, of possessing the honesty to share our fears and our hopes, of expressing solidarity by helping others without hesitation, of co-responsibility in the creation of a better world, and of self-criticism to amend what we do and change our minds when we recognize our mistakes. It is in and as a collective that we can see the evolving nature of our selves; it is through others' eyes that we can see ourselves unfold into plenitude. In this way we can appreciate love: the source and glue of a collective-self. As Humberto Maturana says, to love is to recognize the other as a legitimate other with whom to coexist; and therefore the mother force of societies.

Love is transferred from generation to generation, and thus we become human beings. My mother and my father are the source of the love that lives in me and which I share with whoever crosses my path; my sister is the incessant giver of love; and my wife the partner for the reproduction of an enduring and creating love. Rodeemos el Dialogo ("Let's Surround the Dialogue," or ReD) is the milieu in which we transform ourselves and put our commitment to create a friendlier world into practice. It creates the environment in which we can see that love is not a gift, but a given in our existence. And then we realize that we are just too busy doing to see that love is not-doing. In ReD's spaces we don't make plans to change the world, we meet to engage in conversations about solving the Colombian armed conflict and nurturing peace through dialogue, to recognize our humanity and the love that brings us together, making the world in which we live a safer place.

ReD was born in London in 2012, when the negotiations between the Colombian government and the Revolutionary Armed Forces of Colombia (FARC) started. It was created by a group of Colombians and friends of Colombia in an effort to offer moral support in favor of the peace process. We started our work in Bogotá in 2014. Even though we have campaigned for peace, we have not been able to stop the killings of social leaders in Colombia, which in the last two years, since the signing of the Havana Peace Agreement, amounts to 300. We have not been able to persuade a large majority of Colombians to work for peace; as of today, 50 percent support politics of hatred. We have not reduced the levels of polarization in my country; Colombians are divided across party lines and political leaders that deny the wrongdoings of the past, and those who seek to bring the perpetrators to justice. However, we are the change we want to see. We meet every week to drink a hot chocolate and hear stories of the efforts for peace taking place all around us, and the work of people committed to social change. We listen in detail, we reflect critically, and we offer honest and generous feedback; in so doing we affect the environment we live in, and ourselves. We give life to a shared security in which our right to dream, to act, and to defend equality and freedom is possible.

Shared security is not a branding that promotes the securitization of our identities. On the contrary, it deconstructs the very idea of self and other. Alterity becomes the very source of our security, because security is only possible when shared with others. We do not pretend to be global citizens, nor do we aspire to be world leaders. We are not even activists, we are only human beings unfolding through the encounter with the other; thus, in love and joy we find our security and the security of others, because shared security is the only security possible.

 *Jayathma Wickramanayake is a former member of the Sri Lanka Administrative Service, and currently the UN Secretary General's Envoy on Youth. She will play a critical role in realizing the 2030 UN Agenda on Sustainable Development, which places a significant emphasis on including youth at the center of crisis prevention. She served previously as Secretary to the Secretary-General of the Parliament of Sri Lanka, and the Youth Lead Negotiator on the International Youth Task Force of the World Conference on Youth 2014. She has worked to transform the youth development sector, notably through her advocacy for a cohesive movement for civic and political engagement of young people named "Hashtag Generation."*

The Inescapable Relevance of Youth to the Process of Shared Security
Jayathma Wickramanayake

Generation after generation, centuries-old thinking sees young people as a demographic that must be nurtured and built up to take over tomorrow's leadership in line with the norms of the generations that preceded theirs. We, the youth of this world, know that this is no longer the case. A highly volatile world is rapidly changing what constitutes normative societal behavior, most times even before the next generation has reached comparative maturity.

These days, leaders talk of empowering us and facilitating our participation. Sometimes meaningfully, sometimes symbolically. Are they doing this because there is a genuine insight into the potential of youth as agents of transformation who can rephrase policy based on contention to one based on cooperation? Or are they terrified that if we are not heeded we will turn against them? For many of them, youth are a ticking time bomb. They are frightened by the fact that 41 percent of the world's population is under the age of twenty-four and a full 51 percent is under the age of thirty. Eighty percent of us are in Africa and Asia, with the combined youth populations of the South Asian countries of India, Bangladesh, and Pakistan amounting to the largest in the word. The sheer number of youth who have been given step-motherly treatment yesterday terrify the leaders of today who feel unable to provide them with a quality education, decent jobs, or opportunities for advancement. They look in fear at such peer-coordinated movements as the Arab Spring and wonder, not if, but when, such fast, seismic and status-quo destroying responses will visit their own nations with youth at the vanguard. They therefore reduce us—the energetic, the visionary, the potent—into a problem that needs to be "solved."

The truth is far different. I would like to ask the world: who in their right minds would, in the prime of their lives, wish to live in hate, anger, fear, and doubt, flinging bombs, killing people and being killed in return? Very few, and even those few, resort to it not because of choice but because of a desperation born out of the lack of hope. They do so as a response to the pressures visited upon them by conflicts and circumstances triggered by aged and aging leaders in all sectors of society, and monstrous political institutions that exclude young people instead of including them. That small group of violent youth are reacting aggressively to conditions they were not instrumental in creating.

So, let us be clear here: rather than youth being a problem, or the potential cause of national instabilities as is commonly believed, the vast majority is simply refusing to acquiesce to untenable injustice and deprivation and pushing back *against* violence that has been done to them and their future. The classic narrative that youth are troublemakers is both stale and fallacious and must change. Therefore, it is mandatory that youth must play a significant, if not the largest, part in securing our world. The key to making this necessary perspective shift is that youth are recognized as smart, energetic, forward-thinking human beings who can, and should, be represented in the highest echelons of the governance hierarchies of the world. This, at the present time, is unfortunately not the case.

Let us take a look at the way in which global efforts to mainstream youth is currently working. For me, the statistics are both disheartening and deeply disturbing. It is a little-known fact that 73 percent of the 178 member countries of the Inter-Parliamentary Union have age restrictions on running for public office. Just 2 percent of world parliamentarians are under the age of thirty. The average age of a parliamentarian is fifty-five. The issue is also compounded by the fact that most political parties across the world have age restrictions on youth leadership. This eventually leads to a situation where not only national but intergovernmental bodies are manned by older people who are there simply because they hold higher office in their respective countries, thereby conducting discussions which become exclusive. Most such leaders have difficulties with the realities of a changed world, are alienated from youth, and are not capacitated to speak on their behalf. Yet, they still insist that we are denied the direct representation we need and deserve at every level of governance. This is why, inspired by the youth organization in Nigeria named YIAGA, my office—the Office of the United Nations Secretary-General's Envoy on Youth—scaled up the Not Too Young to Run campaign and strengthened advocacy with all governments to remove outdated age barriers.

It is an uphill battle also within the United Nations. The UN hierarchical system has not changed at all from the multilateral structure that was set up seventy-plus years ago. Hence, with most countries preventing youth from participating in governance, youth are automatically shut out of participating in the UN process. Despite this legacy, things are changing.

The UNSG is very vocal about where youth must be positioned within the global decision-making matrix and is very supportive of my office. In 2015 following the adoption of resolution 2250 on Youth, Peace, and Security, the UN Security Council asked the Secretary General to produce a report on youth empowerment, participation, and ownership and once Graeme Simpson and his team completed it, I was able to address the UNSC directly along with two other youth representatives and make our voices heard in the name of global youth. I saw here, for the first time, the United Nations system really taking up the matter of youth with the focus and commitment it deserves, and I was heartened to hear almost every nation was in agreement with the findings of that report, all of which confirmed the critical importance of including youth in all issues of societal change.

Despite the fact that the evolution of the UN and my own job description is still a "work in progress" and that the process is still not quite at the stage where my office can be as relevant a global advocate for youth as I believe is required, there are some substantive and progressive steps being taken in that direction. This is a happy thought, for it provides both credibility and energy to my work, though I keep sight of the fact that the efforts that get us in front of the inter-governmental bodies are not member-state mandated or funded. Funding for youth-lead or youth-focused initiatives in both international and national contexts remains a challenge including the peace-building support for young people. This highlights the gap between desire and commitment. Goal 16 of the Sustainable Development Goals (SDG16: Peace, Justice and Strong Institutions), was created specifically for purposes such as those for which I advocate both inside and outside the UN system. Yet, we have hardly touched that goal and explored the dynamic between Peace and sustainable development. I believe I know the reason for this recalcitrance, it is because the language of that goal clearly directs us to relinquish the ideologies that support inequity, exploitation, indiscipline, aggression, corruption, and marginalization of certain sectors of population. Goal 16 cannot be even casually touched without substantive sustainable, inclusive approaches, attitudes, and commitments. When one looks at such Goal 16 targets as significantly reducing all forms of violence and related deaths everywhere, ending abuse and exploitation of children, significantly reducing illicit flow of finance and arms, broadening and strengthening participation of developing countries in global governance, ensuring responsive, inclusive, participatory, and representative decision-making at all levels, and so on, that fact becomes abundantly clear. If one wishes for a reason for the comparatively sluggish and slow awakening of the world to the real importance of youth in shared security, one need look no further than the reciprocal tardiness in engaging Goal 16.

Looking over all the efforts of many people though, there is sufficient reason to believe that we are in the home stretch of the transition phase from industrial-age digression to sustainable-age progression. However, this is not sufficient. We must *know* we are in the home stretch. Toward that end, my office uses whatever resources and powers it has to optimal effect in achieving critical mass on real, lasting, youth empowerment. From exercising the power of my office to convene, all the way through to direct, on-site engagement of youth in every type of sociopolitical, sociocultural, and political scenario imaginable, we do not what we can, but rather, what we must. In some cases, regardless of the system.

For example, the high-level political forum on the Sustainable Development Goals (SDGs) sits under the UN Economic and Social Council (ECOSOC). My office then exercises its power of convening to co-convene the ECOSOC youth forum to discuss SDGs annually. The forum usually comprises young people, youth organizations, civil society, and academics but we open it to youth ministers as well so there is a greater practical representation of youth. Together we collate youth-lead reporting on the SDGs. Then we feed our findings to the high-level forum through an extensive lobbying process. We are young. We are relentless.

Another way of getting youth voices heard is to use the fact that as a representative of the UNSG, I am received at the highest level by every nation. I get to engage with the leaders of nations at a level that their own youth rarely have an opportunity to do. I therefore make it a point to go deep into the country and speak to the youth and obtain a clear idea of their most pressing fears and insecurities, and then I use the recognition of my position to put these youth directly in touch with their leaders or to bring their issues to the table. These types of efforts help, at least to some extent, to even out the imbalance, position youth in their rightful place, and take a step toward achieving the foundation targets of global aims such as Goal 16 of the SDGs.

While all of this is of importance to global progress from hate to peace, from uncertainty to security, the real question that needs to be answered is if these efforts are valid when you consider the widely disparate norms under which societies, communities, and nations live. Yet, translating this understanding into practical action is difficult because such a change in approach ups the ante vis-à-vis the sum effort required. Resource allocation and distribution, oversight, and impact assurance methodologies all need to be carefully rethought in order to accommodate the diversity of our world. We must recognize that development or progress must be culturally, nationally, demographically, regionally appropriate, and only pursued with a highly localized understanding of what constitutes collectives, comforts, fairness, and safety.

That sort of effort is not possible simply by convening high level fora. That requires all of us who advocate for a better way of living together to get down on the ground, drive our hands into the diverse soils of this world of ours, smell the air around it, taste the water that runs through it, and at least empathize, if not embrace the realities under which its human beings, plants, and animals find ways of harmonizing themselves within its differences, contentions, and complexities.

What drives me each day is the desire to truly know the extent of the victimization and pain suffered by human beings right down to the smallest group or individual who have been affected by processes that have been mistaken for civilized behavior by generation upon generations past. It is what drives all of us who are young, to whom understanding issues precedes looking for solutions. In this process that we favor as a group, we can see how young people have taken charge of their own peaceful destiny, working with no funds or mechanisms, just going out there and doing whatever they can. It is only when we see the outcome of those efforts that we can truly know that the phrase "taking control of our own future" is not mere rhetoric for the youth of our world. Rather, it is a practical reality.

When I can be a part of such quiet heroism; when I see how I can leverage my office and facilitate these astonishingly beautiful young people to intermesh their varied cultures, ideas, attitudes, and approaches into a recognizable whole; when I see how they reliably default to mutual understanding of disparate ideas and insights; when I see them resolve repeatedly to work together to peacefully address and overcome the complexities and differences of origins, traditions, and cultures to create an unbreakable latticework; when I see them arrive at a collective third space unified and capable, then the sleepless nights of worry, the daily stress of doing what I do makes the doing worth its while. When I see the outcomes of these exercises, I see then the truth of the adage "If one cannot expend all of one's energy to succor a single human being, then one has lost the right to work on behalf of humanity."

So, working singly, working collectively, we, the young of the world, know that the mere absence of violence does not equate to peace. Peace for us is the ability to express ourselves. Peace for us is the ability to marry the person we love while understanding and embracing the idea of another set of people who want their parents to find them their life partner. Peace for us is to feel completely safe, secure, and unthreatened by anyone else. Peace for us is contentment and evenness in the living out of our lives. In this, we like to believe we distance ourselves from those generations that went before and the way in which they created the norms and the ideals of civilization that has brought us to this dangerous juncture in human history.

And yet, by our own proclamation of mandatory empathy, we do not reject or marginalize those people who also live on this earth and who are no longer young. We know that we all deal with the situations that we are handed when we are born. We empathize with our older people in that respect as well. We also recognize that among the older, there are guides and mentors. Despite the criticisms of the UN system, despite the fact that we live in a world where after all its efforts, there have been more than fifty conflicts occurring simultaneously over the last decade, despite the fact that death by war has risen by over 400 percent and death through terror has risen by almost 300 percent in that same period, the UN remains the single largest unifying force among nations. In the end, it is the only truly global entity that has a chance of ending conflicts now and forever. At securing security for now and forever. Its effort may seem snail paced and anathema for a volatile world of human beings living 200-miles-an-hour lives. Its impact may seem as invisible as a line drawn across the sky with a finger. Yet, let us remember that it was born out of the most insecure, vulnerable, and world-damaging era in the history of human civilization and that it has withstood the travails and turmoil of a world rapidly spinning itself out of control. Its mere presence on this planet has acted as a resistive counterforce in human beings bent on destroying the world and themselves. For every failure that can be laid at its door, there are a dozen instances where the UN has succeeded in keeping our vision telescoped on that beautiful place that is visible through the windows of peace, harmony, and security. I can say this, merely by dint of the fact that we are still here. Still wanting harmony. Still desiring peace. Still working for unity. That does not merely count for something. It counts for everything.

 *Matilda Flemming leads the Search for Common Ground's European Affairs team, where she ensures strong relationships with the European Union, governments, and other partners. She is a member of the UN Advisory Group of Experts for the Progress Study on Youth, Peace and Security. She has worked for the European Women's Lobby, strengthening the role of women in decision-making, and the United Network of Young Peacebuilders, leading the civil society campaign for Security Council Resolution 2250 on Youth, Peace and Security. She was co-chair of the UN Inter-Agency Network on Youth Development's Working Group on Youth and Peacebuilding and a member of the Council of Europe's Advisory Council on Youth. Matilda is from Finland and holds a master's degree in Development Studies from the International Institute of Social Studies in The Hague.*

Patriarchy Is (Almost) Everywhere
Matilda Flemming
Brussels, June 24, 2018

This is what I believe: Patriarchy is everywhere. In the home, in the streets, in institutions, in the workplace. We will not be able to transform our societies to be sustainable, just, peaceful, and open, unless we fight patriarchy, unless we as societies find different ways of understanding and organizing power—away from patriarchal power and control.

The Merriam-Webster Dictionary defines patriarchy as "control by men of a disproportionately large share of power" and "a society or institution organized according to the principles or practices of patriarchy." The problem with patriarchy is not only about men dominating power, and it is not only about men oppressing women. Patriarchy as a system of organizing power in society is ineffective, and it is bad for everyone involved—for women, for men, for young people, for everyone. Narrow gender roles, men's violence against women and men, and institutional gender biases are all present in varying degrees in every society on the globe, and are destructive on an individual level as well as on a communal and societal level. In May 2018, a World Bank study, "Unrealized Potential: The High Cost of Gender Inequality in Earning," synthesized the research of economists Quentin Wodon and Bénédicte de la Brière, who set the cost of inequality to 160 trillion dollars.

Having been involved from the very conceptual stage of the UN Security Council Resolution 2250 on Youth, Peace, and Security (YPS), and having worked closely with the Women, Peace, and Security (WPS) agenda, I feel strongly that these global agendas offer a necessary challenge to patriarchal power.

Peace and security have long been the definition of patriarchal power and hard politics. The politics that really matter. The sort of politics you need vast experience of a certain kind for, in order to get involved and to have a say. An arena in which men with gray hair seem to be the only ones with the relevant experience, who literally call all the shots. Men with gray hair defined what peace is (no war, peace through superior fire-power), and what security is (state security). A definition that excludes the lived experiences of the vast majority of societies: the violence that women are facing in their homes; the violence that young people are facing at the very hands of the institutions that are supposedly there to protect them, the state security forces.

Understanding and organizing power

The YPS and WPS agendas are not about tweaking the way we currently do (or don't do) peace and security work, but about radically rethinking what power means and what peaceful societies mean. As the Independent Progress Study on Youth, Peace, and Security, a study for which I served on the advisory board, and which was released by the United Nations this year states, "The systems that reinforce exclusion must be transformed in order to address the structural barriers limiting youth participation in peace and security." I would argue that patriarchy is one of the foundational structural barriers that must be overcome.

Traditionally power has been understood as power *over*. A controlling power. Men's power over women. State's power over citizens. Institutions' power over young people. Hierarchy. What I would describe as patriarchal power.

Feminist thinking, as for instance articulated in the Strategic Framework 2016–2020 by the European Women's Lobby, offers us a new understanding of power: transformational forms of power— individual power ("power within") and collective capacity ("power with")—to empower or positively transform oneself and others ("power to"). Understanding patriarchal power in action means applying a gender and inclusion lens to our understanding of the world. It's about asking on any given issue, *Who is not being heard? Who is not in the room? Who has the power?* The Independent Progress Study on Youth, Peace, and Security also confirms that inclusion is a primary concern for young people: "Systematically addressing the violence of exclusion is the best means to prevent violence."

People in power will not give it up. That's how patriarchal power works. But by organizing and mobilizing people, women's movements, youth movements, and civil rights movements have time and time again shown that power *can* be redistributed. The WPS and YPS agendas offer an opportunity to challenge power and leadership on issues of peace and security. While there is an obvious rights-based argument to be made—women and young people have a right to take part in decision-making on peace and security— research on power and leadership in other fields shows how ineffective and detrimental the dominance of patriarchal power and leadership can be.

Study upon study shows us the poor outcomes of patriarchal leadership, leadership that doesn't listen, is hierarchical and closed to feedback from "below." A study undertaken by Aalto University Professor Timo O. Vuori and Professor Quy N. Huy from Singapore's INSEAD University who studied Finland's once-shining star Nokia's transformation during 2007–2013, shows that they lost their market leading position overnight as a result of the fear of lower levels of the hierarchy speaking up to the leadership.

In an article in the *Harvard Business Review*,[1] Tomas Chamorro-Premuzic, Professor of Business Psychology at University College London, and Columbia University, New York, argues that by "misinterpreting displays of confidence as a sign of competence, we are fooled into believing that men are better leaders than women," since men much more often display this type of hubris. He goes on to talk about humility as a foundational characteristic of a good leader: "arrogance and overconfidence are inversely related to leadership talent."

A study at the London School of Economics[2] points out the prevalence of mediocre men in politics, and shows how more women in politics threaten this mediocre elite as it increases the overall competence level of politicians. According to the study, "Mediocre leaders have a strong incentive to surround themselves with mediocre followers, so as to bolster their chances of remaining in power."

Transformational leadership

Policy makers focusing on peace and security need to understand that hierarchical power structures often do not deliver desirable outcomes, that what we see and know as competence often is a flawed understanding, and that mediocre leadership attracts mediocre leadership.

For too long, too many mediocre old men have had too much power *over*. To be able to tackle the complex challenges our societies are facing—the changing nature of conflict, climate change, income inequality—we need to open the rooms of power to new voices and build new spaces of power. We need to foster transformational leadership with a feminist understanding of power that is inclusive of the practices, experiences, and resources of young people and women, and that elicits pride and respect from followers, effectively communicates vision, mentors and empowers, and problem-solves in a creative and flexible way.

Notes

1. Tomas Chamorro-Premuzic, "Why Do So Many Incompetent Men Become Leaders?" *Harvard Business Review,* August 22, 2013. Accessed September 12, 2018. https://hbr.org/2013/08/ why-do-so-many-incompetent-men.

2. Tim Besley, Olle Folke, Torsten Persson, and Johanna Rickne, "Gender Quotas and the Crisis of the Mediocre Man," *LSE Business Review,* March 13, 2017. Accessed September 12, 2018. http://blogs.lse.ac.uk/businessreview/2017/03/13/ gender-quotas-and-the-crisis-of-the-mediocre-man/.

 *Kessy Martine Ekomo-Soignet A geo-politician by training, Kessy is a community leader, peace-building practitioner and founder of URU, a youth led organization committed to increasing the engagement of youth in locally led conflict prevention and reconciliation efforts in Central African Republic (CAR). She has worked as a consultant on field surveys and data analysis on issues related to youth, community security, and recovery, and access to information on the CAR Special Court for the population. She completed the Mandela Washington Fellowship for Young African Leaders in 2014, and was appointed by UN Secretary-General Ban Ki-Moon as an expert for the Progress Study on Youth, Peace, and Security, as mandated by Security Council resolution 2250. She serves as a correspondent for the British Organization Peace Direct in CAR.*

The Art of Seeing
Adansonia digitata: The African Baobab
Kessy Martine Ekomo-Soignet

I am often asked why I decided to leave my stable life in Paris to return to a conflict-ridden Central African Republic to work with young people. To tell the truth, I never really know how to arrange my words, my ideas, to give a coherent answer, as my decision to return to work for my country was visceral. Have you ever felt the "evidence?" Like when you fall in love and your heart understands but your brain is trying to rationalize things. The crisis environment in which I live in the Central African Republic forces me to be rational, but what allows me to get up every morning—and join my peers to do at least one action that will make a difference—is that sense of obviousness that peace-building needs personal, collective, and constructive commitment and that I must act now.

Peace and security have taken on a special meaning since I worked with my peers. It goes beyond the theories, UN resolutions, political talks, forums… It is mainly about accepting that each person *is* a person (*Zo kwe zo* in our national language), a person full of fears, dreams, hope, and projects.

Young non-Muslims and Muslims enjoy the same dream of living in an environment where they can flourish and become the people they dream to be, to write their personal legend. While the media tends to highlight minorities who hope to realize their dreams by using violence, my experience in the field allows me to say that a large segment of the population, mostly young people, are against violence and try their best, with or without support from the international community or the government, to bring peace where they live. My eyes and my hopes are fixed on them daily.

Creating an environment where young people can meet, be valued, engaged, and collaborate beyond their community and religious affiliation, is planting a seed of hope like the one of an *Adansonia digitata* tree, also called the African Baobab. This slow-growing tree is exceptionally long-lived, and it is common to encounter specimens nearly 2,000 years old.

In other words, it is a question of accepting that change does not come overnight, but of being patient and above all continuing to create spaces where we celebrate our oneness, diversity, and humanity.

I do not think I will live long enough to fully enjoy the fruits of this work, but I think that we are doing our part in the relay of life by laying a solid foundation for the generations of Central Africans who will come after us. The torch will pass one day from our capable and vigilant hands into theirs.

Thus, like the African Baobab, the most useful tree in the Sahel, these young people will produce new generations united by strong common values that will make our country a peaceful, inclusive, and indivisible land.

Jimmy Carter served as the 39th President of the United States from 1977 to 1981. He was awarded the 2002 Nobel Peace Prize for his work to find peaceful solutions to international conflicts, to advance democracy and human rights, and to promote economic and social development.

Excerpt from Speech to the Nobel Committee
Jimmy Carter

Throughout the years of his presidency, from 1977–1981, Jimmy Carter worked to advance his strongest belief: conflict must always be resolved with communal harmony, through cooperation, and with respect for international law and human rights. While he made great strides in bringing conflicting parties to the negotiating table, his life after leaving office has been dedicated to being a relentless, and relentlessly optimistic, advocate for an inclusive understanding of peace. For almost four decades, The Carter Center, which he established with the goal of making a "fundamental commitment to human rights and the alleviation of human suffering," has been at the forefront of non-partisan peace-building efforts throughout the world, including addressing traumas resulting in poor health, lack of access to basic resources, environmental degradation, and increasing capacity for democratic political processes, and access to education and information. When asked to write something for this anthology, he asked us to choose, instead, something from among the works he has already written. We have chosen two excerpts which exemplify the integrity and decency with which he approaches his work. The following is an excerpt from his words to the assembled audience at the Nobel Prize Ceremony. The excerpt on his efforts in North Korea, which follows in the next section, is a significant reminder of how much further we would be today if we had been able to embrace his vision and his actions a quarter of a century ago.

Excerpt from Jimmy Carter's Speech
Accepting the Nobel Prize for Peace in 2002

...I thought often during my years in the White House of an admonition that we received in our small school in Plains, Georgia, from a beloved teacher, Miss Julia Coleman. She often said: "We must adjust to changing times and still hold to unchanging principles."

When I was a young boy, this same teacher also introduced me to Leo Tolstoy's novel, *War and Peace*. She interpreted that powerful narrative as a reminder that the simple human attributes of goodness and truth can overcome great power. She also taught us that an individual is not swept along on a tide of inevitability but can influence even the greatest human events.

These premises have been proven by the lives of many heroes, some of whose names were little known outside their own regions until they became Nobel laureates: Albert John Lutuli, Norman Borlaug, Desmond Tutu, Elie Wiesel, Aung San Suu Kyi, Jody Williams, and even Albert Schweitzer and Mother Teresa. They and others have proven that even without government power—and often in opposition to it—individuals can enhance human rights and wage peace, actively and effectively.

The Nobel Prize also profoundly magnified the inspiring global influence of Martin Luther King Jr., the greatest leader that my native state has ever produced. On a personal note, it is unlikely that my political career beyond Georgia would have been possible without the changes brought about by the civil rights movement in the American South and throughout our nation.

On the steps of our memorial to Abraham Lincoln, Dr. King said: "I have a dream that on the red hills of Georgia the sons of former slaves and the sons of former slaveowners will be able to sit down together at a table of brotherhood." The scourge of racism has not been vanquished, either in the red hills of our state or around the world. And yet we see ever more frequent manifestations of his dream of racial healing. In a symbolic but very genuine way, at least involving two Georgians, it is coming true in Oslo today.

I am not here as a public official, but as a citizen of a troubled world who finds hope in a growing consensus that the generally accepted goals of society are peace, freedom, human rights, environmental quality, the alleviation of suffering, and the rule of law.

During the past decades, the international community, usually under the auspices of the United Nations, has struggled to negotiate global standards that can help us achieve these essential goals. They include: the abolition of land mines and chemical weapons; an end to the testing, proliferation, and further deployment of nuclear warheads; constraints on global warming; prohibition of the death penalty, at least for children; and an international criminal court to deter and to punish war crimes and genocide. Those agreements already adopted must be fully implemented, and others should be pursued aggressively.

We must also strive to correct the injustice of economic sanctions that seek to penalize abusive leaders but all too often inflict punishment on those who are already suffering from their abuse.

The unchanging principles of life predate modern times. I worship Jesus Christ, whom we Christians consider to be the Prince of Peace. As a Jew, he taught us to cross religious boundaries, in service and in love. He repeatedly reached out and embraced Roman conquerors, other Gentiles, and even the more despised Samaritans.

Despite theological differences, all great religions share common commitments that define our ideal secular relationships. I am convinced that Christians, Muslims, Buddhists, Hindus, Jews, and others can embrace each other in a common effort to alleviate human suffering and to espouse peace.

But the present era is a challenging and disturbing time for those whose lives are shaped by religious faith based on kindness toward each other. We have been reminded that cruel and inhuman acts can be derived from distorted theological beliefs, as suicide bombers take the lives of innocent human beings, draped falsely in the cloak of God's will. With horrible brutality, neighbors have massacred neighbors in Europe, Asia, and Africa.

In order for us human beings to commit ourselves personally to the inhumanity of war, we find it necessary first to dehumanize our opponents, which is in itself a violation of the beliefs of all religions. Once we characterize our adversaries as beyond the scope of God's mercy and grace, their lives lose all value. We deny personal responsibility when we plant land-mines and, days or years later, a stranger to us—often a child—is crippled or killed. From a great distance, we launch bombs or missiles with almost total impunity, and never want to know the number or identity of the victims.

At the beginning of this new millennium I was asked to discuss, here in Oslo, the greatest challenge that the world faces. Among all the possible choices, I decided that the most serious and universal problem is the growing chasm between the richest and poorest people on earth. Citizens of the ten wealthiest countries are now seventy-five times richer than those who live in the ten poorest ones, and the separation is increasing every year, not only between nations but also within them. The results of this disparity are root causes of most of the world's unresolved problems, including starvation, illiteracy, environmental degradation, violent conflict, and unnecessary illnesses that range from Guinea worm to HIV/AIDS.

Most work of The Carter Center is in remote villages in the poorest nations of Africa, and there I have witnessed the capacity of destitute people to persevere under heartbreaking conditions. I have come to admire their judgment and wisdom, their courage and faith, and their awesome accomplishments when given a chance to use their innate abilities.

But tragically, in the industrialized world there is a terrible absence of understanding or concern about those who are enduring lives of despair and hopelessness. We have not yet made the commitment to share with others an appreciable part of our excessive wealth. This is a potentially rewarding burden that we should all be willing to assume.

Ladies and gentlemen:

War may sometimes be a necessary evil. But no matter how necessary, it is always an evil, never a good. We will not learn how to live together in peace by killing each other's children.

The bond of our common humanity is stronger than the

divisiveness of our fears and prejudices. God gives us the capacity for choice. We can choose to alleviate suffering. We can choose to work together for peace. We can make these changes—and we must.

From South Sudan to Palestine

Malual Bol Kiir is a South Sudanese Peace and Human rights activist; He co-founded the African Youth Action Network (AYAN), which recruits youths to work together as agents of peace and conflict prevention. He participated in UNHCR's Global Refugee Youth Consultations that brought together youth from twenty-two countries to discuss the most pressing challenges they face and their recommendations on how to best address these challenges. Malual is also a member of the advisory group of experts for the 2015 UN Security Council Resolution 2250, a mandated progress study on youth, peace, and security. Malual is an honoree for the Women's Refugee Commission's 2017 Voices of Courage Award and a recipient of the Right To Play 2018 Champion for Children Award. He was born in 1993.

The Art of Choosing:
At Which Side Would I Throw My First Stone?
Malual Bol Kiir

I am a South Sudanese peace and human rights activist and a former war child. My experience is that of an Israeli boy whose mother is a Palestinian and who has grandparents from both sides of the border. I am a product of two ever-fighting tribes, Dinka and Nuer, the largest ethnic groups in South Sudan. Their wars first broke out inside my family!

Born in a contested area of Abyei between Sudan and South Sudan, and now a native of the border community of Mayom (Nuer), I was born a Dinka and made a Nuer.

This conflict is even aggravated symbolically in me by the three-piece Dinka names of my identity, including the namesake of the ruling president who is blamed for the massacre of my Nuer people, just as Riek Machar is blamed for the massacre of my Dinka people.

However, my dualism in the face of the polarizing conflict in the world's youngest nation is a blessing in disguise. I had to stand for both, and for all, throughout the first war of independence in Sudan and the current war based on a power struggle in South Sudan.

At the beginning of the conflict, in 2013, the war in South Sudan was perceived to be simply between the Nuer and the Dinka people—represented by President Salva Kiir Mayardit, a Dinka and nemesis of the Nuer people and former Vice President Riek Machar Teny, a Nuer considered the nemesis of the Dinka people. This was inaccurate because, although there were tribal elements to the war, and these two tribes had battled each other over resources and land since the nineteenth century, and though politicians were using ethnicity as a tool of mobilization as well as assassinations, it is a conflict that has grown to involve the entire region, with outside parties supporting various warring parties based upon their own economic and political interests. It has been alleged, for instance, that the political leaders and elites of both Uganda and Kenya are allies of the South Sudanese factions—due to the fact that Kampala and Nairobi-based companies benefit from the war, and that Uganda, in particular, has had interests in preventing Sudan from expanding its Arab and Islamic influence southwards from Khartoum—and that they have, therefore, supported the opposition in South Sudan. Even Ethiopia, where most of the peace agreements have been signed, has been tarnished by allegations that its leaders merely want to leverage their involvement for the purposes of gaining international and regional prestige, simultaneously brokering peace in Addis Ababa while also supporting the opposition in South Sudan.

The most affected victim of this conflict is not myself but my grandfather, the spiritual chief of Bul Nuer community. He has never left his homestead throughout the three wars that have taken their toll on his community since 1955. Approaching his ninetieth birthday, married to over twenty Dinka women and over thirty Nuers, he loses a child, a grandchild or a relative on both sides of every battle. He mourns with the Nuer as well as with the Dinka simultaneously. Yet, he is not alone in this scenario.

Having survived the two wars, one in which I participated as a child soldier in the late 1990s, and the ongoing one in which I am on the receiving end as a peacemaker, I have good reason to change these dynamics but there is more to my story than that. I must bury my grandfather during peace, unlike my father, who passed on by the end of the war of independence.

My country, among others, was midwifed by the United States of America in 2011. Unfortunately, no one gives the US and the regional stakeholders any credit today. One refugee woman puts it this way in Uganda, "We do not mention in a lullaby a midwife that would cheer on while the baby is being cut into two by the co-wives in front of Solomon." The international community and regional players are doing just that!

Ultimately, the fight is ours. With or without the world beside us, peace, unity, and development must come to South Sudan through my generation. Yes, I have no side to throw a stone at, and more than that, I am not prepared to throw stones at anybody!

As a young person born in conflicts, raised in conflicts, still living in conflicts, and a victim of Africa's longest civil war, I am very interested in global peace. I don't want to see more people go through the brutality of war that I have experienced, and I need a world where people live in peace and harmony and with love. I would like to see a world where the number of refugees is reduced to less than one million. A world where we focus on handling climate change instead of idling by and waiting to handle the humanitarian crises resulting from wars that arise out of deprivation, hardship, and crimes against humanity. I was forced to be in a boarding school where guns were given to us as child soldiers at the tender age of seven years. This story and many others of children in wars and conflicts have inspired me to work for peace in this world. I was forced to be a child soldier, I have chosen to be a soldier of peace.

Cindy Corrie is the mother of human rights activist Rachel Corrie, who was killed March 16, 2003, in the Gaza Strip. Cindy has made innumerable visits to Israel, the West Bank, and Gaza, including as a co-leader of three Interfaith Peace-Builder delegations. She is President of the Rachel Corrie Foundation for Peace and Justice, and a co-recipient with her husband of a Human Rights Advocates of the Year Award from Seattle University's Human Rights Network and a Pillar of Peace Award from the Pacific Northwest Region of the American Friends Service Committee. In October 2012, they accepted the Lennon Ono Grant for Peace on behalf of their daughter.

Craig Corrie is the father of Rachel Corrie and a founding board member of the Rachel Corrie Foundation for Peace and Justice. He currently volunteers as Treasurer for RCF. He has given talks on peace and justice throughout North America and other parts of the world. He has accompanied Cindy in her travels to Israel/Palestine and had the honor and privilege to make many friends in the area. In previous lives, Craig was a life insurance actuary in an executive capacity with several insurance companies, and spent 1970 as a squad leader with the US army combat engineers in Vietnam.

They Are All Our Children
Cindy & Craig Corrie

Our daughter Rachel was born thirty-nine years ago. In the hour after her birth, her dad, Craig, held and talked to her. He told her she would be loved, that she would not be a rich child, but that she would have a rich life. He shared that while she might not like every aspect of our parenting (particularly when she became a teenager), she had a big brother and sister to love her, to show her the ropes, and to have her back when arguments inevitably should arise. Craig told baby Rachel, honestly, that life would not be perfect, but that it would be all right. She was our third child. We had some experience raising children. Craig welcomed our baby daughter into the world and told her we knew how to do this.

When in 2003, at twenty-three years, Rachel went to Gaza, she took all our family with her. Through her preparation, with books and articles she shared about Israel/Palestine, and most especially through her phone calls and emails home, she connected us to her journey and to the story and people of Gaza, and we learned. We read Rachel's reports about large-scale demolition of Palestinian homes by the Israeli military, about a 10-meter-high fence they were building between Rafah and the Egyptian border, and about "ceaseless shelling" from IDF tanks stationed along the outskirts of Rafah. We read about "the sense of invisibility" people in Rafah felt, and about the Palestinian children who had almost no contact with the outside world and had only seen Israelis inside bulldozers, tanks, and sniper towers.

In our many conversations since Rachel's death, with people throughout the United States and the world, Craig often shares a very simple expectation and truth. At the very least, we should be able to love each other's children, no matter where they live in the world, no matter their ethnicity or religion. He adds that they are *all* our children. It follows, then, that we must genuinely want for them, all that we have wanted for the children we, ourselves, have borne and nurtured.

With the support of an engaged and generous community of family, friends, teachers, and neighbors, Craig and I raised our kids to think and relate globally. This was before either they or we had the privilege of any significant travel. We raised them, too, to eschew violence, in all its forms, and to severely question proponents of violence in the name of "security," since far too often the results of violent actions, no matter how justified, are unbearably damaging to all involved.

The piece that follows is Craig's reaction to learning of the Israeli court decision in the case of seventeen-year-old Nadeem Nowarah, a Palestinian youth killed in 2014 by an Israel Border Police officer at a Nakba Day protest near Ofer Prison in the West Bank. It is a reminder that we must remain alert to the continuing injustices that threaten the safety and security of children everywhere and of all the oppressed in Palestine, but that also threaten the safety and security of young oppressors and all of us—injustices in which we are too often complicit. Craig regularly wears a Rachel Corrie bracelet and also one with Buddhist beads (a gift from a mother in South Korea). They are reminders that we need to stand strongly, consistently, and lovingly for peace with justice.

Since Rachel propelled us into action on Palestine, we have been privileged to travel and to meet people from throughout the world. It is incredibly heartening to find that wherever we go, and in sometimes unlikely places, there are those who share and strive for the same values we treasure, despite enormous differences in our histories, cultures, traditions, and opportunities. During the past year, we spent a week in Busan, South Korea, with young people who are studying and talking about Martin Luther King, Howard Zinn, and Rachel and who look forward to a future that includes their North Korean relatives. We joined a conference in Beirut where organizers from sixty-five countries shared their creative actions in support of Palestinian rights. In Istanbul, we met a young man who walked from Sweden to Turkey, educating about Palestine as he traveled, and a young Palestinian from Nablus whose resistance takes the form of climbing the world's highest mountains. We met a young Indonesian mother who assisted the injured on the Mavi Marmara (part of the 2010 flotilla that set out to break the blockade of Gaza) and the parents of Mohammed Abu Khdeir, the young East Jerusalem boy who was burned to death by Israeli settler youth. All of them are inspiring, and are inspired to seek creative paths to justice, peace, and ultimately security.

I am struck as I write, that the US Supreme Court just handed down a 5–4 judgement upholding the current administration's travel ban that, shamefully, opens the door for keeping *out* of the United States persons from countries like those where Craig and I have been warmly and generously welcomed. Are there dangers in embracing openness? Yes, of course, because ours is an imperfect and sometimes dangerous world. But we refuse for the borders of our lives to be dictated by fear, bias, and racism.

After Rachel was killed in 2003, Craig and I followed her to Gaza and met the friends she had made there. We were privileged to experience their hospitality and to witness their struggle. We wondered at their steadfast determination, under the most threatening circumstances, to forge for their children the same sort of future Craig had promised Rachel on her birth day.

There have been many trips since to all of Palestine—to Gaza, the West Bank, and Israel. On each of these, it is the promise we find in the ongoing, day-to-day work of many colleagues there that sustains our energy and confidence that there are solutions and that something better is possible. There are the committed Jewish Israelis who join Palestinian-led protests in West Bank villages against the pervasive occupation; the Palestinian and Jewish attorneys who at great odds continue to demand accountability from the Israeli court system; the legal and human rights organizations in Gaza, the West Bank, and Israel who year after year document, report, and challenge the injustice and oppression; the Women in Black in Haifa who stand every Friday; and the Palestinian families who stand proud, demanding and providing life for their children. All of these give us faith.

As we move into the winter of our earthly journey, we are taking time together to quietly explore our own country. That led us recently to eastern Oregon's Wallowa Valley to the land of the Nez Perce. The peaceful tribe welcomed the Lewis and Clark expedition in 1803 and the settlers who followed, but were pressured to leave their land for reservations, and were sometimes killed. Part of the tribe eventually fought back before surrendering near the Canadian border where their leader Chief Joseph said, "I am tired. My heart is sick and sad. From where the sun now stands, I will fight no more forever." We are guided by this man who in a later speech to officials in Washington, DC, pleaded for tribal members to be allowed to return to their homeland, and uttered these words: "The earth is the mother of all people, and all people should have equal rights upon it… I hope no more groans of wounded men and women will ever go to the ear of the Great Spirit Chief above, and that all people may be one people."

Cindy Corrie
June 27, 2018

Reflections on Nadeem Nowarah[1]

Outrage, but not surprise, is what I felt when I heard the news from the Israeli high court Wednesday. A sentence of nine months and 50,000 shekels (less than $14,000) for the killing of seventeen-year-old Nadeem Nowarah makes a mockery of any sense of justice.

I remember well sitting in Olympia with Nadeem's Palestinian father, Siam Nowarah, watching over and over again the video of his son being shot and killed by an Israel Border Police officer, Ben Deri. It is a sickening thing to watch. Not just the killing, but the necessity of Nadeem's father being forced to participate in the forensic display of his son's death in an attempt to create public outcry and an eventual trial of the officer that killed him. As I sat and watched, I could not bring myself to tell Siam what I was thinking: "You don't go to the top of the hill looking for water, and you don't go to the Israeli courts looking for justice."

I know also the almost guilty feeling of privilege that comes with knowing that your child's killing has received some notice, when that of so many Palestinian children does not. My daughter Rachel was an international. Siam's son Nadeem's killing was filmed by *CNN*. Both cases eventually forced internal Israeli investigations, but ones that started with Israeli government spokesmen giving ever-changing false accounts, and continued with examinations sloppy to the point of cover-up rather than mere incompetence.

In Rachel's case, no criminal charges were ever filed against anyone, and at the end of our civil case in Israel, the court found, not the IDF (Israel Defense Forces), but Rachel, responsible for her own death. For Nadeem, his killer was found guilty, but by a court that reportedly described the shooter, Ben Deri as "an excellent police officer who was conscientious about orders." The judge did allow, however, that his "degree of negligence was significant and calls for prison time."

Negligence? Look at the video of Deri steadying his rifle on the wall as he lines up the killing shot. Can such deliberation be negligence? Conscientious about orders? What orders, and who gave them? Certainly the order to kill an unarmed civilian is an illegal order, and I'm told that an Israel Border Police officer or IDF soldier's duty is—as it was for me in the US army—not to obey an illegal order. So if an order was given, why is the officer who gave it not also in the docket? What message does this court send to the snipers and their officers now shooting unarmed protesters along the barrier in Gaza?

And what about Ben Deri's sentence then? Let's compare it to the sentence originally handed down to three teenage Palestinian boys this month accused of throwing rocks at, and causing great damage to, the wall next to their West Bank village of Bil'in. You know Bil'in. You know the wall that separates the village from its own cropland; and you know Iyad Burnat, the father of one of the boys arrested. You know them all from the film *Five Broken Cameras*.

I've seen that wall. Ain't no stone gonna hurt that wall, much as I wish it would. The three boys were originally sentenced to two years in jail and fined 50,000 shekels apiece for the unproven accusations. The court also stipulated that if the fine was not paid by last Sunday (April 22, 2018), that the incarceration would be extended an additional four years.

The Israeli military courts, where this case was tried, may not be fair, but they are very efficient. They have a conviction rate of over 99 percent! The boys agreed to a plea bargain, reducing their fines to 18,000 shekels each, with time to gather the fine extended, and their jail terms cut to nineteen months. A reasonable bargain for these children, only if you consider the alternative.

So on the one hand, you have an Israeli soldier given a seven--month jail sentence and 50,000-shekel fine for deliberately killing an unarmed Palestinian boy, and on the other, you have three Palestinian boys forced to plea bargain to over one-and-a-half years in prison and 18,000 shekel fines each for allegedly throwing stones at an inanimate wall.

If you must choose one or the other, go to the top of the hill looking for water!

Craig Corrie
April 27, 2018
Washington, USA

Notes

1.   This article first appeared on May 4, 2018, on the Rachel Corrie Foundation blog. https://rachelcorriefoundation.org/blog.

John Freeman is an American writer, poet, and literary critic. He was the editor of Granta, *and the former president of the National Book Critics Circle. His writing has appeared internationally including in the* New York Times, *the* UK Guardian *and the* Guardian, *and translated into twenty-two languages. His books include* The Tyranny of Email, How to Read a Novelist, Tales of Two Cities, Tales of Two Americas: Stories of Inequality in a Divided Nation, *and* Maps, *his debut collection of poems. He is editor of the eponymous literary journal,* Freeman's, *and the executive editor at Literary Hub. He teaches at the New School and New York University.*

"Visitors"
John Freeman

"Visitors" are so often seen as threats to our safety, I wanted to look at it a different way. Each year I spend about two months in Paris, teaching and living just below the Luxembourg Gardens. I stay on a small cobblestone street where William Faulkner lived for a year, paying the equivalent of one euro a week for room and board. He used to write in the gardens, sitting up with a typewriter in his lap. I often wonder what he would make of the park today, tidier than ever, but also a temporary home each day, for a few hours, if that, of the poor and of refugees, whom I've seen sitting on benches or in shadows or under trees. You don't have to look hard to see them. In the last few years, as terrorism attacks multiplied in Paris and Macron was elected, the police have become ever more aggressive at moving them along wherever they turn up in Paris, people whose lives have been smashed by the brutal civil war in Syria. There have even been reports of law enforcement chasing these refugees into the Alps, men in flip-flops and shorts, families. Paris parks are living monuments to their principles, open to all for an astonishingly long time; even English travelers marveled in the eighteenth century at how the public could take their leisure in such stately gardens. And yet today every time I enter a park in Paris, or anywhere for that matter, I cannot help but think about those who are kept out, in the name of security, based upon their nation-states of origin. So I wrote this poem. It is part of a book around these issues called *The Park*.

Visitors

I've counted
six sides
up Vauigard, across Guynemer
a short bit on D'Assas,
the long stretch up
Rue de Auguste Comte
then over Blvd Saint Michel
down the hill of rue
de Medicis past
Cafe Bonaparte
and the Senat
where the guards stand
with self-conscious weaponry.
One side features
blown up photographs
of polar bears on ice,
like all animals captured
in the moment
of being animals,
bewildered
annoyed
saddened, one might think
by our need to record
what is obvious:
they're at home.
What our looking
has done to them—
they are elegies
to themselves.

In the park
this violet hour,
dawn, walkers
runners,
in the shadows
of trees men with backpacks and
darting eyes look out
sideways
with a similar glance,
don't want
to be seen,
need to be
seen, so we
feel ourselves feeling
their predicament,
two hours here,
while the shadows
remain, then
they'll move on.
On the other side of Paris
an exhibit
depicts them
home
which is nowhere.
By nine, the
Norwegian walking club gathers with
smart cross-country polls and
bulging retirement portfolios,
they'll be gone
across the city
no exhibit,
a man or two,
dirty enough
to creates the kinds of shadows that
make it easy not to see him.

 *Aye Sandar Chit, who is in her late thirties, is a Burmese Muslim woman born and living in Yangon (also known as Rangoon), Myanmar's cultural and commercial hub. With a master's degree in English, she runs a small language school for Myanmar children and is also one of the co-founders of a Muslim women's group that aims to empower Muslim women to participate in Myanmar's nation-building and increase understanding across ethnic and religious groups. She is involved in different initiatives for conflict management and interfaith peace-building with both Muslim and non-Muslim groups in Yangon.*

Speaking with a United Voice
Interview with Aye Sandar Chit

What does shared security mean to you?

If I reflect on my life and what I'm seeing, the condition of Myanmar Muslims is getting very difficult. In the past there was discrimination—in job opportunities with government for instance—but it was not that prominent and we didn't feel quite so insecure. In the last ten years, propaganda and hate speech is getting very obvious and the impact is huge on every Muslim. It's difficult to be proud to say that I'm a Muslim in Myanmar because there are some people—not all—that feel that Muslims don't belong to this country. This puts us in a very difficult situation because Myanmar is our country and we love Myanmar but are told "you don't belong here." The discrimination is growing in many areas—politics, education, job opportunities, religious rights, ethnic rights, business practices, and social life. Some of the discrimination is because of rules and regulations but not all of it. And the degree differs according to the place. What's happening in Rakhine is different to Rangoon but there are still a lot of limitations here. We fear that [the violence] which happened in Rakhine might happen in the central and main cities. We also believe that these things are happening mostly for political reasons and that there are many citizens who are not Muslim but they do not hate Muslims. They understand the situations and stand with us. Of course, there are also people who misunderstand Muslims. I have heard so many stories about "you Muslims are like this or like that." They get the wrong messages, and they are worried about us or begin to hate Muslims. But, not everything they've heard is right.

So when I think about shared security, I think of shared responsibility. Security is normally meant for the government, but I understand that it is the responsibility of citizens too to create security in their community. I remember what happened in 2012, there were tensions in Rangoon due to the riots in Rakhine. People here were feeling insecure. Then, the men in our community said, "We have to protect our streets." They felt it was their duty to protect their homes, so they patrolled. No one gave them that duty, they just did it themselves. The interesting thing is that security groups included Muslims as well as Buddhists. It's not only physical security though, security in heart is also important. Although nothing might happen to our houses, we may still feel insecure. In my case, because I wear my headscarf, I sometimes feel afraid to be on the bus alone late at night in case people attack me—I think this kind of insecurity is experienced by many other people as well. This is one of the main reasons I want to work together with people from different religions and beliefs. I can learn how they feel, what their worries and concerns might be, and I can share the concerns of my community. When we get to know each other well and understand each of our concerns, then we can work together to reduce the insecurities between our communities.

How did you first begin thinking of a way to engage with the issues you cared about?

What I care about most are peace and educational development. I began working as a teacher and came to know that the educational standards of our children were quite low. Then I realized that this was because of the systems and policies in place. And, I also realized that we cannot have better education without peace. What is disturbing our development and creating poverty in our country? We have so many conflicts, tensions and riots—so if I don't work for peace then we won't ever have educational development in our country. This was my journey to becoming a peace-builder.

What gives you the courage to do this work?

The condition of our country. I love Myanmar but when I was in other countries and studied their development I felt like "Why can't our people enjoy this—why should our children suffer?" This encourages me to work for the country. I'm not interested in only working for the Muslim community—in my eyes everyone is a human. I'm from Myanmar: I want to see development in our country for all people and I want to see all the people secure and prosperous and happy. These things inspire me.

Who walks beside you?
There are many people… to name one is difficult. I have a friend, he is a Buddhist and he leads a CSO. Although he is a Buddhist what he does and what he speaks about are never meant only for the Buddhist or Burmese community. He is quite fair and speaks the truth… If a minority is right he stands on their side and for justice, he even gets attacked by his own people. His example walks with me.

What is your biggest, wildest dream for your community? For the world?
What I want to see is real peace and justice in Myanmar. I don't want equality but I want equity. I want to see a community in every part of Myanmar where people are not discriminated against because of their race or religion or sex. We'll have a community where people share love, where different minorities and the majority will work together for peace, development, and justice and fight together against bad people through peaceful resistance. I want to see our country celebrate the beauty of its diversity, enjoy different cultures and not see diversity as a weakness but as a strength. The same idea applies to the world. We all are human. And, by sharing and caring for each other, we can build a better world.

 *Andrés Álvarez Castañeda is Dean of the School of Social Sciences at Universidad del Valle de Guatemala. An Anthropologist and Sociologist, he has won scholarships from Fulbright, Chevening, the Organization of American States (OAS), the German Academic Exchange Service, the US State Department, and the Swedish International Development Agency (SIDA). One of the youngest Heads of Department and Deans in the History of the Universidad del Valle de Guatemala, he has more than sixteen years of experience in academic, governmental, and non-governmental environments. His research interests include early warning of conflict, social and political conflict prevention, security sector reform, human security, and peace education.*

The Fable of the Three Brothers
Andrés Álvarez Castañeda

I. Introduction

Guatemala endured a gruesome civil war through the second part
of the twentieth century. In 1985, a new constitution was approved
and elections were held, giving way to the Cerezo Presidency, the
first legitimate and democratic one since the US-led intervention in
the country in 1954. A decade later, comprehensive peace accords
were finally signed between the government and left-wing guerrilla
groups. The country was left deeply scarred after so many years of
dictatorships and violence. At least 200,000 dead, most of them
indigenous non-combatants, a broken economy, international isolation, and a very weak and fragmented civil society were some of the
most obvious consequences of this conflict.

From 1996 to date, Guatemala has undergone several processes
that academic literature usually refers to as disarmament, demobilization, and reintegration, truth commissions and the promotion of
historical memory, and Security Sector Reform (SSR). Of these, this
last one has been the most complicated, and the one with which I
have been most involved.

In this essay I wish to establish some of the critical issues in
reimagining security in a post-war country. In order to do this, I will
use a song by Cuban songwriter Silvio Rodríguez, "Fable of the Three
Brothers." I will first give a little background on my work in SSR in
Guatemala, I will then explain the story of each of the brothers in the
fable, and I will finally propose a way out of this situation.

2. My Background in SSR

I first got involved in Security Issues in Guatemala in 2001, when I was hired as an analyst in the Strategic Analysis Secretariat. The institution was a relatively new one, and until very recently it had been in the hands of the military. Secretary Édgar Gutiérrez Girón, appointed by President Alfonso Portillo, began a sweeping reform process that included researching, analyzing, and making public the old military-intelligence databases, hiring new staff with academic (non-military) backgrounds, and establishing new protocols for intelligence work within a democratic framework.

For three years I had the privilege of serving alongside a young, vibrant team of political scientists, psychologists, sociologists, economists, journalists, and experts in agriculture, conflict resolution, and foreign affairs. This is also when I began studying conflict resolution with Fundación Propaz, through an Organization of American States Scholarship. During these years I got to know closely the institutional framework of security in Guatemala.

I later took a two-year sabbatical away from work, to study for an MSc in Social Sciences, with emphasis in Political Sociology in the Facultad Latinoamericana de Ciencias Sociales (FLACSO). My research topic, inevitably, had to do with the social construction of the idea of security in the rural areas of the country.

I eventually returned to Security Sector Reform (SSR), mainly through the National Security Advisory Council. A product of the Peace Accords, the Council is comprised of members of civil society, the private sector, and academia, and its main objective is to advise the President in security policy. During the nine months I worked there, our main objective was to establish a National Security System, with clearly defined functions for each institution, but also—and this proved harder to implement—communication mechanisms between institutions in order to truly shape a viable system.

I went on to study conflict resolution at the University of Bradford, the final step toward truly understanding the profound human nature of the phenomenon of in/security. It was also an opportunity to analyze different topics such as Conflict Transformation, SSR, and Prevention from a global perspective. My time at Bradford went by quickly, but it was one of the most enriching experiences in my lifetime.

Upon returning to Guatemala in 2006, I got involved in what I believe has been the country's best effort in reforming security toward a more human paradigm. Under the vice-presidency of Eduardo Stein, a national system for conflict prevention was established. Led by Carmen Ortiz, a renowned political analyst, the system was in charge of preventing violent social conflict. The challenge was huge, since we had to design the system from scratch. It is important to emphasize the wide success of the system because of its inclusive, human-security-centered approach. The main idea of the project was to gather timely information from local governments and leaders, as well as NGOs working on the field. This information was then processed using conflict analysis tools and decisions were made as to where, when, and how the government should intervene. Political problems soon ensued when other security bureaucracies saw their influence diminished. This system effectively reduced violence, prevented future conflicts and, in the end, saved lives.[1] From 2007 to date my experience in SSR has been less intense, given my administrative posts at Universidad del Valle de Guatemala (UVG), although I stay passionate about the topic. During these recent years I have participated as a consultant for UNDP, attended two prestigious training workshops (the Top Level Seminar on Peace and Security, Uppsala University, and the ICAR course at George Mason University), promoted research on these topics from UVG, and sat on the board that selects the candidates for the Rotary Peace Scholarships.

3. The fable of the three brothers

Silvio Rodríguez Domínguez, the famous Cuban singer, wrote "The Fable of the Three Brothers." It is included in his 1980 LP *Rabo de Nube.* It tells the tale of exploring, pioneering brothers, each one with a specific outlook on how to find his way. As a former practitioner, and now an academic involved with security issues, I believe we can better understand the challenges to SSR through this song. Through these years I have encountered many representatives of each of the three brothers. Most of them are well intentioned, passionate civil servants, activists, and academics.

a. The First Brother

"Of three brothers, the eldest left to conquer, so he would never make a mistake, he was wide awake, observing his path. After walking in this position for a long time, his neck got stuck watching the ground, and he became a slave of his own precaution, growing old with his short-vision."

The first brother represents the proponents of a "hard line" in security in Guatemala. They believe that the police should be trained, equipped, and given legal liberties to suppress the various security threats in the country, but especially youth gangs, drug cartels, and common crime. From their worldview, youth problems have more to do with a particular crisis and with values than with broader, structural issues. Some of them were trained with a counterinsurgency mentality and are stuck in the years of the Civil War. They are constantly frustrated with human security policies, since these are seen as "utopian" and "unrealistic." Social conflict is always viewed as manipulated by "invisible" political entities (international socialism, for example). Some of the proponents of this view are well embedded within the State Security System. Others work as spoilers, be it as lobbyists or as opinion makers. It would be harsh and irresponsible to consider all of them as members of organized criminal groups, though some have been known to have these connections.

b. The Second Brother

"Of three brothers, the middle one left to conquer, so he would never make a mistake, he was wide awake, observing the horizon. But this smart boy couldn't see the rocks and holes that would eventually surrender his feet. And he spent most of the time in the ground. And he grew old, wanting to go far, but always falling near."

The second brother represents the proponents of the human security paradigm. They are fixed in a long-term view of the world. Many of them are social scientists and got involved in security matters through activism. With time, they have learned the more technical aspects of security. In general, they prefer to work within the framework of preventive policies and steer clear of criminal investigation and crime-fighting issues. The main term used by this group is "prevention," but it is used in very broad terms. Only recently have there been some efforts emphasizing monitoring and evaluation that will eventually yield data in order to determine what constitutes "good" prevention practices. For this group, youth is to be protected from structural violence, but they have failed to implement viable solutions to gangs and other ever-growing problems. They are good at talking the talk, but have fallen short of walking the walk, in regard to reducing homicide and crime rates (much of the violence in Guatemala is perpetrated by young people against young people).

c. The Third Brother

> "Of three brothers, the youngest one left to conquer, so he would never make a mistake, he had one eye on the horizon, and one on his road. And he explored farther than his brothers, with an eye on today, and an eye on what will come. But when time came for him to rest, his gaze was lost between being and going."

Although the third brother also lost his way in Rodríguez's song, eventually losing his mind, I believe that a variant of this brother is what we should aspire to be within the Security Sector in Guatemala. We need to work simultaneously in the short and the long term, in preventive and reactive strategies. The gap between short and long-term world views has been mentioned before by other authors. Specifically, in Guatemala, Héctor Rosada has been very vocal about this topic.[2]

What we are lacking is a concrete, prioritized list of tasks and policies to start implementing simultaneous and complementary short-term and long-term actions. And all of this without going crazy, as in Silvio's song. At the risk of sounding too arrogant, I will allow myself the theoretical exercise of proposing the following prioritized agenda:

Short Term, Reactive	Long Term, Preventive
1. Invest in criminal investigation techniques including forensics, urban tactics, and criminal intelligence (civilian controlled).	1. Emphasize monitoring and evaluation in all crime, violence, and conflict prevention projects, in order to construct a robust database. This will in turn allow us to:
2. Continue with the good work of fighting against impunity.	
3. Work in local security plans that will allow neighbors to internalize community problems and become a part of the solution.	2. Define future policy from an evidence-based perspective.
	3. Implement peace education in the K–12 curriculum. This requires thinking beyond the traditional National Security System, to include the Ministries of Education and Social Development. From this base, special attention should be placed on:
4. Implement laws, regulations, and policies aimed at creating a stable career path for civil servants in general, but especially in security institutions.	
5. Establish stricter controls on guns and on private security companies	
6. Acknowledge that other forms of violence, such as gender violence and child labor exploitation are part of a larger mechanism of structural violence, that can and will eventually feed homicide and crime rates.	4. Creating after-school programs for marginalized youth. Sports, Arts, and other forms of expression can greatly ease the angst they feel, and reduce the temptation of getting involved in gang activities.
	5. Work on a culture of peace, from a multi-institutional perspective, involving ministries, the private sector, and academia.
7. Approach drug policy from a more integral perspective, including the public health dimensions of drug use and the creation of viable alternative economies for those currently involved in the drug business.	6. Implement a comprehensive policy for reconciliation. To date, the main findings of the truth commissions are still questioned by the extreme right, who have a very powerful propaganda machine that continues polarizing society.

4. Conclusion: How can we be the third brother without going mad?

The fable in Silvio's song indicates that if we try to concentrate on both things, the immediate and the long-view, we will eventually go mad. A solution would be for the third brother to facilitate the work of the other two. He could do this by communicating good practices between the operatives working on short-term results and the policy makers thinking about the long term. He could them meet in common places and view each other as integral pieces of a larger system. This is the only way forward in my opinion in order to build a safer, more human, and inclusive country for everyone.

Notes

1. Andrés Álvarez Castañeda, "Conflict Early Warning Systems: The Guatemalan Experience." Conflict Resolution Institute Working Paper #7. Josef Korbel School of International Studies, University of Denver, 2012.

2. Héctor Rosada Granados, "Guatemala, 1996-2010. Hacia un Sistema Nacional de Seguridad y Justicia." *Cuadernos de Desarrollo Humano*, 2010. PNUD Guatemala.

Li Yingtao is a professor and doctoral supervisor in the school of International Relations and Diplomacy, BFSU, and deputy executive director of the Center of Gender and Global Studies, BFSU, and has been engaged in research on the history of international relations, non-traditional security, the UN, gender and international relations, and feminism peace studies. Major works include International Politics from a Gender Perspective, Feminism Peace Studies, Feminism International Relations, Global Environmental Issues from a Gender Perspective, *and so on, and she mainly teaches history of international relations, art of negotiating study, feminism, and international relations. Major awards include "Beijing Outstanding Teacher Award," and "March 8th Red Banner Badge." She is also the lecturer of an excellent open video course evaluated by the Minister of Education, "The Art of Negotiating."*

Understanding Shared Security from a Gender Perspective in the Chinese Context
Interview with Li Yingtao

What does shared security mean to you, as a global citizen, as a practitioner, as a world leader, as an activist, or as an advocate?

As a scholar of gender and international politics, and an advocate for gender equality, I focus my attention on the security of women and girls. Back in 2003, I published a book in Chinese titled *International Politics from a Gender Perspective*,[1] in which I reviewed the issues that women face in terms of security. In this book, I noted that "security cannot only include traditional concepts of military and political security, but must include security of employment conditions, and security from war, all forms of violence, and economic or environmental threats. At the same time, state security cannot be constructed on a foundation of the oppression and exploitation of women." In an article I published later, "The Security of the Little Mermaid,"[2] I proposed the concept of "women's human security" in a plea to international political researchers and practitioners to place more emphasis on the interests of vulnerable groups, including women and children, and to listen more closely to their voices, so that they are no longer voiceless or invisible like mermaids.

In Chinese academic circles, the concept of "Gongxiang Anquan" or "shared security" was first proposed in 2014 by Zhejiang University Professor Yu Xiaofeng in an article titled, "Shared Security: A New Type of Non-Traditional Security."[3] He emphasized in his writing the non-traditional aspects of security, proposing a security concept centered on the value of human life, which is principled on a peace shared by all of humanity, and which is realized through the practice of mutual trust and cooperation toward the achievement of win-win ideals as an objective. The essential value of non-traditional security then is "shared security." In Wei Zhijiang's view, a theory of "shared security" might be constructed through a positive discourse around the creation of a theory and narrative of international security with Chinese characteristics. Wei argues that the concept of "shared security" has deep roots within ancient Chinese philosophy, drawing on the Book of Changes, which speaks of the "maintenance of the supreme harmony," and the philosophy that "All nations live side by side in perfect harmony." It is a form of security that is collectively established, maintained, and shared.[4]

From a perspective of gender equality, I believe that "shared security" represents a security that transcends national boundaries, and which encompasses global security, national security, community security, and individual security. It is a view of security that transcends the distinction made between traditional and non-traditional security, and a state in which all men and women can be safe and secure at all levels. Far more than the passive notion of "no internal fear, no external threats," it is a security which promotes the equality and development of all people, and which can be enjoyed by all; it is a positive form of security, which grants power and rights to all vulnerable peoples.

How did you first begin thinking of a way to engage with the issues you cared about?

I was first awakened to feminism by my mother, with my academic interest in the field of gender and international politics being sparked by my participation in the Fourth UN World Conference on Women.

From my early childhood days, my mother would often complain that she did not want a daughter, not because she harbored any prejudice against women, but because she felt that the world simply was not fair to women, and that women's lives are too miserable and too difficult. But for me, growing up in so-called different times, with a narrative of "men and women are equal," I never reflected very deeply on my mother's comments or on the realities of life for the women of her generation.

In August and September of 1995, I had the good fortune of being able to participate in the NGO Forum of the Fourth UN World Conference on Women, which was hosted in Huairou, Beijing. The Forum helped open my awareness of the importance of equality, development, and peace for women globally, and made me acutely aware of the gap in my own knowledge when it comes to gender equality and women's empowerment. It was at this conference that I determined to pursue a PhD, and study feminism in international relations from the vantage point of Chinese history and the Chinese national context.

On the basis of my PhD dissertation, I published my first book in 2003, *International Politics from a Gender Perspective,* which also happened to be the first full volume in Chinese on feminism in international politics. I later published a book titled *Feminist Peace Studies,* an edited volume *Feminist International Relations,* and two more books titled *Global Environmental Issues and the Sociology of Gender,* and *The Sustainable Development on Gender Equality.* I am proud to say that my experience in the Fourth World Conference on Women is recorded in these books and articles.

What gives you the courage to do this work?

It is my mother and my co-workers who give me the courage to work as a researcher of gender and international politics and an advocate for gender equality.

In 2002, my mother came to Beijing to help me look after my newborn child. She knew that I had participated in the Fourth World Conference on Women, and that I was engrossed in research on women's issues, and she would occasionally discuss with me the status of women in China. At that time, my PhD dissertation had already been accepted for publication by an international politics series put out by the Shanghai People's Press, and I needed to revise it based on expert opinions, so I went right back to work after giving birth. My mother was terrified of me doing this, as in China, the month after giving birth, a woman is to "Zuo Yuezi" or be confined for a month for recuperation. Failure to go through this recuperation period is said to result in the onset of postnatal disease. To prevent this, she took close care of me throughout, but also emphasized that she wanted to be supportive of my dreams so I could publish my dissertation as soon as possible. I was touched by the way that my mother supported me, and took this as a source of motivation.

Through my work, I have interacted with many talented, gender-aware, and courageous scholars, practitioners, and advocates. These include scholars from other countries, representatives of international organizations, officials from within the Chinese government, members of the All-China Women's Federation, and grassroots organizers. In particular, I have tremendous respect for Professor Cynthia Enloe, Ms. Zhang Youyun, Professor Li Xiaojiang, Professor Du Fangqin, Professor Liu Bohong, Professor Wei Guoying, Editor-Professor Tan Xiuying, and Professor Feng Yuan. Their efforts have given me the courage to move forward.

Who walks beside you?

In terms of my current work, I collaborate with a very diverse group of people. First, in 2018, I was honored to be invited to join the editorial team of the International Feminist Journal of Politics as an associate editor, and to begin working with one of the pioneers of the field of feminist international relations theory, Cynthia Enloe, and other international scholars. As the only member of the editorial team from mainland China, I feel both proud, but also a particular responsibility.

Second, as a scholar of gender studies, I collaborate regularly with China's largest women's organization, the All-China Women's Federation, including the Beijing branch of the Federation. Third, I work closely with other scholars of women's studies in China. I worked with editor Professor Tan Xiuying, who is one of the founding editors of *International Security Studies*, to initiate a biennial Forum for Chinese Women Scholars of International Relations. At the same time, I am also attracted to grassroots organizing, and work closely with community organizations, which enable me to feel the power of unity.

What is your biggest, wildest dream for your community? for the world?

As I mentioned already, my first interaction with the World Conference on Women was in 1995. At the time, I was deeply impressed by the theme of the conference, "Equality, Development, and Peace" and its core principle: empowering women, because "the rights of women are human rights." Later, I saw this start to come to fruition at the international level with the passage of UN Security Council Resolution 1325 on Women, Peace and Security. In the millennium development goals passed by the UN in the year 2000 and the 2030 sustainable development goals passed in 2015, achieving gender equality and empowering women and girls are both identified as core objectives. The process of realizing gender equality and empowering women and girls is really the process of the world progressing toward equality, development, and peace—or stated in other words, the process of every person obtaining "shared security." This is both my dream for China, and my dream for the world.

Notes

1. Li Yingtao, *International Politics Under a Gender Perspective* (Shanghai: Shanghai People's Press, 2003), 210.

2. Yingtao, "The Security of the Little Mermaid," *World Economics and Politics* 2 (2004): 19.

3. Yu Xiaofeng, "Shared Security: A New Type of Non-Traditional Security," *Journal of the Humanities and Social Sciences of Zhejiang University* 2 (2014): 199.

4. Wei Zhijiang, "The Roots of 'Shared Security' in Non-Traditional Security Research," *International Security Studies* 3 (2015): 52–67.

 *Khine Thurein, in his early thirties, is an ethnic Rakhine civil society activist from the Rakhine state in western Myanmar. He has been a student, a political leader, taught English to relief workers in disaster-hit areas, worked with political parties ahead of the historic 2015 national elections, mapped changing dynamics in the CSO community in Rakhine, and he remains committed to working to overcome the many challenges Myanmar faces.*

The Strength of Shared Work
Interview with Khine Thurein

What does shared security mean to you?

When I hear about shared security, I think we are living in this world and sharing its resources—the material, natural, and knowledge. It's a human morality. We have collective and individual rights. Collectively as a group—ethnic or national—we have the right to protect and maintain ourselves but at the same time we are responsible for the security and wellbeing of others.

When I discuss the issue of the Rohingya within Rakhine society,[1] there are so many differences between people over how to see this problem and solve this issue—now it's also becoming a global issue. I believe no one is happy with the conflict but when we consider how to solve this problem everyone just talks about identity and land rights. The way people in the communities—Muslim or Rakhine—see things from different perspectives triggers many more problems. The conflict is getting bigger and larger day by day. We need a new strategy and approach not only from the military and National League for Democracy but also from the local and international communities.

[As for Rohingya returning to Rakhine from refugee camps in Bangladesh] I have no idea about when they will return. But it's not just about returning—it should have a systematic process in line with international standards and existing laws; at the same time, we would need to have proper housing and healthcare and livelihoods for them. But throughout history in Myanmar, the government and military treated us differently in Rakhine. Rakhine is like a separate place rather than a part of the whole Union [of Myanmar]. If there is a law, it should be extended equally to the whole country, but the law is different from state to state. For example, if you have the NRC (National Identity Card) then you should have the right to travel, but often people are not allowed to travel because they are Muslim. This is not the right way—there should be freedom of movement for all citizens. I worry that when they [the Rohingya] return, nobody will be able to guarantee their wellbeing, and the security of other peoples, including Hindus. Who can guarantee that bloody conflict will not happen again? The authorities are responsible and must take accountability for everyone's security and wellbeing.

One of the critical points in this conflict is about the naming; "Rohingya" is how many of that group self-identify, but is a highly contested term in Myanmar, with the government using the term "Bengali" to imply that the group is not indigenous to Myanmar but rather illegal immigrants from Bangladesh. When someone asks me if I accept the name I cannot say yes or no. If I say yes, that will be against the Rakhine community's values and concepts. At the same time, it seems to me that the term Rohingya is a new name. That's why I don't really get into arguments about this naming game. At this stage, rather than supporting each other, attempts to resolve the conflict stop at naming and arguments about history—"Which name is right?" "Who are Rohingya?" "There are no Rohingya!" "There have been Rohingya in Rakhine for 500 years!" All different narratives. I think the government and military—also some of the Muslim and Rakhine political and religious leaders—are responsible for the way we see each other. So, we need to see differently than we do at the moment. If we see each other as rivals or enemies then we can fight until the end of the world but never solve this conflict. I think both communities (Rakhine and Rohingya) would be better off if we worked together—we have to find a way to understand each other and this is what I understand by shared security.

How did you first begin thinking of a way to engage with the issues you cared about?

I was born in a poor village in Rakhine state and in our society we always felt that we were neglected by the rest of the Union—in every sector like education, security, employment, infrastructure we are very poor so our natural instinct compels us to fight for our people and the development of our community. I think this is a common value that we all share in poor and isolated corners of the world. When I was sixteen or seventeen, after I finished high school, I got involved in underground work with some friends, producing and distributing political pamphlets. During the 2007 Saffron Revolution (where Buddhist priests were at the helm of many demonstrations), we helped the monks to organize meetings. At this time there were no active political parties in Rakhine but when I came to Rangoon I met many old great politicians—including many leading members of the Arakan League for Democracy, the National League for Democracy, and the Shan Nationalities League for Democracy—and I had the opportunities to meet many of the senior politicians and listen to them. I believe in politics and I always wanted to be a politician when I was at university, but later I realized I wouldn't be a good politician because rather than focus on power I was interested in knowledge, in academics!

What gives you the courage to do this work?

I have many good friends, so when we conduct any activity we hardly do things alone—I work with other community members and friends… contributing as part of the community team. My friends and my community give me the strength and courage to get involved in social and political works.

Who walks beside you?

I have many politicians I admire, from Daw Aung San Su Kyi to Arakan politicians. I admire U Aye Thar Aung, the current deputy speaker of the parliament, and have listened for a long time to his ideas about federalism in Myanmar. I respect many of the 88 Generation. I also regard U Win Tin as a great politician, activist, and journalist—he spent nearly twenty years in prison, sacrificing a lot of his life before his death. In Rakhine state I respect the Arakan Army (an ethnic Rakhine armed group fighting with the Myanmar military) because Arakan (the name for Rakhine in its native language) is a very old kingdom and was independent for many, many centuries… the Arakan kingdom collapsed in 1785, about the same time America gained its independence! Many Arakanese dream that Arakan will again be an autonomous state one day—like a real federal state in the Union. The Arakan Army are giving hope to the Rakhine people who feel very hopeless—they carry the lost dream of Arakan and are the only institution in Rakhine now with a vision for the future and ready to take risks to make peace and development in Rakhine state.

What is your biggest, wildest dream for your community? for the world?

Since I was young, I have two words in my mind: "peace" and "green"… I love the name Greenpeace! I want my state, Arakan, to be the land of peace, and to stop the civil war in Myanmar. I want to see the world as a green environment and living in peace. Peace is not only for ourselves but for all humanity, without being manipulated against each other. We see that there is a lot of political manipulation in our country, so I really want everyone free from this manipulation. People should have access to their basic rights, and education and benefits should not only be reserved for powerful people.

Notes

1. Rakhine state was made internationally infamous in late 2017 and early 2018 due to the Myanmar military's "clearance operations," which violently displaced around 700,000 Rohingya people who fled into neighboring Bangladesh.

Thevuni Kotigala is a member of the Advisory Group of Experts for the Progress Study on Youth, Peace and Security, mandated by the UNSCR 2250. She is a researcher, peace-builder, and a trainer in youth empowerment, peace-building, and active citizenship. Thevuni is the Co-founder and Director of Open House, which is a human-centric organization that was founded with the ultimate objective of serving grassroots-level communities particularly targeting young men and women. Over the past years, she has worked with young people directing all her work toward creating resilient and peaceful communities.

The Art of Listening:
Parallel but Unequal Lives
Thevuni Kotigala

I was born into war and I've lived my life in a country ravaged by fear, pain, and bloodshed. A decade after the war ended, I'm still waiting to experience the true peace that comes not only from the absence of war, but from the presence of trust and a shared vision for our country.

I struggle...

As a Sinhalese Buddhist, I belong to the ethnic and religious majority and that comes with a sense of extreme privilege. I have access to spaces, opportunities, and a feeling of belonging that translates into a sense of freedom. Yet on a daily basis I see people who don't share my identity and suffer discrimination—whether perceived or real—or move with less comfort in the same social spheres we both have to occupy.

We all have our inner struggles: we struggle for fairness, for justice, for the right to live our lives fully. But I feel that the struggle of those who are discriminated against is much greater, because often not even their existence is acknowledged as a result of being considered the "other." There are many social hierarchies and structures that focus on "differences," which divides us deeply to the core, and sometimes these differences are elevated above our much more accessible and prevalent commonalities; particularly that of being human. Thus, we are asked, or forced, or choose to continue to live our lives within a framework that emphasizes an "us" against a "them."

Working with different communities, I've had many moments where I've sat down to listen to someone's story and shared their grievances and sorrow because I know the importance of listening. I remember the day that I understood this. I was nineteen years old and was listening to a friend recount the life he was forced to live, as opposed to one he might have chosen to live. A young teenage boy belonging to the Tamil minority, he recollected what it felt like to flee gunfire during the peak of the war in Sri Lanka. He had been running with his younger brother beside him, trying to escape both gunfire from the Sri Lankan armed forces and the LTTE. He told me how at one point he panicked and felt heavy and unable to move while trying to drag his little brother along. In that moment, a bullet struck his brother, piercing his skull, making that the last memory he would have of his sibling. At that juncture between life and death, he was forced to choose. He chose to take one last look at his little brother and leave the breathless body in the middle of the war fields while he kept going, running desperately to save his own life. Those few seconds have haunted him, making him die inside again and again, though on the surface he is a living human being. From that day on I always tried to look beneath what people presented, to try to reach their inner hurt as well as their hopes.

Instead of noting our differences, *if we try* we could see each other in terms of the lives that we've lived. We would realize that our origins, aspirations, and struggles are more familiar to each other than we might have imagined. Within that realization, we would understand that no one person's grief is superior or inferior to another's—it's a painful feeling that we all struggle to bear. We all feel hurt the same way. But human nature is such that we overcome our painful grief and move on, *hoping* that tomorrow will be better. This "hope" carries us through and beyond all our suffering. Hope is the key factor that helps us to facilitate resilience at all levels—as individuals and communities who try to overcome our worldly struggles.

I hope…

Hope is what fuels me.

We live in a world where our issues are so complex and intertwined that we cannot solve them overnight. All my efforts are directed toward reaching into people's hearts, believing that their goodness will multiply someday—changing one young person at a time, hoping that my work will someday be carried on by others. I'm hopeful that the younger generation will finally understand their potential for greatness and progress and become the sculptors of a better tomorrow. Change is inevitable; it is the only constant that we can count on. I believe we need to direct our energy to make sure that this *change that is going to happen* will benefit humanity.

This is my belief.

Waging Peace: North Korea
Excerpt from *Beyond the White House*
Jimmy Carter

The Carter Center involvement in North Korea was perhaps the most controversial and important of all its efforts. For almost four years, beginning in 1990, Kim Il Sung, the dictatorial communist leader of the Democratic People's Republic of Korea (DPRK), had requested that I find some way to visit Pyongyang. His contacts with me were usually his nation's representatives to the United Nations, and the US government imposed a twenty-five-mile limit on their travel. Usually they made arrangements to meet me on my visits to New York, and on two occasions they managed to gain approval to come to Georgia. Increasingly, their messages were focused on the growing crisis caused by the prospect of the DPRK's reprocessing of nuclear fuel rods removed from their antiquated power reactor, which used carbon as a moderator.

They knew of my background in nuclear reactor design from my Navy days and claimed that they wanted to avoid any confrontation with the United States and other concerned nations. The basic problem was that our country had outlawed all direct communications with the leaders of North Korea. President Bill Clinton was responding to this challenge by seeking UN Security Council approval of economic sanctions even more restrictive than those that had been in effect since the Korean War. With a vote in the United Nations pending, my concern was increased by some Chinese visitors who told me the result might very well be another war on the Korean peninsula. They said that the sanctions would be interpreted as an international condemnation of the North Korean government and a personal insult to North Korea's revered (almost worshipped) leader, and that the only response from the isolated and paranoid people would be to launch a massive attack on South Korea.

On June 1, 1994, I called President Clinton to express my concerns, and he said that he was leaving for Europe in a few hours but would send a senior official to Plains to brief me. Two days later I was informed that a junior member of the White House staff would give the briefing, but it would have to be postponed for a few days. I expressed my displeasure to the president's chief of staff, who promised me an immediate briefing from Ambassador Robert Gallucci, coordinator of an interagency group dealing with the Korean Crisis.

Our Center's director of programs, former ambassador Marion Creekmore, joined me and Rosalynn at our home for an excellent three-hour presentation by Gallucci, who seemed to share our trepidation about Pyongyang's likely reaction to sanctions. He said that the president was committed to impose sanctions on the DPRK because they had not complied with commitments of the Non-Proliferation Treaty. There could be no communication with leaders in Pyongyang except intermittently through their UN ambassador, Ho Jung, and no real assurance about whether the messages were delivered. The entire situation was a comedy of errors, and the administration was divided on what should be done.

When Gallucci left, I began considering the consequences of going to North and South Korea just representing The Carter Center, with or without approval from Washington. In effect, this would be a small nongovernmental organization going against the policies of the government, with tremendous momentum already having been built up to induce other nations to follow the US lead toward sanctions—and a possible war.

I first received assurances from the North Koreans that their invitation was still firm, that it was personally from their "Great Leader," and that I would be permitted to go directly from Seoul across the Demilitarized Zone (DMZ) to Pyongyang. Then I sent a letter to President Clinton stating that I had decided to make the trip. The president was still in Europe to commemorate the fiftieth anniversary of the Normandy landing, and my letter was directed to

Vice President Al Gore. He convinced me to change its wording to "strongly inclined to go," with a promise to use his influence to get approval. I urged him to bypass the State Department, and the next day he called and said that Clinton had approved our trip, although he was certain the State Department would resent it.

Before going to Washington with Marion and Rosalynn for a briefing, I wrote out a series of questions for use in North Korea, including information from on-site inspectors on the nuclear issue, possible easing of US–DPRK relations, mutual inspection of military installations, presence of US nuclear weapons in the area, US obligations to South Korea, the status of joint military exercises between our two nations, and circumstances under which US officials would deign to speak to their peers in Pyongyang. We had a brief meeting at the airport with National Security Adviser Anthony Lake, who was on his way to his home in New England and did not seem interested enough to spend much time with us or to see us at the White House. Our subsequent briefings from the CIA and State Department were superficial and in conflict with information that the Center's interns had gathered from Billy Graham, some university professors, CNN news reporters, and a few others who had visited North Korea in recent years. When I questioned the accuracy of statements from CIA and State Department people, they explained that no middle- or high-level US official had ever visited North Korea and that they got their information from South Koreans and satellite observations.

We went home with many unanswered questions, including how we could communicate securely from Pyongyang to Washington without returning to South Korea; who would make the final decisions in North Korea—Kim Il Sung, his son Kim Jong Il, or military leaders; and who were the hawks and doves in Washington and what was their relative influence. I talked directly with those previously interviewed by our interns and an expert on nuclear engineering from Georgia Tech. At least I felt that I understood the basic agreements the United States desired to obtain from North Korea.

Before I left the next morning, I drafted a final list of questions to be answered in North Korea and ideas on how the crisis might be resolved. After I had read these to Bob Gallucci and obtained his approval, I decided to list a number of additional requests to be made of Kim Il Sung that might be "frosting on the cake."

We left home on Sunday, June 12, with no official status. We were on our own. We were welcomed to Seoul by US Ambassador James Laney, a close friend and former president of Emory University. He had arranged talks with President Kim Young Sam and his top advisers, who seemed somewhat troubled about our planned visit to Pyongyang. One minister, who was in charge of reunification talks, seemed to be more objective about their northern neighbor and was quite helpful. Assuming a North Korean perspective, he gave us his assessment of the reasons for their troubling policies. General Gary Luck, commander of all US and South Korean military forces, was deeply concerned about the consequences of a Korean war, which he thought was imminent. He estimated that the costs would far exceed those of the 1950s. He told us that he had given the same assessment to the president and top leaders in Washington earlier, but that his warnings were not received seriously, and military decisions were being made in Washington without consultation with him.

Colonel Forest Chilton told me that he could not work out an agreement for joint US and North Korean teams to find and recover the remains of Americans killed in the Korean War. He believed his experts knew precisely where three thousand bodies were buried while our troops occupied the territory. I promised to discuss this with Kim Il Sung.

The crossing at Panmunjom was a strange and disturbing experience. For more than forty years, Koreans and Americans had stared across the Demilitarized Zone with suspicions, and often hatred and fear. We were the first persons permitted to cross the DMZ to and from Pyongyang since the armistice was signed in 1953! As we approached the precise line, a concrete pad about a foot wide, our aide Nancy Konigsmark stepped just across it to take our photograph. Instantly, she was grabbed by burly security guards and returned to the proper side.

North Korean vice foreign minister Song Ho Kyong was our host during the two-hour drive over an almost empty four-lane highway. He explained that his country did not produce luxury cars but made only buses, trains, subway cars, and trucks. We were to find a superb mass-transit system in Pyongyang, with an especially beautiful subway system (no graffiti) more than three hundred feet underground. Throughout our visit, our hosts were open, friendly, and remarkably careful not to make abusive or critical comments about the South Koreans. They often expressed concern about misunderstandings and lack of progress on the peninsula but would acknowledge that these had been caused by mutual mistakes.

We stayed in a beautiful guesthouse in a garden area adjacent to the Taedong River, and the North Korean officials readily agreed to our suggested schedule of discussions. Our first meeting was with Foreign Minister Kim Yong Nam, who was polite but whose responses to my proposal on how to end the impasse were quite hard-line. He had an apparent fixation on a round of talks with US officials as a prerequisite to any affirmative actions. It seemed obvious that the threat of sanctions had no effect whatsoever, except as a pending insult, branding North Korea as an outlaw nation and their revered leader as a liar and criminal. This was something they could not accept.

Economic sanctions had no meaning for them, since their basic philosophy—almost a religion—is *ju-che*, meaning "self-reliance." In a practical sense, what was being proposed in the UN Security Council would not be damaging because North Korean trade with the United States and its allies was almost nonexistent and UN agencies provided the country with little benefit. Although the minister's comments were moderate in tone, it seemed quite likely that this country would go to war rather than yield to international condemnation and economic pressure, and he seemed uninterested in the specific proposals I had prepared.

I got up at three the following morning to try to decide what to do. Constrained by my agreements with Washington, I finally decided that Marion Creekmore should drive to Panmunjom to send a secure message from South Korea to inform Washington to seek authorization from President Clinton to propose a round of talks to defuse the crisis. In addition, I suggested that Bob Gallucci consider a visit to Korea. I woke Marion, he accompanied me into the garden to avoid any listening devices, and I gave him my message with instructions not to send it until I could meet later that morning with President Kim Il Sung.

When this meeting took place at the palace, Foreign Minister Kim and Vice Foreign Ministers Song Ho Kyong and Kang Sok Chu also attended. The latter was Gallucci's counterpart, responsible for negotiating with the United States on the nuclear issue.

President Kim was eighty-two years old but vigorous, alert, and remarkably familiar with the issues. He consulted frequently with his advisers, each of whom bounced up and stood erect while speaking to the "Great Leader." There was no doubt that Kim Il Sung was in full command and could make the final decisions. After thanking me for accepting his four-year-old invitation, he asked me to speak first.

I described my unofficial role, my briefings, and my visit with South Korean President Kim Young Sam, and then made the presentation that I had prepared before leaving home. I outlined the entire situation to be sure that he was fully aware of all concerns about North Korean nuclear policies. On occasion, he would nod or ask me to pause while he talked to his advisers. Richard Christenson, our State Department interpreter, later reported that Kim was obviously not thoroughly briefed on one important problem: International Atomic Energy Agency (IAEA) inspectors being expelled.

Finally, in effect, the president accepted all my proposals, with two major requests. One was that the United States support North Korea's acquisition of light water reactor technology, realizing that the funding and equipment could not come directly from America. (He had been promised a two-thousand-megawatt reactor by President Brezhnev in the late 1970s, but the Soviets had defaulted on this promise after Konstantin Chernenko became leader.) This was actually something we would have wanted the North Koreans to have because the enriched fuel would have to be acquired from foreign sources and the production of weapons-grade plutonium would not be so easy as in their old graphite-moderated reactor, which could use refined uranium from their own mines. Kim's second request was that the United States guarantee there would be no nuclear attack against his country. He wanted a third round of US–DPRK talks to resolve all the outstanding nuclear issues. He was willing to freeze their nuclear program during the talks and to consider a permanent freeze if their aged reactors could be replaced with modern and safer ones. I was surprised to find Kim familiar with these detailed issues.

I assured him that there were no nuclear weapons in South Korea or tactical weapons in the waters surrounding the peninsula, and that I believed the United States would want to see the DPRK acquire light water reactors. He agreed with me that the entire Korean peninsula should be nuclear-free. Since I now felt that I had gotten everything we needed, Dick Christenson called Marion Creekmore to tell him to return to Pyongyang without sending any message to Washington.

After lunch, we moved to talks with vice Minister Kang Sok Chu, the North Koreans' chief negotiator on nuclear questions. He went through the history of the nuclear issue from their point of view, which seemed reasonable in some respects. He was meticulous in his description of what had happened, and I could understand the correlation of events from totally disparate perspectives. On occasion, he deviated from what Kim Il Sung had committed to do, but when I asked him each time if he had a different policy from his "Great Leader," he would back down.

Kang claimed that they had delayed unloading the spent fuel rods from their Yongbyong reactor more the six months after the normal date and had been surprised by the IAEA's announcement to the UN Security Council, backed by the United States, that they had violated their agreement. He claimed they had made a reasonable proposal to resolve the issue, to which they never received a response.

Minister Kang informed me that when I arrived they had already decided to expel the inspectors and disconnect surveillance equipment in response to the abusive sanctions language announced by UN Ambassador Madeleine Albright and Bob Gallucci. Also, he said, "All the people in the country and our military are gearing up now to respond to those sanctions. If the sanctions pass, all the work you have done here will go down the drain." He said the North Koreans were convinced that the spent fuel rods could still be assessed by the IAEA and were willing to be flexible if this conviction should be proven wrong. He maintained that noted physicists in Europe and the United States agreed with their position. We discussed a number of other technical points. I saw no reason to argue with Kang on these points but just endeavored to protect the agreement I had reached with his president.

After supper, I called Bob Gallucci on an open line to report the apparent agreement with President Kim. He said they were having a high-level meeting in the White House and would "consider" my report. I notified him of my plan to give CNN an interview but to refrain from speaking for the US government, and he had no objection. During the end of my live CNN interview, I was informed that National Security Adviser Tony Lake wanted to talk to me, and we finally got him on the phone. After I answered a few questions, he asked me to call him back in an hour for the US decision. I did this, and he asked for three more hours to consult with other nations. This brought us to 5:30 a.m., and I understood that they would accept the terms I had worked out. Lake then read a statement they proposed to make, and he agreed to a few of my suggested changes. It was understood that the North Koreans would free their nuclear program through the new good-faith talks. In fact, it would be several months before the rods were cooled down enough for reprocessing and President Kim had agreed to "freeze" the nuclear programs, as I suggested.

Later that morning (Friday in North Korea, Thursday at home), Rosalynn, Marion Creekmore, Nancy Konigsmark, and I were invited to go on a long boat ride with President Kim and his wife, from Pyongyang down the Taedong River to the "Barricade," a remarkable five-mile dam built by North Korean soldiers. An ingenious system of locks and dams permits shipping and the flow of fresh river water to the sea but impedes the influx of salt water. The CNN camera crew were also onboard. I advised Kim that, in my opinion, full implementation of our agreement would mean that the sanctions efforts would be held in abeyance. (Unfortunately, part of this comment was picked up on camera and came out as though I were speaking for our government and declaring the sanctions issue to be dead.) I explained to the interpreter the meaning of *abeyance*.

We discussed removing the remains of US soldiers buried during the war, and after I explained that this would avoid later arguments and be a significant goodwill gesture to the American people, the president listened to the comments of his wife and then agreed to permit joint teams to find and return these bodies, provided the United States paid the expenses. I urged him not to let this joint effort become bogged down in debates.

Things were going well, and I decided to push my luck. I asked him to agree to immediate summit talks with South Korean President Kim Young Sam to plan for reunification of the peninsula, to consider mutual reductions in military forces with joint inspections to confirm compliance, and to withdraw heavy armaments far enough from the DMZ to forgo a preemptive attack on Seoul. He agreed to all of these proposals.

Kim said that for forty years no progress had been made, and he asked if The Carter Center would be willing to provide our good services to bridge the existing gaps and to help ensure the success of North–South talks. I promised to mention all these things to President Kim Young Sam on my return to Seoul.

We found Kim Il Sung very open toward Christianity, having been saved from a Japanese prison in China by Christian pastors. Also, he was an avid hunter (claiming to have killed two bears and two hundred boar during the past year) and quite interested in fishing. He and his wife argued about which of them was the better hunter. He said that after the Japanese were expelled from the country in 1945, the families along the rivers tried to kill all the "Japanese fish." He knew they were rainbow trout introduced before 1910 by American miners and had maintained a large program since then to stock the streams from several nurseries. We agreed that I would send in some biologists and fly-fisherman to analyze North Korea's fishing opportunities, and I let him know that Rosalynn and I would like to be among the first to fish the streams. After visiting the Children's Palace and seeing a remarkable performance of the young people's skills and talent, I finally went back to the guesthouse for some sleep.

The next morning we returned to the DMZ, where we had a press conference and answered questions from CNN, the North Korean news media, and reporters from China and Russia. Then we traveled with Ambassador Laney to Seoul, where I gave a full report to President Kim Young Sam. At the US embassy, we were amazed to discover that our actions in North Korea had been met by criticism and partial rejection in Washington. I discussed this negative response on a secure telephone with Vice President Gore and told him I would like to come to Washington before going home to explain the results of my trip in more detail. I considered all my actions to have been in accord with the policies of the administration. Apparently coached from the sidelines, he made it clear that I should return directly to Plains and not brief the administration. After a discussion with Marion and Rosalynn, I decided to go to Washington anyway. It was obvious that either they did not understand what Kim and I had decided or their preference was some kind of further economic or military confrontation.

I held an extensive press conference at the US embassy, during which Ambassador Laney informed me that President Kim Young Sam had agreed to the summit meeting. I explained the nuclear situation to the best of my ability, answered questions, and made it clear that I was still speaking as a private citizen representing The Carter Center.

When we landed in Portland, Oregon, to change planes, I had a call from Tom Johnson at CNN. He faxed us an incredibly negative article from *The Washington Post*, with quotes from top officials in the Clinton administration, such as, "We have no way of knowing why he thought what he thought, or why he said what he said." "Carter is hearing what he wants to hear, both from Kim Il Sung and from the administration. He is creating his own reality." The article also said that "when Carter first informed Washington of his desire to accept the North Korean invitation, officials were divided about whether to try to talk him out of it."

Marion Creekmore and I returned to Washington via Atlanta, while Rosalynn went home to Plains. No one met us at the airport or when we arrived at the White House, and we never saw the president, vice president, or any cabinet member. An usher took us to Tony Lake's office, where we found him, Bob Gallucci, Deputy National Security Adviser Sandy Berger, and Assistant Secretary of State Winston Lord. There was a strain in the air. I reminded them that I was well informed about the issues, not gullible, loyal to my president, and reasonably intelligent. I then read them the trip report I had written on the way home and answered their questions.

They explained that the remarks in *The Washington Post* (which they all denied making) were based on fragmentary information from Pyongyang. However, there was a more fundamental difference. The administration had been committed to what I considered a disastrous course of action—to browbeat North Korea publicly and to seek UN sanctions. I was doubtful that the Chinese would have permitted the resolution to pass and convinced that North Korea would not have yielded to this pressure, causing great danger of another Korean War.

Once the news report saying that, in my opinion, Kim Il Sung had responded adequately to US proposals was broadcast, the sanctions movement was dead in the water. Influential people, both Republicans and Democrats, including Senator John McCain, were still calling for military action against North Korea. President Clinton, however, had made no criticism of me and had approved my trip over the objections of some of his top advisers, particularly in the State Department.

When I talked by secure phone to President Clinton, who was at Camp David, everyone left the room except Tony Lake. Clinton said he was grateful for my trip and appreciated the results, and I replied that he was the first person in the government who had said this. I briefed him for about thirty minutes, and when I hung up, Tony seemed distressed. He kept the door shut as we leveled with each other. He swore his friendship toward me, said he had approved my trip to Korea, and denied any responsibility for the criticisms. I repeated my differences with the administration and said I resented the White House decision that I should return from Seoul to Plains and not to Washington. When I made a brief report to the news media upon leaving the White House, Tony stood by my side to indicate support for what I had to say.

At my hotel I met with about a dozen reporters to give them basically the same report. Although most of the news stories were beginning to be more positive, I felt that I had to repair the potential damage of unanswered questions. After another extensive interview on CNN, I returned home. I had forgotten it was Father's Day.

South Korean Ambassador Han Seung Soo informed me that his country was assembling a top-level ministerial group to arrange for the summit meeting. Jim Laney called to say how grateful the South Koreans were for our defusing the crisis. Before my visit, people there had been flooding the stores to stock up on groceries and goods, and had held unprecedented air-raid drills and announced that 6 million reservists were being put on alert. After I came back to Seoul, everything had returned to normal.

There was still obvious skepticism in the White House and news media about my report of Kim Il Sung's commitments, so on Monday I sent Kim a letter, with a copy to Clinton, enumerating them all. He responded to me in writing on Wednesday, with a copy to the White House, confirming everything. I called Clinton, and he promised to announce that if the commitments were confirmed, there would be no need for sanctions.

A month later, Kim Il Sung died, and his son, Kim Jong Il, wrote to tell me that he would honor the commitments made by his father. Subsequently, Bob Gallucci was able to negotiate an official agreement with the North Koreans that confirmed the nuclear deal, and Secretary of State Madeleine Albright later visited Pyongyang. Kim Young Sam and his successor, Kim Dae Jung, were making good progress on reconciliation with North Korea.

And then a new administration came to Washington. President George W. Bush derided the North–South peace effort and, in effect, canceled the nuclear agreements with North Korea. He also ordained that there would be no face-to-face discussions with Pyongyang officials, and meetings with them would be confined to a six-nation forum. Any commitment to forgo a military attack on the DPRK was out of the question until all other contentious issues were resolved. The North Koreans were accused of having a secret program to enrich uranium, a process that is very slow and requires an enormous facility of gaseous diffusion equipment or centrifuges. The North Koreans expelled the IAEA inspectors, renounced their commitment to a Non-Proliferation Treaty, and began processing spent fuel rods from the old Yongbyong nuclear reactor. They now have what is believed to be enough nuclear material for seven or eight bombs, and have demonstrated their capability with one detected explosion.

Joyce Ajlouny has served as the general secretary of the American Friends Service Committee (AFSC), since September 2017. Prior to joining AFSC she was employed by Friends United Meeting and served as the director of the Ramallah Friends School in Palestine, where she led a diverse staff of over 170 educators and administrators for thirteen years. Before that, she worked in international development focusing on minority and refugee rights, gender equality, economic development, and humanitarian support. She served as the country director for Palestine and Israel with Oxfam Great Britain, chaired the Association of International Development Agencies there, and worked as a program officer and project manager at various United Nations agencies. Joyce holds a master's degree in Organizational Management and Development from Fielding Graduate University in California.

The Courage to Engage Each Other
Joyce Ajlouny

*Speech to the Conference for the 18th Anniversary
of the "6.15 Inter-Korean Summit"*

Ladies and Gentlemen,

When the wind and sun competed to see who would have the traveler remove his coat, the force of the wind had the traveler wrap his coat even closer to his body, but the gentle sun persuaded him to take off his coat as his body gradually warmed. "Persuasion is superior to force" was the moral of Aesop's fable "The North Wind and the Sun," which inspired President Kim Dae-jung to refer to the South's softened policy toward the North as the Sunshine Policy.

Eighteen years ago, Kim Dae-jung took a bold and courageous step by engaging North Korea through a policy of gradual persuasion. It was a moment of bold, practical, and moral leadership. We should always celebrate when leaders demonstrate the courage to do what's right.

Now is a perfect time to reflect back on the Inter-Korean Summit of 2000 and the courage that propelled Kim Dae-jung and his cohorts to further the Sunshine Policy that led to the Summit. This is indeed a moment to lift up as an example of the ongoing fruits that come from courageous leadership. I hope that all of us here can work together to affirm the power of persuasion over war and spread more sunshine on the Korean peninsula.

Now is a fortuitous time to join with other Nobel Peace laureates and many friends in this reflection and celebration. I am honored to be here, representing the American Friends Service Committee, a Quaker organization that has worked for more than 100 years to heal the wounds of war and prevent violence by addressing its root causes. AFSC's peace and justice efforts span seventeen countries and its quiet diplomacy through convenings continues to bring differing views closer together.

Led by the Quaker ideal that every human being possesses that of the divine and their dignity must be respected, the American Friends Service Committee continues to work effectively to create bridges of connection and reconciliation where others see division and enmity. To ease tensions and build understanding, we supported people-to-people delegations between the United States and the Soviet Union during the Cold War; we also performed humanitarian work without respect to military "sides"—as an American group helping feed Germans after World War I or helping Vietnamese civilians in the North and South who needed artificial limbs, for instance. Through our history, we have also stood by the side of just causes which led us to take bold stands against all forms of violence and oppression—particularly wars and militarization—and against systems and policies that divide us—so we were an ally in the struggles against racial segregation, against apartheid, and now against Israeli occupation of Palestinians.

Today, through our regional programming, we have accompanied communities who have been victims of oppression and marginalization and supported their peace-building and social cohesion efforts. In Myanmar for example, our humanitarian effort in response to the plight of the Rohingyas comes through our local partners who bring Muslims and Buddhists together to provide much needed humanitarian support. In Zimbabwe where I was last week and in Burundi, we encourage communities from opposing tribes and political parties to find ways to engage and cooperate. Vocational training, micro-credit, and job creation projects are an entry point to rebuild cohesion and mend differences. This is yet another opportunity to emphasize that to restore prosperity and dignity to all, persuasion—the sun—is indeed superior to force.

Our belief in the value of each person and that everyone can be a peace-builder led us to work in North Korea, where we have engaged in both humanitarian work and people-to-people diplomacy.

AFSC worked on the Korean peninsula since 1953, when we arrived to help with reconstruction and refugee aid projects. We have been working in and with North Korea since 1980, helping facilitate people-to-people exchanges. We were the first US public affairs organization to send a delegation to Pyongyang. Since 1996, we have worked on food security and have had a great deal of success by partnering with Korean farmers to improve agriculture in the North. A significant AFSC success story is the use of plastic trays for seedbed cultivation which we had first introduced on AFSC farms in 2007. Their use increased rice yields by 10–15 percent. The trays are now being used throughout the country, and AFSC has supported efforts to produce trays domestically. AFSC also contributed to the introduction of greenhouses in North Korea and trained greenhouse managers who happened to be women. This project had a positive impact on the livelihoods of farming communities.

AFSC is an example of a small private US NGO that has realized substantial results over the long term in the DPRK, even while operating under significant administrative constraints and with relatively limited resources. Key to AFSC success is working in close partnership with North Korean counterparts. Relationships that have developed between AFSC staff and local farm managers, agriculture scientists, and government officials have, over time, facilitated a degree of trust and openness in discussions around shared goals and have afforded continuity in activities year to year.

More effective than short-term humanitarian aid, long-term assistance projects that address real human needs in a pragmatic and respectful way have the potential to produce tangible results in the DPRK, by building trust, supporting change, and benefiting ordinary Koreans.

So, my perspective on what works in peace-building is influenced by the experience of my organization. We have demonstrated, like many likeminded international NGOs with us, that engagement with the so-called "enemy" does work. Sadly, engagement is not always the strategy of choice to address global conflicts—even if it is the only one that truly leads to lasting peace.

Not only is engagement more effective, we are also seeing

signs of significant popular support for it. The wave of excitement generated when the two Korean teams walked united in April this year was evident.

Public opinion in the United States and both Koreas approve diplomatic engagement. While we don't have a poll of North Koreans, my colleagues recently returned from a delegation there just two weeks ago. Our DPRK partners expressed optimism about the recent improvements in relations between their country, the US, and South Korea. They expected the result of the summit to be good—things will improve for them, they will have a chance for economic development and a better life. The impact for agriculture will also be good.

***

We live in a time when far too many of our societies are dominated by the politics of anger and resentment. We see it every day in the news, in our communities, in our politics. Politicians and influential people in the media blame other groups for our problems, saying they are a threat, the so-called "others" are dehumanized, they are called animals, terrorists and criminals, they are not as good as us, not as worthy of the respect and dignity we enjoy. Too many of my fellow citizens in the US blame immigrants, Muslims, and entire communities of color as threats to "our" well-being. I myself, a Palestinian-American, lived for decades in Palestine under military occupation, as part of a people dispossessed and collectively dehumanized and defined—every single one of us—as a threat to Israel's security. In the Korean context, I see repeatedly how people in the US do not understand DPRK realities. The prevalent lack of understanding of the conflict in the US has allowed the US government and media to portray the DPRK as a senseless, backward, and rogue state. These are far from accurate depictions of the farming communities we know.

This culture of anger and dehumanization is rampant in our societies today and leaders' rhetoric dangerously encourages acts of xenophobia and racism. It leads us to self-destructive actions, like the squandering of our prosperity on weapons, prisons, and walls with the false claim that they protect us, instead of investing in education, health, innovation, and peace-building. This culture has real ramifications for our collective human security. Our entire society becomes worse off as inequality, insecurity, and incivility rises.

We urgently need a moral renewal, a cleansing of hearts and minds. There is a surefire cure for the culture of resentment, and while it's not easy, it has succeeded in many different contexts in human history. It is what we in the American Friends Service Committee call "shared security."

Shared security is the simple concept which emphasizes that each of our human destinies are intertwined. In our increasingly interconnected world, our security is equally joined. For security to become a reality for all, we need to collectively achieve freedom from fear and want, we need to address security as a common right for *all* people followed by an intentional practice to build just societies and inclusive communities, and finally we need to recognize our shared responsibility to achieve it.

And here, we faithfully believe, there will not be true and lasting peace on the Korean peninsula until everyone feels secure. Kim Dae-jung, late in life, remarked that "The South and North have never been free from mutual fear and animosity over the past half-century—not even for a single day," He added, "When we cooperate, both Koreas will enjoy peace and economic prosperity." I couldn't agree more. Cooperation is the key to moving from mutually threatening to mutually thriving.

Once we understand that true peace comes from achieving shared security, nonviolent engagement becomes the approach of choice. Threats that are seen as harmful would then be replaced with active listening, dialogue, and empathy. We see that success can only be achieved by a policy of sustained "proactive engagement" rather than continuing down the path of hostility, war games, and sanctions. Engagement (not "maximum pressure") is the key to peace on the Korean peninsula.

Here, the words of another courageous leader, Nelson Mandela, come to mind. He said: "If you want to make your enemy your friend, then work with your enemy. Then he becomes your partner."

It is important to remember that engagement with our so-called "enemies"—and not just through humanitarian assistance programs, but cultural activities, people-to-people programs, athletics, and other exchange programs—historically has been used to build understanding and mutual trust, and lay the groundwork for higher-level diplomacy on other issues. For one, ping-pong diplomacy certainly helped set the groundwork for US–China official diplomacy.

As a Quaker organization, we understand that peace doesn't just "break out." Peace—like war—takes sustained effort: preparation, strategy, investment, and ongoing practice. AFSC's programs, and those of many like us in the excitingly growing peace-building world, provide important models for a US–DPRK engagement strategy that would promote relationship building between North Koreans and Americans, a US engagement strategy that would improve security for all stakeholders on the Korean peninsula. Such a strategy requires a collective effort to positively transform current cycles of tension and conflict.

It's encouraging that leaders leaving this recent summit understand that this is not the end, but a beginning of a process. A declaration remains worthless if not followed up by sustained action to implement the agreement. As we've heard, people in the US and throughout the Korean peninsula are hopeful for change and we want to make sure the long work of peace-building continues so those hopes do not get dashed. We have seen far too many examples of how inaction on agreements fuels more conflict and renews feelings of distrust and desperation by those who were counting the hours to reclaim their freedom and dignity. I personally remember how quickly my feelings of optimism and my dreams of a better life for my children were crushed after realizing that the courage and political will were absent in implementing the Oslo Peace Agreement. Decades later, with many other devoid declarations that followed, peace remains farfetched for Palestinians and Israelis and the so-called signed agreements are nothing but pieces of worthless paper collecting dust in the safety vaults of our governments. I know firsthand that nothing hurts more than the feeling of being let down by leadership and to hesitantly—almost in denial—be forced to retract to an even darker place of desperation and hopelessness than where you originally started. I would hate to let down the hopes of all those Korean and Korean-American families who look forward to a reunion.

This is where humanitarian efforts link in. They are a concrete way to keep generating the persuasive sunshine for engagement between North and South and between our countries. They work. They relieve suffering. They create channels of interaction and confidence-building that pave the way for better relationships and conditions in the future.

And we have many areas for potential cooperation. AFSC has been working with Koreans in the US and on the peninsula to develop recommendations for our leaders to follow, and I'd like to share a few insights.

Despite governmental attempts to sever people-to-people links, there remain connections between the US and DPRK that cannot be regulated away. I speak of thousands of Korean Americans who are part of families divided by the ongoing war between the US and North Korea. In the past, these families were free to visit the DPRK to search for their loved ones. Many of them were able to locate and reunite with long-lost relatives. Today, these families are prohibited by US travel restrictions from going to the DPRK simply to reunite, if only briefly, with a family member they may not have seen in decades. Within this tragedy of family separation, however, there is opportunity. Opportunity to restore living links between the US and DPRK and to advance a sincere diplomacy—one initiated with an embrace and based on enduring love, rather than a policy of aversion driven by fear. Some families, however, will never be afforded the opportunity to embrace each other once more—and yet, their love endures. Families of the over 5,000 US service members whose remains were left in the DPRK after the war are still searching for their loved ones today. From 1996 to 2005, the US and DPRK carried out joint operations to locate, collect, and repatriate the remains of these US service members. A successful exercise in cooperation that is *still* bringing closure to families today as the remains are identified and the families are located. This is an area for potential collaboration.

We just need political leaders to seize this opportunity and it seems that the joint declaration this past Monday did just that. This is indeed a welcomed and encouraging step.

While family reunions and service-member remains are not seen as urgent security concerns, they offer, though, some easy wins to begin de-escalating tensions, shining the sunlight of engagement, and reconciling wounds. Policymakers, then, neglect these issues not only at the expense of individuals and families but at the expense of international security. We need the US government to continue and deepen the path to international cooperation and shared security. Immediately, we need travel and humanitarian restrictions lifted, since these methods, by working together to solve mutual problems, pave the way for other engagement to work.

In 2016, the UN Development Program reported that about 18 million North Koreans were in need of some sort of humanitarian assistance. Just one year later, an independent UN expert reported that *even* UN agencies were having difficulty with shipments of humanitarian aid due to sanctions. It was noted that equipment such as wheelchairs and cancer medications were being denied entry. While sanctions are getting in the way of wheelchairs, we must bear witness that sanctions are having an indisputable and detrimental impact on humanitarian assistant in the DPRK, despite assurances from US government officials that sanctions are not meant to hurt ordinary North Koreans.

Humanitarian efforts are some of the sunshine that lights the way of collaborative engagement. We need to change policies that block needed humanitarian work.

It is wonderful to share these experiences and thoughts with you today. Before I close, I want to ask everyone here a question. As supporters of diplomacy, we know the steadfast work and courage it takes to engage other people to resolve tensions. What can we do to create a culture that sees the value in every human being and rewards the courage to engage? What stories should we be telling to celebrate this courage? We need all the leaders we can to reach for the light of reconciliation, as Kim Dae-jung did with the Sunshine Policy—when he chose warm persuasion over the gushing force of the wind.

As we share our experiences and reflections today, let us take back to our communities the message of action; action to make sure that our leaders choose the courageous path of promoting shared security rather than militarism, threats, and war. If we can share this message far and wide, we will make a difference that will last for generations. Thank you!

 *Khaled Mansour is an independent writer, consultant, and a professor of practice on issues of human rights, humanitarian aid, development, and communications. He was a journalist for 10 years in Egypt, South Africa, and the USA. He served for thirteen years in the United Nations including for UNICEF, peacekeeping missions, and the World Food Program. He led the Egyptian Initiative for Personal Rights in 2013–2015.*

(In)Securing Each Other
Khaled Mansour

Beirut, 2006. My adrenaline level shot up so high that I felt every part of my body down to the tips of my toes in a state of alert, as I walked deeper into the cavernous neon-lit parking lot and away from the half-glass entrance that I had just bolted. I had just strongly advised, or almost ordered, a French security officer to put away his loaded gun and immediately back off from the locked door. Angry protesters had earlier stormed the ground and upper floors of the UN headquarters in Beirut.

Half an hour earlier I was sitting in my office. If I looked through the window from my sixth-floor office I could see the demonstrators growing more agitated. If I turned toward the flat TV screen on the wall, I could see their faces up close on live coverage from Al-Jazeera and a few other channels. I turned to my computer and resumed writing my report when a security officer almost yanked me and hurried me down the stairs. We had made the last turn toward the car park as the first demonstrator broke open the entrance to the ground floor a few meters away.

We watched our impending doom live on a couple of TV screens in the basement as the pounding and breaking noises shook the ceiling above our heads. I called several TV stations. "We are over 100 humans still in the building that angry protesters seem to be setting fire to," I said. "Our death would not return to life the hundreds of Lebanese who have been killed by ceaseless, indiscriminate, and disproportionate Israeli air raids and bombardment in the past couple of weeks. We are not the enemy... there is no sense in taking revenge against an institution because it could not help you and because you cannot retaliate against a powerful opponent." My fear was mixed up inextricably with anger and disgust at all parties, including the protesters. For some few minutes I gave up on it all, on even trying to make sense of it. Maybe it was my repeated indignant pleas, but more probably interventions by senior officials and top Hizbollah politicians, one of them coming in person to the building, that finally calmed down what could have turned into the last day of my life, together with that of many others. Such a possible "last day" had gone by several times in my life, and it might have contributed to a sense of false security at times, but at most other times it caused in me an abiding anxiety that led to an obsession with security while continuously drawing me toward insecure places.

Earlier that week, I had visited Tyre, Qana, and other communities in southern Lebanon from where hundreds of thousands of residents had fled the Israeli onslaught, a massively disproportionate revenge attack after Hizbollah killed three Israeli soldiers and kidnapped two in a brazen operation in mid-July 2006. During that visit, I saw families exhuming the bodies of loved ones from makeshift tombs on roadsides because it had become relatively safe during one day of ceasefire to finally move them to their eternal resting place in a cemetery. A UN relief aid team whose coordinates were known to the Israelis and to the Lebanese was jolted by aerial bombardment that hit a couple of hundred meters away. This complex, sad, and extremely disproportionate fight between the unchecked power of Israel and the angry, justified—albeit manipulated, and at times self-defeating—acts of resistance or revenge by militias from Lebanon, had been recurrent since 1978. Invariably the material and human losses were dramatically heavier on the Lebanese and Palestinian sides.

I was born in Cairo one year before the 1967 Six-Day War in which Israel occupied vast tracts of land in three Arab countries, and brought all the Palestinians who still lived in the Gaza strip, the West Bank, and Jerusalem under its rule—but not as citizens. More than 50 years later, millions of Palestinians suffer an apartheid-like system, with conditions legally worse for those who live in the occupied territories.[1] Israel's ceaseless search for security—exclusively for its

Jewish majority—has taken it into five or six wars, not to mention innumerable incursions and raids on several neighboring countries and the untold tens of billions of dollars spent on armament, defense, and attack capabilities. All these policies have systematically generated deep levels of multi-faceted insecurities for the Palestinians and for people in neighboring countries.

To make matters worse, so-called geopolitical and security concerns—from Tehran to Riyadh, Abu Dhabi, Sanaa, and Cairo—and the intervention of regional and international powers (Turkey, Iran, Russia, and the US to name the main players), have been creating unprecedented levels of insecurity for the people who live in this region and beyond.

The Syrian Baathist regime, long known for its cruelty, now occupies a place of dishonor among murderous regimes with a macabre record of gruesome killing, bombing, torture, disappearances, and ventures into new terrains of bestiality toward humans. In the past seven years, aided by Russian forces, Iranian soldiers, and Hizbollah fighters, the regime has killed over half a million Syrians and displaced half the population of the country, 10 million people, inside and outside their homeland. Intervening countries either back Assad, kill their own enemies, or (especially from Sunni Gulf countries until recently), bankroll some of the most nihilist versions of jihadi Islamist militias for their own geo-strategic interests. What started as peaceful uprisings against a kleptocracy turned into a complex war by proxy in which some of the long brutalized are now running wild either under the banners of ISIS or as pro-Assad vigilantes.

***

Since I graduated from university in 1988, I have traveled a great deal in many African and Asian countries (visiting or living for long periods of time in places like Sudan, South Sudan, South Africa, Pakistan, Afghanistan, the occupied Palestinian territories, Iran, Lebanon, Syria, etc.). I also had the great experience of reporting on the making of US foreign policy from Washington, DC, in the late

1990s and approaching the upper echelons of the United Nations system in New York for a few years in the early 2010s.

In all these places I either witnessed, worked on, or reported on extreme forms of man-made human suffering. I met survivors and murderers, interviewed bereaved women, spoke with vengeful bloodthirsty men, got mistreated by child soldiers, looked away from the heart-rending scene of malnourished children, kept my cool and professional demeanor in the presence of frightening generals and unhinged soldiers, and broke down one or two times in a demolished refugee camp in Jenin or a children's cemetery in Hirat.

Like many journalists, aid workers, and human rights professionals, I saw how the need for security, justice, revenge, dignity, domination, protection, and peace intermingle, shape and reshape our daily lives from airports in the West to wedding parties in Yemen and Afghanistan (with all of them being targets or their activities turned into occasions for anxiety and trepidation rather than anticipation and joy). I had slowly installed a glass barrier between my feelings and reality in order to protect myself from continual exposure to inhumanity and degradation.

In 2003, I survived an attack by a massive car bomb targeting the UN headquarters in Baghdad. The explosion, which killed more than 20 of my colleagues, also cracked this barrier between myself and the scenes of abject poverty, inexplicable deaths, and looming menace to which I had come so close for many years. I went through emotional hell for many months as I stood at the brink of my abyss of dark and bloody memories, reexamining scenes from a flattened refugee camp in Jenin, to scary stories by former political prisoners who have been tortured in countries I lived or worked in, to encounters with displaced people in Pakistan and Iran, to quick interviews with women in Kabul, Taliban members in Kandahar, defense officials at the Pentagon, UN heads of operations in New York, and government officials in Western and Eastern capitals. That was when I decided to take several months off and away from such scenes to re-process and slowly submit to my emotional turmoil in order to tame my own demons. In less than a year I was back in "action," better prepared but also believing that one never completely heals on his or her own but within the "normal" stream of life.

Fifteen years later, this brink no longer scares me, nor do horrifying events unfolding around us; they do not egg me on to clamor for revenge or express rudderless indignation (at least not beyond the first few human hours of justifiable anger). I still experience a sense of impotence sometimes, but I quickly channel this into something useful for myself or people around me, focusing my contributions on small civil organizations working in the fields of rights, aid, and advocacy. I take occasional depressive attacks and waves of sadness as signs of my own humanity and healthy vulnerability. I no longer believe there is an innate good or an ingrained bad nature in any single human being.

There remains, however, a sense of an ethical and moral world that we all should strive for. I believe in the power of empathy and the virtues of compassion, and think, despite all the mayhem around us, that we can become what we work for, collectively. For me, this means at both individual and communal levels that one group or individual's security does not come from the insecurity of others, and that most of the threats communities or states face can be largely addressed not by barriers (glass or otherwise), from behind which one can send drones or missiles or barrel bombs, but through genuine and creative engagement. Yes, at one time or another you may need to use force, but there are huge distances to be covered and many compromises to be made before that decision might be taken.

The most important challenge is to redefine the question, What is our security? What do we want to secure? Against whom? And why? And what does the other (that menace and source of insecurity) want from us? And is there any sense in what they are demanding? Can we talk? Can we compromise? What is non-negotiable? What can we share? And who are the "we" that we seek to defend?

The increasing inequalities, oppression, humiliation, and erosion of commonalities within and among countries are, for me, the primary cause fueling anger, insecurity, and alienation. Ultimately, these forces push millions of people into the hands of violent groups or institutions that seek revenge, security, domination and/or forcing their way of life on others, often under the pretext of saving them or serving a higher purpose. This is a world of rationality of means and utter irrationality of ends.

Reams of studies and articles claim that people around the globe are becoming more populist, more protectionist, even chauvinist and nativist. They are bent on ensuring security for themselves and their own. If they have functioning systems of justice and some minimum social and economic rights, then all of that is for their own kith and kin to enjoy while not only shutting away others, but even going as far as justifying inhuman and extrajudicial measures against them to allegedly protect their own privileges and entitlements. For example, a recent study by Counterpoint has shown that in the UK the deployed frames of thinking and the messages they launch on rights issues shape the values and positions of their readers. In the British press, the study found that there was a "substantial opposition… to applying the fundamental principles of human rights to everyone; instead, minority groups such as foreigners, criminals, or prisoners were regularly presented as undeserving of human rights protections." Let us assume the media deployed other frameworks of looking at the world that support and nurture equality, social justice, and human rights. I would agree with the study, that this could possibly end in more "support for the values and principles that underpin" universal human rights.

Despite the dominance of neoliberalism in our planet, I still believe that the challenge is to convince more people that social and economic rights do not stop at borders and that the other, who is not protected as a citizen of the country, and also that other who belongs to a minority in your own country, needs to be included in one form or another. Until this is satisfactorily done there will be neither peace nor security.

The same evening of that frightening experience in the UN offices in Beirut, I agreed to a request from a TV channel to attend a live group interview in the public square in front of our offices. The station and the anchor who was pro-Hizbollah bused in about twenty people from different families who had lost loved ones under

Israeli raids in the previous few days. It was tense, confusing, and made worse by the anchor grandstanding and inciting comments. At one point, he looked at a seventy-something-year-old father and asked him, "what do you have to tell the international community?" pointing at me. The man, who had lost his son, barely spoke two words and then started to choke on his tears. The sensationalist anchor was fired up. It was good TV after all. He looked at me and said, "so what is your answer?" I just stood up and walked across to the old man, helped him to his feet, hugged him tight and walked him away—slowly, away from the floodlights for a short private conversation. This may sound melodramatic to some, and dreamy to others, but it is this man and his harrowing loss, and many women and men like him, who inspire me and many like me in our ceaseless search for genuine common security. It is because of him and his son whom I never met that I remain committed, that I continue to struggle in my own small ways for social justice, and for us to reconstruct a humanity in which people are more empathetic and freer to realize their own collective and individual potential. In my everyday work, I try to translate this into working with individuals and organizations that advocate in concrete ways for such an existence, in small steps. I always remember this bereaved man from south Lebanon and many like him that I met from Darfur to Mazar-i-Sharif and from Juba to Berlin. I know quite well whose interests I am pushing and why, because without empathy and the power of compassion, we end up in-securing each other and adding more fuel to an engulfing fire.

Notes

1. About 20 percent of Israel's citizens, or 1.7 million people, are descendants of Palestinians who were given Israeli citizenships after they refused to leave or were not forcibly removed in 1948 when Israel was created on Palestinian land that was previously under British mandate.

*Nigel Nyamutumbu is a media develop-
ment practitioner, currently heading the
Media Alliance of Zimbabwe (MAZZ), a
coalition of nine media support organizations. He has been involved in media and
journalistic work in various capacities
over the last decade. Before that he was
the Programs Manager of the Zimbabwe
Union of Journalists (ZUJ) and has had
stints with the* Daily News, *the* Zimbabwe Independent, *and currently
writes for the* Standard *newspaper. He earned his media and international relations qualifications at the University of Witwatersrand, South
Africa, where he was awarded a First Class Certificate in Media Studies
and served in various student leadership capacities. Nigel is an alumni
of the International Visitors Leadership Program (IVLP), which is a
United States of America (USA) Department of State premier professional exchange program.*

Challenges and Opportunities for Peace Advocacy in Zimbabwe
By Nigel Nyamutumbu

Since gaining independence in 1980, the dominant political and socio-economic narrative in Zimbabwe has been violence in various forms. Prior to independence, there had been violent confrontations between the state, then led by a white minority government, against nationalist movements that not only represented the interests of the black majority, but also popular democratic aspirations for equality, constitutionalism, and accountability.

The state has been at the center of violence in Zimbabwe in both the pre- and post-independence eras. Any form of opposition to the current government has been met with a violent response by the ruling party with the aid of state security institutions, particularly the police and intelligence officials—whether one analyzes the violence that rocked the southern parts of the country in what was termed Gukarahundi when at least 20,000 civilian lives were lost in the 80s or subsequent violence against opposition political parties in the form of the Zimbabwe Unity Movement (ZUM) in the 90s and the Movement for Democratic Change (MDC) in the 2000s.

Reasons for this violence are varied but largely revolve around power, allocation and/or distribution of economic resources, particularly land, and the people's desire for freedom and self-determination. Other factors that account for violence in Zimbabwe include racism, tribalism, and patriarchy.

Thirty-eight years after independence, Zimbabwe remains at a crossroads. Violent confrontations seem to be on the decline, thanks to a number of peace interventions carried out over the years:

various advocacy peace campaigns, training programs and dialogues that promote peace among political parties, religious and traditional leaders have been convened; and the government of Zimbabwe established a task force made up of the three main political parties and set up a peace, reconciliation, and national healing department in the office of the president and cabinet. Nonetheless, more needs to be done to ensure that peace prevails within this relatively small Southern African country.

When I joined the civic movement for democracy in Zimbabwe in 2010, the country's main political parties, the Zimbabwe African National Union Patriotic Front (Zanu PF) and the MDC had agreed to work together in a government of national unity (GNU), whose main purpose was to ensure a peaceful transition to democracy in Zimbabwe through the development of a new constitution that would allow for the holding of free, fair, and credible elections.

This was indeed an opportunity for me to contribute to this significant process in our country's history and if there is anything I take pride and joy in, it is that I was instrumental in mobilizing colleagues within the media and information sector in the process of crafting a new charter. The Parliament of Zimbabwe set up a Committee with representatives of three political parties represented in the legislature to spearhead the Constitution making process. This committee would convene consultative public meetings to solicit views on people's expectations on the new Constitution.

I worked to bring journalists and media practitioners from both the state controlled and private media together to develop a media policy framework for the country. I further submitted position papers before the parliamentary committee tasked with developing the Constitution.

This was a particularly thought provoking and learning experience for me as I encountered people of varying cultures and diverse views. I often found myself in the middle as a negotiator, trying to convince people, and the drafters of the constitution, on the need to entrench journalistic and media freedoms in the new constitution.

The new constitution set Zimbabwe on a new democratic trajectory, with an expanded bill of rights, which recognized citizens' rights, something that had not been provided for in the Constitution that the country adopted at independence.

Several attempts had been made by both state and non-state actors for the country to adopt a new charter, which were unsuccessful. For example, in 2000, the majority of Zimbabweans voted against a proposed constitution and in 2007 there was another draft. In 2013, however, the country was united in this agenda and, although the development of the Constitution was spearheaded by political parties represented in Parliament and thus not independent of the ideologies of the government of the day, the people of Zimbabwe had the final say.

The adoption of the new constitution in a way marked a new chapter for the country that had for long been riddled by violence.

Although the time that I have been directly involved in democratic policy dialogues, particularly within the media and information sector, was characterized by a remarkable decrease in the cases of physical violence compared to the pre-GNU era, there are structural issues that continue to pose threats to obtaining peace and stability in Zimbabwe.

These structural challenges operate on at least four levels, which include policy and legislative, restriction of space for citizens to access information and express themselves, lack of media diversity, and the unsafe working environments for human rights defenders. The four mentioned challenges and other related impediments are key strategic priorities if Zimbabwe is to realize democracy.

Impediments to freedom of expression and free media in Zimbabwe are predominantly caused by restrictive legislation and policies, which enable political interference in the information sector and criminalizes free expression. In working around this strategic priority, I, working together with a number of free speech advocates that make the Media Alliance of Zimbabwe (MAZ), have been focusing broadly on advocating for the entrenchment of freedom of expression and access to information as guaranteed in Sections 61 and 62 of the new Constitution. We have done this through active engagement with media and information sector stakeholders advocating for legal reform as well as alignment to new constitutional provisions. A part of this objective is also anchored on strengthening networks/alliances that combine forces and synergies in furtherance of democratic legislation and policies.

Moreover, we have been focused on ensuring that there is a pluralistic and diverse media based on the assumption that this type of media, in quantitative and qualitative terms, ensures an expanded range of information and views for the public, especially for marginalized groups in society. Media diversity and pluralism in Zimbabwe would entail the development of public, independent, and community media, as well as the development of alternative forms of media and information.

In order to realize optimal contribution and equitable value addition from all human rights defenders, including practicing journalists and media practitioners in general, it is imperative that their security is guaranteed. To that end, we have been spearheading various campaigns against sexual harassment, and stigma and discrimination against persons with disabilities, in spaces such as newsrooms and tertiary training institutions. Again, in the interest of protecting citizens, activists as well as journalists and media practitioners in times of instability, we have been continuously carrying out interventions that enhance their safety and have put in place response mechanisms that ensure victims of violence get adequate support.

All the above mentioned challenges and interventions that I and other media advocates have been implementing are indicators of how Zimbabwe is generally a restricted space. The main factors inhibiting space include restrictive legislation, violence and intimidation, and withholding information that is in the public interest.

Beyond the interventions that we have been carrying out, the November 2017 political developments, which ushered in a new government through an intervention by the military, pose both threats and opportunities for realizing sustainable peace and democracy in Zimbabwe.

On one hand the entrenchment of direct military involvement in subverting a constitutionally elected government is certainly regression and poses a threat to the work that myself and other peace practitioners have been doing over the years. Yet on the other hand the peace that is currently prevailing in the country, and the various channels for open discourse and engagement with government, present an enormous opportunity for joint action in instilling democratic values of equality, respect for the rule of law, and peace. The country is experiencing peace, partly because the military backed government is desperate for legitimacy, particularly from the international community. As such, in these international reengagement efforts, the government is leading the process of ensuring peace and stability, more so as the country prepares for elections slated for July 30, 2018. The opening up of spaces, albeit incrementally, is partly due to the advocacy interventions that we have been carrying out over the years, and also the desperation for international legitimacy.

Going forward, there is need to consolidate the gains we have attained thus far in opening the space for citizen participation and ensuring peace in Zimbabwe. The processes we have gone through in building national consensus during the constitution making process and the creation of strategic synergies with key state and non-state actors in advocating for peace could serve as a lesson for peace advocates working throughout the world, particularly in restricted spaces.

I personally envision a world in which people are able to respect each other's diverse views and backgrounds, a world that appreciates that the only way out of any conflict is through negotiating and finding common ground. I am committed to playing a part toward attaining this global vision, beginning in my own home, church, and within my social circles.

I will use my influence within the African region, particularly in Southern Africa where I am a member of various networks and committees, to ensure that in all the work we pursue there is need to upscale advocacy for peace. By the same measure, I will continue to take a keen interest in my country, where I am currently serving as a development practitioner. I will continue to add my voice at policy dialogues and play a watchdog role to ensure that values entrenched in our constitution are respected and there is a deliberate attempt by all to ensure there is sustainable peace in the country.

It will not be easy, but it is certainly attainable. Yes, sustainable peace is possible in Zimbabwe.

Sue Williams has been engaged with reconciliation and peace processes for thirty years, both as a political mediator and as a teacher/trainer. She and her late husband, Steve, were representatives of Quaker Peace & Service (British and Irish Quakers) in Botswana, Uganda, Kenya, and Northern Ireland, and independent consultants in a number of countries. They are the authors of Being in the Middle by Being at the Edge: Quaker Experience of Non-Official Political Mediation.

From Unilateral Actions to Reciprocal Security
Sue Williams

"The good we secure for ourselves is precarious and uncertain until it is secured for all of us and incorporated into our common life."
—Jane Addams, from *Twenty Years at Hull-House*

Security, as I understand it, is both emotional and systemic; that is, security can refer to an internal or an external state. In this article, I will focus on experiences of working to build shared security in situations of violent conflict.

Underpinning everything else, my sense of security rested on faith, both in God and in people. "The Lord is my light and my salvation. What, then, shall I fear?" (Psalm 27:1).

I do derive security from internal certitudes, from the inside out, as it were. But I do not believe, as many seem to, that only inner security is necessary as a foundation for shared security. For many people in the world, much of the time, feelings of insecurity come from forces outside themselves. In given circumstances, this might be the case for any of us. Once threatened, we cannot seem to feel secure alone, yet we do not feel secure in the presence of those around us. If we are not internally secure, are we doomed to a life of mutual threat? Or, if we cannot generate a sense of security from within, can we build one together from without?

The Case of Uganda

As representatives of British and Irish Quakers in Uganda in the mid-'80s, my husband, Steve, and I lived in a context of civil war, with six armies competing for control of the country. People were being killed at such a rate that the newspaper could not keep up with listing the deaths, even devoting two pages per day to the list.

In one sense, there was no security to be had. The violence brought an urgency to everything and gave rise to superstitions and magical thinking. One example was the adage: Never be the first person to go down the road. Magical, yes, and circular, yet it also described that degree of vigilance one developed in noticing whether a shop was closed, or the children were not playing outside the school. Everything was uncertain, but being alone was ominous.

This was also an indicator that security is a group state, ideally, each person contributing to the security of others. Or, in a polarized and violent situation, each person unsure whether others made them secure or insecure, and tending to seek security amongst those most like themselves.

Our work was to promote peace and reconciliation in any way possible. This developed into support for a variety of small groups of people doing all sorts of constructive things, sometimes inventive, sometimes dangerous. In addition, where possible, discreetly, we engaged with army commanders and "rebels."

Armed groups (whether legal or illegal) tend to be insular, isolated, dependent on their own group, and not trusting of others, especially others who are armed. So, to get to negotiations, or any kind of communication, the process of building security had to begin where they were. In Uganda, we were eventually able to make contact with a particular armed group and the commanders of the part of the national army that was fighting them, as well as a designated member of the government.

They did not trust words, so it always began with action. They refused to negotiate with their enemies; that might give them legitimacy. So, the first actions were unilateral. In this case, the rebel group said: "We are not saying anything to the army or the government. But we will demonstrate good will toward the local community, and command of our forces, by stating that we will stop conducting night raids." We made contact with an army commander, who had noticed that night raids seemed to have stopped, but had not seen it as an

intentional demonstration of control. "I don't care what they're doing, but our army does care about local people caught in crossfire. So
we will confine our troops to barracks at night." Both groups made
these unilateral gestures in the expectation that the other side would
continue as usual, in which case they would go back to business as
usual themselves. But, if the other side did something unexpected,
then it presented a dilemma.

We came to understand that our role at this stage was primarily
as interpreters, pointing out changes in behavior and the intentions
behind them as they had been revealed to us. Both groups tested each
other, and they tested us. Slowly, there was progress in the form of
indirect communication leading to the possibility of direct meetings.
The talks began to focus on where to meet (Geneva was eventually
chosen) and how the rebels would get there without depending
on the government for funding or passports (Quaker foundations
would fund; UN travel documents would be provided.) Without
acknowledging it, they were building together toward a process that
might provide shared security.

At just that moment, the Ugandan government was also in
negotiations with a rebel group in a different part of the country. An
amnesty was offered, and some of the rebels surrendered. They were
killed while in government hands. Not surprisingly, the rebels we
were dealing with immediately canceled plans for Geneva and went
back to full-scale fighting.

As this example shows, the infrastructure for shared security
extends beyond the conflicting parties. Though parties in conflict
can work toward some way of making their situation more secure,
they do not have complete control over it. Building a process leading
to shared security depends on the resilience of the process, and on
developing broadly shared understanding and support of what is
being constructed. And those, in turn, depend to some extent on
whether people believe that security is possible together. In our case,
it was important that fighters on the ground come to understand that
their security could be guaranteed by their opponents in a process of
reciprocal security: We are safe if you are safe, and conversely. These
groups do not trust easily, and continue to test processes and results.

At the same time, the broader society also needs to be brought along with this way of thinking. Governments rarely let their people know that something is changing, until the ceremony to sign the agreement. This makes it difficult for people to understand or accept what has happened, and why they should trust people who have been trying to kill them. In this Ugandan case, there were civil society groups working hard to re-frame people's understanding of possible changes, in ways that complemented the mediation efforts with armed groups and government. This complementarity seems to me an essential part of building shared security.

The case of Northern Ireland

The second analysis looks at complications of shared security when there are parties involved at multiple levels. These examples are from Northern Ireland, notably in the nineties, when we lived there.[1]

Security was commonly seen as an inverse relationship: what was good for one side was bad for the other. Political actors behaved as though they could make their side more secure, by making the other side less secure. Security was a zero-sum game.

One common pattern among groups who are in conflict, but don't seem to be winning, is to try to expand the conflict to engage actors in a larger framework. This can be thought of as the "big brother" syndrome, turning for support to a more powerful group at a higher level. Each of the two main demographic groups in Northern Ireland had a "big brother." Those who wanted Northern Ireland to be part of the Republic of Ireland,[2] variously identified as Republicans, Nationalists, and Catholics, looked for support to the Government of Ireland. Those on the other side, wishing to remain under the sovereignty of the United Kingdom,[3] who were identified using terms such as Loyalists, Unionists, or Protestants, looked to the Government of the United Kingdom.

Below are graphics showing political and armed actors in conflict at the local level, and above them (on their respective sides) the Governments of Ireland and the UK. The opposing Northern Ireland parties looked upward for support, and in some ways at some times they got it. This instability continued at the international level. For the most part, the position of the Irish side was supported by the United States, while the position of the British was supported by the European Union. One could have years of debate about whether, why, and to what extent this was true, but the point here is that the instability and insecurity in Northern Ireland were mirrored at both national and international levels. This made it even less likely that Northern Ireland parties would look to each other for shared security.

Work went on for many years at and between all these levels, to end the conflict and find reconciliation within the society. Looking back, it now seems clear that one major key that opened possibilities for agreement was the decision of the two governments not to support different sides, but to try to establish neutral positions with respect to the conflict, for the good of the society as a whole.[4] Many things fed into this, others ran counter to it, and nothing proceeded smoothly. Nonetheless, in retrospect, there were both structural and conceptual shifts that gave the parties in Northern Ireland space to try to sort out the conflict.

The first diagram that follows is a graphic representation of the way parties at different levels lined up with the basic two-sided conflict in Northern Ireland (shown at the bottom of each diagram) around 1984. The second diagram shows the line-up in roughly 1995, after the two governments had coordinated their stances. The active groups at the Northern Ireland level line up more-or-less symmetrically. In the middle of the diagram is the centrist political party, Alliance, drawing people of both cultures and focusing on policies, and which drew support from international solidarity. Left of that[5] are the "constitutional" Unionist parties, UUP and DUP, and to their left the armed/extremist wing, called Loyalists, represented by the UDA and others (shaded because they were considered illegal). Moving right of center, SDLP is the main constitutional nationalist party, and to its right the armed/ extremist wing, called Republicans, represented by Sinn Fein and the IRA (shown as shadows, the IRA actually illegal, Sinn Fein running candidates but considered outliers by Unionists).

Broadly, the groups on the left side of the 1984 diagram looked to the British government for support, and those on the right looked to the Irish government. Similarly, the EU supported the British position, particularly its continued sovereignty over Northern Ireland. In a parallel arrangement, the US supported the groups on the right side of the diagram, at least emotionally, and there was considerable financial support by the American public, particularly to Sinn Fein and the IRA.

By 1995, the situation had changed dramatically, in both structural and conceptual terms.

To continue the earlier metaphor, the decision by British and Irish governments to stop being "big brother" threw protagonists

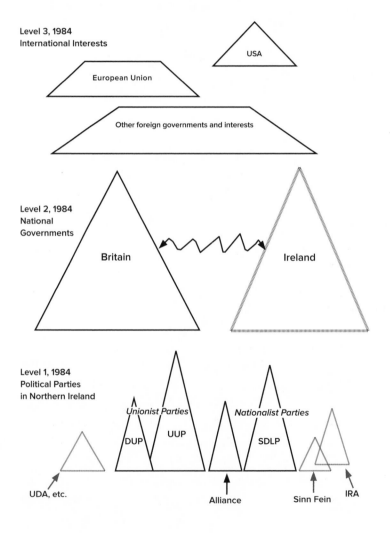

back on themselves in their own context. The new agreement also acknowledged, for the first time, a structural role for the Irish government in matters in Northern Ireland, through the Anglo-Irish structures. The two governments can be understood to have made this decision to ensure the security of both countries. At the same time, it changed the framework and the focus, thus enabling work toward shared security of local actors by local actors. This was a structural change that enabled the work of security-building to take place. Later steps, including a change to the Irish constitution,

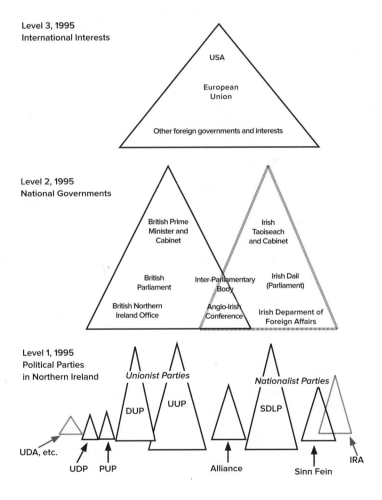

Level 3, 1995
International Interests

USA

European
Union

Other foreign governments and interests

Level 2, 1995
National Governments

British Prime
Minister and
Cabinet

Irish
Taoiseach
and Cabinet

British
Parliament

Inter-Parliamentary
Body

Irish Dail
(Parliament)

British Northern
Ireland Office

Anglo-Irish
Conference

Irish Deparment of
Foreign Affairs

Level 1, 1995
Political Parties
in Northern Ireland

Unionist Parties

Nationalist Parties

DUP

UUP

SDLP

UDA, etc.

UDP   PUP

Alliance

Sinn Fein

IRA

solidified the structural changes.

Another key aspect of the process of security-building is shown by an insight stated by a member of a Loyalist armed group: "We can no longer afford even one more victory or one more defeat." By this he meant that the inverse relationship, the zero-sum game, was finished. If something happened and his side claimed victory, the other side would inevitably see it as a defeat, and conversely, so they must stop claiming victory and defeat. This was emblematic of a paradigm shift. He was the first I heard articulate it, but it was soon seen as the beginning of a sea change. This man, and soon his group and other armed groups, and eventually most of the parties involved, understood their own interests in a different way. And this, also, may be thought of as building shared security from the inside out.

Many individuals and groups in Northern Ireland had maintained contact with politicians, armed groups, even prisoners, in hopes of enabling direct negotiations to take place. In small ways, at different levels, shuttling began to lead to some direct meetings. Activities to promote reconciliation at the grassroots level also began to get some traction, and reduced popular support for violence by any side.

As this paradigm shift took hold, there were glimmers of a recognition that, from now on, security would have to be seen as reciprocal. Still, the first moves were unilateral: the IRA and the UDA declared ceasefires, not together, not explicitly in collaboration with anyone else, but as defiantly unilateral actions. These actions may be seen as steps toward building shared security from the outside in. Political parties and governments met these ceasefires with suspicion. Nonetheless, one step at a time, the building of shared security began. Republicans refused to hand over their arms, seeing this as a surrender. Eventually, they agreed to a complicated formula to put arms "beyond use." Loyalists added to their ceasefire an apology for the suffering they had caused ordinary people. Special commissions held public consultations and "testimony" about people's experience with the violence, with police, and about their wishes for future arrangements. The Irish government was acknowledged to have a legitimate interest and role in Northern Ireland. The Irish constitution was changed, dropping the claim to the North. The peace process was seen to have begun. A referendum was held, North and South, and demonstrated that the majority of both societies agreed to the arrangements coming out of the peace process. In key ways, the EU offered an overarching structure which encouraged cross-border harmonization.

This long process can be seen as an example of building shared security, both structurally and conceptually, from the outside in and from the inside out. That is, people changed the way they thought of security, and there are institutional arrangements to reflect and embody this changed understanding. There are still splinter groups occasionally engaging in violence, but the refusal of "their" side of the population to support them denies a mandate for continued violence. There is plenty of conflict, yet much has changed. If the imperfect peace is to improve, or even to last, these changes will need to be taken for granted, become the norm, and be embedded in the culture. Whether the vote on Brexit can damage this remains to be seen.

The Personal View

Working to help others build shared security is, I think necessarily, an impartial activity. The actors in conflict were polarized and very partisan, and we were able to work with them because we were neither. But to be impartial is not to be lacking in principles or emotions.

We had the good fortune to work in difficult places with extraordinary, committed, inspiring colleagues and fellow workers. We were lucky enough to survive, though many of our colleagues did not, particularly in Uganda. The lessons were hard-earned, and often took on different forms in different places. Still, we learned that if you have any degree of peace and security, you must work to keep it, and you can only keep it by improving, by monitoring any problems or grievances and addressing them. With luck, many groups and individuals will work hard in their own ways to address the issues they see, and the cumulative impact may be better than anyone imagined.

These kinds of situations do test our faith, in our beliefs, our capacities, and the people closest to us. And we are tested in large and in small ways. Steve and I experienced that. Having considered ourselves pacifists, we discovered that, in situations of violent conflict, we felt more secure without weapons, without guards, and so felt we could call ourselves pacifists. And we understood what it meant when we encouraged others to lay down their arms.

No one knows how they will react in unfamiliar situations. No one knows precisely how to build peace or shared security. We try one thing, then another, find allies, learn from what seems to be helping, support others, and look for ways to be useful. It seems that, when we are desperate, we pay more attention to God, to each other, and to the beautiful world around us. It is important to forgive ourselves and each other, to do what we can, and to support the constructive endeavors of anyone willing to try.

Notes

1. There are wildly conflicting views on what happened and why in Northern Ireland, and we encourage people to explore other views. We lived there only twenty years, so our perspective was necessarily limited. For one retrospective, see Niall Fitzduff and Sue Williams, *How Did Northern Ireland Move Toward Peace* (Cambridge, MA: CDA Collaborative Learning Projects, 2007).

2. At that time, this group constituted about 45 percent of the population.

3. At that time, about 55 percent of the population.

4. This change had both explicit and implicit elements, including the Anglo-Irish Agreement of 1985 and the British declaration of "no strategic interests" in 1990.

5. Left and right here are not indicative of political stances, merely a way to show how groupings line up vertically and horizontally.

Raja Shehadeh is a writer and lawyer. His books include Strangers in the House; When the Bulbul Stopped Singing: Life in Ramallah Under Siege; Palestinian Walks: Notes on a Vanishing Landscape, *for which he won the 2008 Orwell Prize for Political Writing; and* A Rift in Time: Travels with My Ottoman Uncle. *Shehadeh is a founder of the pioneering human rights organization Al Haq, an affiliate of the International Commission of Jurists. His most recent book is* Language of Peace, Language of War: Palestine, Israel and the Search for Justice.

Excerpt from *A Rift in Time: Travels with My Ottoman Uncle*
Raja Shehadeh

When asked to write something for this anthology, renowned Palestinian lawyer, activist, and writer Raja Shehadeh turned to a selection of passages from his memoir, *A Rift in Time: Travels with My Ottoman Uncle*. That book chronicled his journey as he retraced the footsteps of his great-uncle Najib Nassar, an Ottoman journalist, as he lived and then escaped from occupied Palestine. During his own lifetime, and certainly as he made this journey, Raja Shehadeh notes that the struggle for freedom has been as unending as the enduring beauty of the landscape upon which these struggles take place. As we accompany him for a while on this quest, the borders drawn on the topography of Palestine as well as our own psychologies shift to open our minds to the other, more tenable necessity of peace.

***

The crust of the earth is subject to so many tensions and stresses that sometimes it breaks. A fault then develops. Blocks slip off the earth's crust along great ruptures or cracks. Distinctive landforms are associated with faulting: where a succession of tension faults occurs, a series of troughs or rift valleys may result. The Jordan Valley is one such depression. Driving further down into the Rift Valley, we decided to park the car by the side of the road and observe the markers which characterize this amazing geological feature, one of the longest faults on the surface of our planet.

Looking north along the road leading to the valley, it is possible to see hills with strata that had once been parallel to the ground now pointing downwards, providing visual proof of how the land collapsed into itself when this great fault was formed. To my right as we stood by the road was the Dead Sea, which lies like a basin, bordered on either side by sharply cut cliffs and mountains. It is both mysterious and seductive, poetic and lethal, alluring yet treacherous, with many superstitions and fears associated with it. It was once thought to exude noxious fumes that would kill anyone who got too close. And many perished trying to survey and sail it…

…The sea shimmered so peacefully in the morning sun. I felt a strong desire to follow the great fault, traveling through the Rift Valley starting north in the Syrian plains, through Lake Qaraoun in Lebanon and down to the Dead Sea and Lake Tiberias, examining how it developed from geological pressures on the tectonic plates far below the surface of the earth. Regardless of Palestine and Israel, British colonialism and the geopolitical realities, I still want to travel through this valley, imagining it as it had once been, all one unit, undivided by present-day borders. But until the political problems of this region are resolved—a prospect unlikely in my lifetime—a trip like this will not be possible. For now, all I could manage after crossing four of the five checkpoints along my way to the Galilee was to take a moment to contemplate the view in my unceasing attempts to assert my freedom.

Leaving the Dead Sea, we made a left turn and began our trip on the road north, with the scanty waters of the river trickling down some distance to the right. Presently we came upon the secondary road that turns eastward to the Allenby Bridge, the main crossing point for Palestinians into Jordan. My heart began to beat faster as my fears were aroused by the sight of a long line of cars and buses halted along the road, waiting their turn to deposit passengers—hundreds of anxious, sweating Palestinians on their way to Jordan—made irritable by waiting in closed vehicles baking under the hot sun.

On a raised piece of ground on the hillside near the entrance to the bridge terminal, Israeli officials had used small stones to mark out the Star of David and nearby the insignia of the Israeli police, attempting to claim the land by adorning it with the symbols of their state. Like the seal stamped on our documents. This was just another way of indicating that the area was no longer considered occupied territory; it has been annexed de facto to Israel and placed under the jurisdiction of its Ports Authority. Driving from Ramallah, we had passed numerous other borders, borders within borders within borders. Everywhere I looked I could see borders, barbed wire and watch towers.

The best antidote to the claustrophobia we Palestinians feel while attempting to cross the many borders Israel has created is to focus our attention on the physical expanse of the land. Israel is attempting to define the terrain, to claim and fragment it with wire fences, signposts, gates and roadblocks staffed by armed soldiers backed up by tanks. I am but one of the millions of travelers who have passed through over the ages. I lifted my eyes and beheld the wonderful valley created eons ago as it stretches far and long, north to Lebanon and south to the Red Sea and into Africa, utterly oblivious of the man-made borders that come and go.

Rethinking Paradigms

Victor Ochen is the Founder and Executive Director for the African Youth Initiative Network (AYINET). Born in northern Uganda, he spent twenty-one years as a refugee and transformed his experiences into leading the anti–child soldiers' recruitment campaign amidst the war in northern Uganda. He is one of the most important figures in Africa in the struggle for human rights and justice. Forbes magazines named Ochen in 2015 as one of the "10 most powerful men in Africa," while Archbishop Desmond Tutu attested that "my heart swells with joy to see Ochen as one of the new hope for Africa." He is the first Ugandan and the youngest ever African nominated for the Nobel Peace Prize in 2015.

Between Truth and Feeling, Peace
Victor Ochen

In my interpretation, shared security means communities that do not have to seek justice through retaliation. Anything short of that is some security—not real security.

From my years experiencing violent conflict in northern Uganda, I can say that the most difficult energy to let go is the energy of revenge. I witnessed deep anger when my society got entangled in endless and vicious cycles of pain and suffering. I saw people moved by waves of fear. I began to wonder why on earth the powerful would destroy our communities, kill innocent people, abduct tens of thousands, and displace over three million people. The ensuing atmosphere destroyed the legitimacy of the state in the eyes of citizens. The result was what I regard as a triangle of mistrust between the State, the Citizenry, and the Rebels. The State was accused by the Citizens for its failure to protect them from the Rebels who conducted reprisal attacks on the civilian population.

With so much hardship, daily survival and constant losses within families due to war, our society was flooded with monumental rage. Many utterances contained explosively unforgiving messages, and you could imagine what would happen if those who carried so much anger had weapons at their disposal! But knowing this did not stop repeated massacres by the armed forces, it did not stop people being blown up by land-mines and grenades, and even worse circumstances such as those where children were regularly forced to kill or rape their family members before they were taken by the armed forces as child soldiers.

I remember when I was growing up, I thought I had a dream for Africa, but along the way I have realized that Africa had a dream for me. Today, I guess I can say that along the journey I have experienced the worst in life, and also the best that life can offer. It's been a twister of a journey where beyond the violence I went through I have also found how to be at peace with myself and at peace with the world. This is when I came to realize that dreams require the dedication of both time and attention.

Growing up in my little-known village of Abia in the Lira district of northern Uganda, I can confirm that the message of peace was very unpopular. Yet I can also say in complete honesty that peace was not a known concept. We were a generation born into war. We survived war daily, we witnessed our parents struggling to afford us a meal a day at best. Whatever question we asked, the answer was always war! Why are we not having food? Why don't we ever sleep in our house? Why do we have no schooling? Why we are living in the camps? Why are too many people dying? Why did we not have bedsheets, clothing, or shoes? The answer was war! War defined our lives and fatigued entire communities with suffering. Every child played only war games.

It was indeed a painful experience, where we were forced to confront the significant tragedies that defined our lives, but I always felt we could triumph. My most devastating experience came in 2003 when, after all the years we had spent running away from the rebels, my twenty-four-year-old brother, Geoffrey Omara, was abducted together with my cousins and nieces. Sadly, they have never been seen or heard from again. Heartbroken and affected as I was, there was something in me that, while admitting that my people had suffered greatly, and that perhaps their urge to strike back was driven by an expression of deeper frustration, made me believe that we could overcome. I could understand the feelings of the people around me, but I was equally fearless in criticizing war as our chosen option, as I was tireless in promoting the message of peace and hope among my peers. I remained convinced that we could do things differently.

Living and growing up in a camp for Internally Displaced Persons (IDP) shaped me. Perhaps it taught me forcefully that there was a kind of person I should never be. I remember that after years of living in the IDP camps in northern Uganda, gunshots got louder and closer, panic intensified, and I knew those bullets were targeting us. I knew I could be a victim of abduction and torture, or be killed at any moment, but I never at any point considered vengeance as a viable and practicable response.

Because of the calamities that surrounded us, I valued every hour that I was safe from abductions. I appreciated every day that ended with me still being alive. It was not a question of a tomorrow or a future, it was a question of now. Perhaps because of the faith I had in my choices, my actions, and the discipline my poor and loving parents instilled in me, I developed a certain level of trust in what I might do with my life. I remember, I always asked my mother if life would change and she would proudly say yes; it was about to change, and she would say she also saw me as being part of the picture that could create that change. I got more courageous because my mother inspired in me great love for people who were suffering, and the will to never give up. My biggest sources of strength come from my own identity as someone who was born into and experienced great suffering, but who also was raised with great love. I identify and connect with people and their hardships.

I understand that there comes a moment in every person's life when one's faith and tolerance are sorely tested. I say this from my personal experience. Several years ago, I started the African Youth Initiative Network (AYINET), an organization to support war victims, especially youth who were former child soldiers, and treating war-wounded victims. One day, while on a mission to do community youth counseling, meeting with former child soldiers and hearing their stories as we sought to heal their trauma, I met a young man. He told me his personal stories while he was in captivity. He explained how he had been commanded by seniors to go and attack IDP camps, loot foodstuff, plant land-mines and abduct more children. As we got deeper into our dialogue, he shared with me his experience of how they used to go and attack Abia Camp. Abia is where I was born, and the camp I grew up in, where I'd spent most of my time. He went on to explain one particular experience when they abducted so many youths less than 70 meters away from the government soldiers who were drunk and sleeping in the church. He went on to tell about a particular child—not knowing who he was talking to—and how he was commanded to abduct this boy. How he tied him up, made him carry loads of food. He did not know he was talking to that child's older brother. I did not know what to do, whether I should tell him that he was talking about my brother or not. I struggled to contain myself so as not to let him realize anything. I cut our interviews short and told him we would have it rescheduled for the next day. I drove back to town mentally blacked out. I wondered if I should tell my father or any other family members. I tried to process what to do in vain. After a sleepless night, I decided not to tell any family members, but instead I went back to meet the man the next day. When he continued telling me the stories, I couldn't handle it. I felt weak and told him once again that we would reschedule after a week. I went back pondering the same questions: what to do with him, and whether I should tell any of my family. For a second time I decided not to tell my family members, but when I went back to him after a week, I asked him if he could accept an offer of employment, and if the answer was yes, that I would give him a job. He responded by wondering what he could do since he had never been educated. I told him that "your difficult life journey beats any academic qualifications and I don't mind your lack of education, but only if you could work and provide counseling support to your fellow formerly abducted youth." He said yes, he would take the job if I believed he could do it. I created that job for him. I made him a counselor. I employed my brother's abductor.

It was not until I employed him that I was able to be at peace with myself and at peace with him. From working beside him each day, we built a strong culture of dialogue on humanity, the value of life, and how tolerance and having faith in someone who should have been your enemy can bring peace of mind. I have never told him that he abducted my brother, neither have I ever exposed him to my family. He works very well, he is happy that I appreciate his knowledge, and he gets along well with all of our staff, the majority of whom are also victims of war.

There is no doubt that I took on the work of advocacy in a volatile context. It's true that I didn't have much advanced education, nor was I ever exposed to any international systems and communities. But I feel that I am rich in my exposure to societal suffering. I wasn't working on issues which I had studied or researched, I was working on the life that I lived, trying to reshape the terrible experiences that for a long time I had wanted to simply survive or escape.

I am aware, of course, that I am a part of, and working with, a generation of young people with a strong lineage of resistance, revolution, and war. Even though we seek to increase social cohesion, build bridges between yesterday, today, and tomorrow, it will be difficult. One thing that I found empowering has always been the practice of framing dialogues around our suffering and building a shared vision for our future. I have found that the creation of a culture that drives dialogue on humanity and tolerance, and establishes effective methods of overcoming religious, generational, and cultural differences is much needed work. We are willing to do it.

Ironically, traditional UN and international responses seem to focus repeatedly on women and children, but not on youth. But, working with young people throughout my entire life, I know that they are the generation that will determine whether there can be peace or the absence of peace. I have always told donors not to consider how much you have spent, but how much you have achieved. I always ask youth and post-conflict communities to consider this: that we have buried so many people but that we have never buried the deep-rooted mistrust, intolerance, corruption, and injustice that can lead us down the same destructive paths.

For me, shared security must have a strong human face. It is not the viewfinder on a gun but the sight in our hearts that can put an end to hatred. I do believe humanity can coexist, especially if we are willing to share and care for one another. The world is so rich that some people throw away food while there are people starving. We have accumulated so much money in the banks, yet there are children unable to go to school, and many are dying from diseases because their families can't afford to get them medical care.

For years I have led my dedicated, loyal, and hard-working team at AYINET, the majority of whom were victims of war, with the conviction that we must care for people who suffered at the hands of people who didn't care, or under the watch of authorities who refused to safeguard citizens, and who both only cared about power. Together we have helped bring medical teams to repair the injuries of tens of thousands of rape victims, and those innocent men, women, and children whose faces were deformed by their lips, ears, and noses being cut off. I believe that healing helps bring a desire for dialogue and reconciliation.

It is important to know that when you make an environment so toxic that people fear to discuss the issues that affect them, they'll act silently in negative ways. I am delighted that from the darkness of war and suffering in northern Uganda, we have slowly germinated the seeds of peace and unity. I lead a strong team of youthful war survivors as we create spaces for dialogue, mobilizing critical masses of young people who are hard at work to defuse the motives for rebellion, and who preach peace. Give them a chance to rebuild their nation.

 Nancy Lindborg is President of the United States Institute of Peace. Prior to that, she served from 2010 to 2015 as the assistant administrator for the Bureau for Democracy, Conflict and Humanitarian Assistance (DCHA) at USAID, leading USAID teams focused on building resilience and democracy, managing and mitigating conflict, and providing urgent humanitarian assistance. She led DCHA teams in response to the ongoing Syrian Crisis, the droughts in Sahel and the Horn of Africa, the Arab Spring, the Ebola response, and numerous other global crises. Previously she served as the President of Mercy Corps, where she worked on global relief, development, and peace-building programs. She started her career working in Kazakhstan and Nepal.

Peace is Possible: A Tribute to Landrum Bolling
Nancy Lindborg

The causes of war are manifold, and the pathway to peace is daunting and long. And for those who work to build peace, it often seems a hopeless endeavor, with no ways forward amid the thickets of powerful interests, violence, and politics. But a great teacher in my life taught me— and countless others—that peace is indeed possible.

Dr. Landrum Bolling entered my life in 1996, when he was eighty-two years old and preparing to spend the next two years supporting reconciliation in a Bosnia still raw and rubble-filled from war. His career had already spanned decades and continents, while I was still finding my way in the world of relief and development. Throughout the next twenty-five years, as I came face to face with the ravages of violent conflict and disaster, from the Balkans to Somalia to Syria, Landrum was right there with wisdom and encouragement, never pausing in his pursuit of a better world.

Inspired by his Quaker faith, Landrum saw the humanity in everyone. He was an avid believer in the power of people to transcend hatred and division when they had a chance to share stories, connect at a human level, and find common ground. He would be the first to say that any conversation about shared security must start by recognizing that in a world of 7 billion—or of 10 billion when today's newborns reach middle age—we either share security, or we share insecurity.

Landrum saw the cataclysms of World War II, serving as a journalist on the frontlines in Europe. Once while visiting Landrum in Bosnia, we were gathered in a hilltop restaurant when Landrum recounted his first time in the country. As a young reporter, he managed to tag along as Tito triumphantly returned to Sarajevo in 1945. He later went on to uncover a brutal French massacre in an Algerian village that had been hidden by the authorities. But far from returning hopeless from the seismic ravages of the war, he was of the generation that rallied to meet the challenges of the post-war world. As President Roosevelt noted in 1945, "The point in history at which we stand is full of promise and danger. The world will either move forward toward unity and widely shared prosperity—or it will move apart."

Landrum moved forward toward unity throughout his life. For more than fifty years, he worked to find solutions to end Israeli–Palestinian violence. Despite the persistence of that conflict, he remained dedicated to bringing options, ideas, and people together. He wrote the book *Search for Peace in the Middle East* in 1970, helping to inspire the idea of the two-state solution. He was trusted by both sides as a convener and interlocutor, by diplomats, faith leaders, and students. When asked how he managed to maintain such strong relationships on all sides, he offered a master class in peace-building by responding simply, "I listen."

He left his imprint on numerous institutions and inspired countless individuals to pursue practical action for peace: Indiana's Earlham College, the Tantur Ecumenical Institute in Jerusalem, and the Lilly Foundation. For fourteen years he worked down the hall from me in Washington, DC, at the international nongovernment organization Mercy Corps. He profoundly shaped both the organization and along the way, my life and work, by his conviction that humanitarian work should aspire to do more than save lives. He believed it was vital to connect aid work with reconciliation and in the wake of conflict help rebuild the social fabric of a destroyed community.

One of the early pieces of wisdom I learned from Landrum was that conflicts are never over until people find their own inner peace. He believed the core of peace and reconciliation was the ability of individuals to forgive. Holding onto grievances is the destructive kernel that results in continued cycles of conflict. It breeds hatred that is powerfully corrosive for both people and societies. "Forgiveness means letting go of all hope of a better past," he often said.

To work with Landrum was to constantly discover new stories and connections that bubbled up from the long stream of his life. Unbeknownst to me until I had lunch with Landrum shortly after joining the United States Institute of Peace (USIP) in 2015, was Landrum's role in its creation. Some forty years earlier, while at the Lilly Foundation, Landrum had been the one to provide a planning grant to a group of citizen activists advocating for an American "National Peace Academy."

The result was the establishment of the United States Institute of Peace by the US Congress, championed by senators who were WWII and Korean veterans, seared by their experience on the battleground. Like Landrum, they were convinced the nation would benefit from a greater focus on how to wage peace more effectively. USIP was signed into law in 1984 by President Ronald Reagan, with the mission "to serve the people and the Government... to promote international peace and the resolution of conflicts among nations and peoples of the world without recourse to violence." From that modest planning grant, Landrum planted a seed that became an Institute that has for thirty-four years provided research, training, grants, and practical action for preventing and resolving violent conflict. It has supported and launched a broad network of scholars, practitioners, and policy makers who generate ideas, and turn those ideas into action, in pursuit of a world that shares security for greater peace.

We are once again at a point in history in which the world is full of promise and danger. And more than ever, in a world now shrunken to a fast-paced global village, when conflict within nations has increased levels of violence, when 65 million people are displaced by violence, and new great power competition is on the rise, we will either share the prosperity of security or the contagion of insecurity.

It is tempting to lose confidence in the face of the complexity that propels these prolonged conflicts. But in the spirit of Landrum, I believe peace is possible—because of the many people who choose to act every day on our wider and deeper self-interests rather than our shallow and immediate ones. In 2018, Shi'a and Sunni tribal sheikhs in Iraq are sitting together to broker peace in communities that were shattered and filled with distrust following the brutal rule of ISIS. Young people are mobilizing in Nigeria to challenge an old, corrupt order by running for office. Peace marchers in Afghanistan are fearlessly walking through communities that have been at war for forty years, declaring "enough is enough" to both the government and the Taliban. Youth activists in Libya are organizing dialogues to quell conflicts between cities.

For the last two years I have had the wonderful opportunity to join youth leaders from conflict-scarred countries in Dharmsala, India, for dialogues with His Holiness the 14th Dalai Lama. Each young leader has chosen to work for peace despite experiencing personal tragedies: barely escaping after being pulled from a Nigerian bus by Boko Haram; or being forced by Syria's war into becoming a refugee day laborer in Lebanon instead of heading to college in Aleppo; or traumatized amid an Al Shabab bombing of a sports stadium in Uganda.

For these youth, it is not easy to find the inner strength and resilience to sustain their commitment to building peace. They are often living and working in communities filled with violence and anger. In their dialogues with the Dalai Lama, the youth often ask for political analyses of conflicts in their countries or advice on strategies for action. His Holiness's responses are simple, urging the youth to sustain compassion as their single most important compass. "Seven billion people; one world," he frequently exclaims.

On a warm day in mid-June 2016, Landrum Bolling was in the vaulted hall of the United States Institute of Peace, waiting during a visit by His Holiness the Dalai Lama. His Holiness spoke to an audience about the power and importance of youth and their essential role in building a more peaceful world. But, with his eightieth birthday around the corner, he also had asked to meet some "elder peace-builders." Few wore that mantle more fully than Landrum. His Holiness stepped into the hall to meet Landrum, then a mere 102 years old. I introduced the two, explaining Landrum's career. The Dalai Lama took Landrum's right hand and bowed deeply, touching his forehead to the back of Landrum's hand. He then helped Landrum to a nearby chair, saying, "Compared to you, I am much younger," with his trademark chuckle. "I know your commitment," he said to Landrum. "Ohhh, wonderful!"

After Landrum's death, his wonderful and luminous daughter, Rebecca Pollack, sent me a copy of an undated, handwritten set of comments she found in her father's papers. It is vintage Landrum, and I can hear his smooth baritone voice as I read it. After noting all the questions that won't lead you to an answer to life's great challenges, he writes that the real question is this: "How to take the physical resources we have, the education, knowledge, skill we have and the social idealism we have, and create and sustain a decent world? How do we build a peaceful brotherhood of man?"

Landrum answers that question with this affirmation: "We bet our lives on the possibility it can be done, rejecting the ideas of cynicism and despair which tell us it can't be done." He concludes with an exhortation that he used often as he urged people to connect ideals with action. "You are building it now. Too many people are trying to start, to commence to begin. You are working at the great task of building brotherhood and peace. Now."

 *Khury Petersen-Smith is a geographer and activist who lives in Boston. He completed his PhD in the spring of 2016 at the Clark University Graduate School of Geography. His dissertation,* Pivoting to Asia: Sovereignty, Territory, and Militarization, *focuses on US militarization in the Asia-Pacific region. Khury's research interests include US empire, territory, place, and resistance. His activism is wide-ranging, but has focused in particular on opposing US empire, resisting racism, and solidarity with Palestine. Khury is the co-author of the 2015 Black Solidarity Statement with Palestine, which was signed by over 1,100 Black activists, artists, and scholars.*

American In/Security: From the Plantation to the Military Base
Khury Petersen-Smith

In an 1820 letter to John Holmes, Thomas Jefferson—the slave-own-ing settler known in the United States as a "Founding Father"—wrote the following about the enslavement of Black people: "We have the wolf by the ear, and we can neither hold him, nor safely let him go. Justice is in one scale, and self-preservation in the other."

The wolf, the enslaved Black population, posed a mortal dan-ger. But only to someone who chose to capture it, straddle its back, and hold it by the ear. The question of how this situation arose—in which the wolf did not have a say—goes unasked.

Jefferson never resolved his slave master's dilemma. In the same letter, he did call for the "diffusion" of enslavement by expanding the United States' territory—and therefore the theft of more land from Indigenous peoples and, in fact, the extension of slavery. But he acknowledged that this—the ownership of human beings—came at a price. Not for enslaved Black people or dispossessed Indigenous people, but for the white rulers of the United States. The elite would live in the constant fear that comes with the fact that their existence, and the existence of their state, rested somewhat precariously on the subjugation of a group of people whose liberation lied in the destruction of that edifice.

When officials in the US today claim to take certain measures "for security reasons," their actions are rooted in this history of enslavement and dispossession. Though slavery was abolished, racist state violence against Black people continues, as does the ongoing war against Indigenous people. These groups were far from the last to be punished for the success of the United States project. Rather, our oppression is central to a foundation whose structure has come to include myriad police forces, borders, the military, laws, and legal systems that have ensured the exploitation of the bulk of people in this country. Today, "security" is a convenient heading for a range of state activities directed at control.

"Security" is the watchword that serves as the explanation for surveillance cameras, police presences, and other sets of practices at airports, in subway stations, and countless other places. "Security" is what justifies the policing of all public space, actually, and the monitoring of our private moments, particularly when they are communicated electronically. It is the security of power. And it necessarily comes from the insecurity of those of us restricted from holding power.

Security for some, and its twin, insecurity for others, are not only rooted in US soil and the people who have worked it—those forced from it, and bound to it. They extend the world over.

One night in Okinawa, I was riding in a car to a restaurant with a Japanese friend. It was my first night in Okinawa, and we were eating out to celebrate my trip there, during which I was researching the massive US military presence on the island. As we waited at a stop light, my friend pointed to the car in front of us and called my attention to the fact that its license plate number began with a "Y."

"The 'Y' license plates belong to Americans," she explained. "Okinawans hate to see cars with 'Y' plates."

My friend explained to me that, should Okinawans find themselves in collisions with American drivers—US military personnel or their family members—the police would inevitably side with the Americans, even if they were the ones at fault. Legally, US military personnel enjoy tremendous protections through the Status of Forces Agreement that the United States has negotiated with Japan.

Okinawa, a distinct place and group of people historically entrapped by Japan, is currently jointly colonized by the US and Japan. Okinawa, where the US Department of Defense controls nearly one-fifth of the island's land, enters international consciousness whenever protest follows the crash of a military aircraft in one of the island's cities, or a sexual assault by a US serviceman. But the daily insecurity that comes with negotiating American drivers on Okinawan highways—as powerful behind the wheel as they are in uniform—tends to escape world news media.

Lest one forget, the US militarization of Okinawa does not exist to make the lives of Okinawans dangerous and difficult, though it certainly does that. It has a larger purpose: the projection of US power into Asia, and the Pacific, and throughout the world. The US bases in Okinawa have anchored military operations in and beyond the region since the Second World War. In other words, the bases, a source of insecurity for Okinawans, exist to produce insecurity for people all over the world.

This is how the United States entangles disparate populations into violent realities in the name of "security." This form of security cannot be democratized or otherwise made more inclusive or progressive. It must be ended.

But what about a shared security? What about a condition of safety, in which we can pursue lives that are not bounded by anything other than the wellbeing of others and our planet? That form of security is possible, but achieving it is complicated. This is because insecurity is symptomatic of a world ordered by inequality. Likewise, a shared, radical security would be the expression of a society whose foundations were altogether different.

In Okinawa, I met with Susumu Inamine, then mayor of Nago City. Camp Schwab, a sprawling US Marine Corps base, is located in Nago City, and the US and Japanese governments would like to locate an additional base there. Mayor Inamine was elected twice after campaigning against the bases. He generously took a break from his mayoral duties that day to answer my questions, and I began with my biggest one: how could he, as the mayor of a mid-sized city, located on a small island on the side of the world opposite from the United States, possibly stop the US military from building its base? The mayor's response was immediate. "We cannot stop the US military. Here, in Okinawa, we cannot stop it alone. That's why we need people outside of Okinawa to support us."

Upon hearing Mayor Inamine's response, I understood the

work of Okinawan activists in a new way. Despite the fact that I cannot read Japanese, the history of Okinawa and the contemporary resistance there is easy to access. This is because of the diligent work of Okinawan activists, who have made their situation legible to people very far away.

As with so many stories of oppression and resistance, those of Okinawa resonate far beyond the place where they unfold. In their efforts, Okinawan activists have become networked with those in the Philippines, South Korea, Guam, Hawai'i, and Puerto Rico, among other places. It is US militarization, through the building and maintaining of bases, that has brought people in these places together. Washington has spent decades constructing relationships with Tokyo, Seoul, Manila, and other power centers in the name of "security," at the peril of ordinary people the world over. What if we, as ordinary people, build relationships across communities and borders on the basis of solidarity instead?

To return to Thomas Jefferson's colorful metaphor, the United States has made wolves of many of us. But in our resistance, perhaps we can be guided by a vision that involves overcoming the common sources of our insecurity, oppression, and dispossession. And among ourselves—the different groups of people brought together through entanglement in the same system—we can build relations, not based on marginalization and antagonism, but cooperation, identifying with each other, and mutual interest in liberation. These elements of solidarity can not only guide resistance, but act as seeds for a vision of a new society.

We can imagine the pursuit of such a society—the development and honing of just and respectful ways of interacting—as planting a tree. Locating its home, rooting it firmly, nurturing it with care at times, and giving it space for its natural growth in others. In this vision, shared, radical security is not the tree. It is the shade that emerges as the tree flourishes.

 *Diana Francis is a peace campaigner, writer, and speaker. She is a program associate with Conciliation Resources, convener of the Rethinking Security Council (Ammerdown Group) and a member of the Society of Friends (Quakers). She has many years of international experience in supporting groups of people working nonviolently to address social and political cal conflict and violence, acting as a facilitator, trainer, mediator, and consultant. Currently, her overriding aim is to help promote a movement for change in the way people think about security, starting in the UK, in order to transform international relations policy so that it is no longer driven by the urge to dominate, but by the will to cooperate for the common good.*

The Things that Make for Peace
Diana Francis

I have always been an activist: someone who feels bound to act on
my responsibility to myself as a human being and for others: people,
other creatures, and the earth itself. I do not necessarily speak or
behave as wisely, effectively, or kindly as I might, but I do my best
to put into practice the values I hold. Those values were passed on
to me by my parents, whose tolerant and strong Christian faith and
ethics led them to refuse war service in World War II, and to work
instead to build bridges with "the enemy," help refugees, and bear
witness to the transformative power of nonviolence. To me too, the
Jesus with whom I became familiar as a child was an inspiring and
radical practitioner of nonviolent power: the power of love to refuse,
confront, and transform violence.

When I was fifteen I went to a weeklong youth event, organized
by the Fellowship of Reconciliation (FoR), to which my parents
belonged. There we discussed our beliefs, did role-plays, challenged
each other, and reflected on what we had learned. Then, in the eve-
nings, we visited youth clubs in the area to present our pacifist views
to other young people and engage with them as we were challenged
on our beliefs.

Not long after that week's immersion, I got together with
others at my school to form a youth group of the Campaign for
Nuclear Disarmament (CND) and the following year joined a days-
long protest march, from coast to coast, in the North of England.
From then on, national protests, direct action at weapons bases and
arms fairs, and regular local campaigning were a regular part of my

life. This year, at the Aldermaston nuclear weapons establishment, I joined CND's sixtieth anniversary demonstration and still join a weekly peace vigil at home in the city of Bath.

My understanding of nonviolence was greatly enlarged when I represented my national FoR branch at an International FoR (IFoR) gathering in India. There, I began to learn about what active nonviolence meant to people living in circumstances very different from my own, and from different faith or philosophical backgrounds. In the three years during which I served on IFoR's Steering Committee and my eight years as its President, I traveled widely and learned about the courage and sacrifice of those resisting dictatorship nonviolently, witnessing the power of their action in different parts of Latin America, in the Philippines, and in South Africa, achieving what violence, where tried, had not.

The process of the Soviet Union's disintegration added to the evidence for nonviolent power. As liberated areas began to experience new identity conflicts, all too often threatening or accompanied by violence, it also demonstrated the need to apply nonviolence not in freedom struggles but in resolving conflict and reconciling histories, to provide the basis for peaceful coexistence.

Having completed my time with IFoR and responding to this additional understanding of what nonviolence could require, I trained as a neighborhood mediator, and in turn became a mediation trainer in South West England. However, I was drawn back into international work and for more than twenty-five years have worked in different parts of the world as a trainer, facilitator, mediator, and accompanier, supporting local people who are taking their own action to prevent, transform, or recover from violent conflict. Those people have included grassroots activists, social or political leaders, and representatives of paramilitary groups. Some of them are models of nonviolence in action while others have violent backgrounds. All of them, like me, have their dark and light sides, and have the capacity to change.

Now, in my seventies, I find my convictions unchanged and my values only strengthened by my experience of working with all those people; and most of the skills and knowledge that I have developed through the years has been their gift. They have deepened and broadened my understanding of "the things that make for peace" (Luke 19:41–44), leading me into a process of never-ending reflection, questioning, and reaffirmation. They have also stoked the fire of my passion for change and for communicating to others, in person and in writing, what I have learned.

Despite all the human-generated suffering and destruction in the world, my work with others has given me all the evidence I need of the human potential for good. I have seen paramilitaries in Northern Ireland who had given themselves wholeheartedly to violence, and who had measured their own worth by the numbers they had killed, open themselves to others and to other ways of seeing things, sometimes risking their status and whole identity in order to step out of the cycle of violence and move forward into another life. I was present when sworn enemies from competing paramilitary factions in North East India washed one another's feet.

If people can be transformed, so can societies. I know community activists and civil society leaders who have given everything they have to the work of peacemaking, often for years on end and at risk to their own lives. I have seen them apparently lose the gains that they have made and their own credibility. Yet they have hung on, working in the small spaces left available to them; or they have come back with new vision and energy, mobilizing fresh support with a message of shared responsibility for the future. Together with my experience in the silence and solidarity of Quaker Meeting, it is their resilience and creativity that help me to keep going and give me hope that it is possible to develop a global society where the concept of shared security is embraced and lived.

Paradoxically, while believing that immeasurably greater human security could be achieved within my grandchildren's lifetime, I am also very much aware of the shared, and inevitable insecurity of human beings and all other life forms. The most fundamental facts of our lives are beyond our control. None of us chose our genetic make-up or the circumstances into which we were born; we did not choose the early influences that shaped us. Nothing and no one can secure us against untimely harm or inevitable death. Perhaps equally importantly, we do not choose the fact of our own isolation, each living in our own separate body and unique mental world. In this sense we live and die alone.

I believe that the level of consciousness that human beings have developed, including the consciousness of our own individual vulnerability and mortality, makes our need for others emotionally profound as well as practical, so that we, as a species, have developed a unique capacity to register and act upon our needs, both spontaneously and systematically, giving each other emotional support and comfort and cooperating with each other to achieve common purposes.

Although such cooperative and supportive responses are perhaps strongest among those we know and are related by family, friendship, neighborhood, employment and so on, they very commonly include strangers. If someone falls on the road, they will be quickly surrounded by well-wishers offering help. If someone is struggling to get through a door, someone else will hold it open. Strangers delayed or trapped together in a train will soon begin talking to one another, to dissipate their anxiety, pass the time, or help one another. In some cases, care for others takes the form of extreme altruism—the voluntary sacrifice of one person's life for the sake of another, or the refusal to harm another person, even at the possible cost of being harmed, even killed, in their place.

These human attributes go far beyond the mechanical cooperation of ants, for instance, whose practical sociability is phenomenal.[1] Our traits are genetically developed and are based in kindness, the cognitive and emotional recognition of being "of a kind" with fellow human beings and acting accordingly. They are experienced as empathy and compassion and are the basis for such limited security as we can create for and with each other: mutual or shared security.

In reality, of course, as a consequence of the fact that human beings are not simply programmed, as ants are, to play certain roles, but do have their own individual personalities and formative experiences, compassion and cooperation cannot be guaranteed to all people in all situations. They can be overwhelmed by other impulses and motivations: fear, suspicion, greed, selfishness, jealousy, anger, and hostility. Our "better nature" may also be overcome by fatigue, stress, and mental illness.

These other human attributes and motivations will be familiar and understandable to all of us. They too are part of the human condition and can give rise to acts of unkindness, both relatively trivial and deadly serious. When they are translated into the way societies are structured and into the cultural norms that govern behavior, institutions, and policy, they give rise to deformities such as patriarchy, racism, and militarism, which reduce and sometimes destroy shared security. They also displace cooperation with a contest for domination, violating the humanity of all concerned, and sometimes generating the mass violence of war.

Indeed, as the third millennium gets underway, humanity is confronted by multiple threats that stem from this culture of domination and the "eat or be eaten" approach to collective existence.[2] These different threats to security are interrelated and compounded by each other. For many people (and other beings), around the world, past and present, they have already brought catastrophe.

At the social level, the violence of crime and even terrorism is often associated with poverty and marginalization, which create feelings of powerlessness and motivate the exercise of the negative power to hurt or destroy.

The grievances of poverty and marginalization thereby become causal factors in war, while at the same time war is frequently used to extend economic and political dominance—in other words, for greed.[3] War is the most naked and concerted instrument of domination and counter-domination. It is the ultimate violent power, the power to violate and destroy.

Armed violence is the most common route to political oppression and is used to put down resistance of all kinds. When resisters turn to violence themselves, either they are quickly crushed by the regime or the conflict will develop into protracted civil war, most often lost by the resisters, who themselves are transformed by violence. In such cases, any "success" is achieved at the cost of great suffering and destruction.

No matter what its cause may be, war involves the effective suspension of the most fundamental human rights, including the right to life itself. Furthermore, its impact is not only injury and death, sometimes on an incomprehensible scale, but the creation and exacerbation of poverty, the destruction of property and livestock, the consequent loss of livelihoods—often resulting in forced migration—and the degradation of the infrastructure necessary to economic development. War not only creates poverty but constitutes a monumental waste and diversion of the resources needed for its eradication.

War is also intertwined with the growing environmental crisis. While it may be waged as a function of competition over scarce resources, it destroys, degrades, and pollutes the earth, hastening the further destruction of habitats and biodiversity, and accelerating climate change. Its environmental footprint joins the destructive methods of farming and the wasteful and polluting consumption of the rich to threaten the security of us all.

Yet alongside the grim reality of dominant power and its effects, another, cooperative model of power is already in operation and offers far brighter possibilities ahead. That model is characterized by nonviolent resistance to oppression, constructive and transformative approaches to conflict, human rights protection, economic justice, the sharing and protection of scarce resources, and the safeguarding of our planet.

Much good has been and is being achieved. An understanding of planetary interdependence and shared security is present in the existing attitudes and endeavors of countless people. There are elements in all societies that are positive and caring, at least at the personal level, and in most there are organizations and systems that work well for most people; aspects of government policy that are progressive; individuals who work quietly to bring about change and others who stand up against tyranny; economically advantaged people who want to close the gap between rich and poor; poor people supporting each other and working together to improve their rights; scientists, engineers, campaigners, and politicians working to protect the earth and growing numbers of people who are coming to reject war and focus on peace-building. And, here in the UK at least, the coming generation is far more progressive and compassionate than the ones ahead of them and deeply concerned about all aspects of human security.

Perhaps the greatest obstacle to change is the feeling of powerlessness experienced by so many. Those who live in poverty or in the margins feel they have no voice while those of us who are the material beneficiaries of the current dispensation find it impossible to separate ourselves from what it gives us, or from its injurious impact on others and on the future of all of us. We feel disempowered by the knowledge that if we act alone to modify our lifestyles, while others continue as before and policies remain unchanged, we shall have little impact. Even those who enter politics and other power arenas in order to effect change often feel themselves to be powerless in the face of existing norms and systems.

Those norms and systems must change. Despite our existential vulnerability our human species has enormous resilience and capacity to adapt and invent, born of our gifts of thought and communication. We must wake up, speak, and act together. We must ensure that, as we feel these pressures with increasing intensity, we will act collectively with ever greater determination. "People power" is real and the very urgency of our current global predicament makes this a time of great opportunity. If we can, in ever growing numbers, begin to talk to anybody and everybody about the threats and the need for change; to build bridges of solidarity between haves and have-nots, communities and organizations, civil society and politicians; and build alliances with others doing similar things in different countries, we can rapidly build our numbers and influence to the point where we are transforming minds, hearts, and systems.

For real change we must address the humanity of those who seem to stand in the way of our good goals. Anger and distress may provide the initial impetus for protest and resistance, but we would do well to heed Bertholdt Brecht's warning about anger's potentially dehumanizing effect: "Alas, we who would lay the foundations of kindness could not ourselves be kind." We must learn to speak with passion and truth but not in ways that will alienate those we want to join us. We must listen as well as speak, and make our approach to change as inclusive as the forces that have brought us to this point are divisive. Respect and dialogue must remain at the heart of the journey from here to the world we need to create. Indeed, they lie at the heart of it.

Just over four years ago, frustrated at the way in which the extraordinarily courageous and persistent work of local peacemakers was constantly obstructed and sometimes nullified by the catastrophic impact of geopolitics, a group of "peace professionals" came together for two precious days, to discuss this grim reality and consider how we could use our knowledge and connections to make a difference.[4]

In this first meeting we identified two key problems: a misconceived concept of what security is, and the idea that the hard and often violent pursuit of what is perceived as self-interest will produce it. We saw security in terms of wellbeing and freedom from fear, generated and enjoyed in concert with others, through constructive and cooperative relationships created on the basis of respect and mutuality. We saw insecurity as often generated, rather than prevented, by policy and practice based on the military "solutions" of "defense," as threat or attack.

We agreed that what was needed was a new understanding of security as something that needs to be shared and can be created only together. So the network organization, Rethinking Security was born. Its website, www.rethinkingsecurity.org.uk, tells the story so far. Our approach is to generate a big conversation at the local level, through civil society groups and organizations spanning different security concerns and identity or interest groups, to discuss the day-to-day security concerns they have, from the global to the personal, and the changes in policy they would like to see.

Through these local conversations, paralleled by discussions among the national organizations that support them and represent their interests, we hope to create a broad constituency of support for radical changes in national policy, informing conversations with policy makers, and the proposals made to them by Rethinking Security. (Documents produced for both levels of conversation are available on the website.)

In my local campaigning group we have found that Rethinking Security has given us new energy and a creative framework for engaging and cooperating with others in our city who are concerned with different aspects of human security. It also helps us to reach a wider public than before, enables dialogue between different social sectors, and provides the focus for our local political engagement.

My hope is that this initiative and others like it will contribute to a fast-expanding and radical process of rethinking that can still reverse what seems, at times, to be a rapid descent toward the abyss. If we realize that our old dysfunctional habits have brought humanity to the brink and begin to communicate in earnest; if we can manage our fear, heed our best instincts, and recognize that we will sink or swim together, we can yet avoid destroying each other and our planet and create a safer, fairer world—together.

Notes

1. Edward O. Wilson, *The Social Conquest of Earth* (New York: Liveright Publishing, 2013).

2. Diana Francis, *From Pacification to Peace-Building: A Call for Global Transformation* (London: Pluto Press, 2010), 73–74.

3. Paul Collier and Anke Hoeffler, "Greed and Grievances in Civil War," *Oxford Economic Papers* 56 (2004): 563–595.

4. The American Friends Service Committee and The Friends Committee on National Legislation, "Shared Security: Reimagining U.S. Foreign Policy," American Friends Service Committee, July 2015. Accessed September 18, 2018. www.afsc.org/document/ shared-security-reimagining-us-foreign-policy.

 *Dr. Azza Karam serves as the senior advisor on culture at the United Nations Population Fund (UNFPA), where she coordinates UNFPA-wide outreach with faith-based partners and chairs the UN Inter-Agency Task Force on Religion and Development. Before she joined UNFPA, she was the senior policy research advisor at the United Nations Development Program in the Regional Bureau for Arab States.*

174

Going Beyond "The Weakest of Faith"
Azza Karam

The catcalls by men in the street, the groping in many public spaces, and especially when taking public transport—including by boys younger than me—the glares by some of the veiled women as I walked past (unveiled yet modestly dressed), are memories underlining the deepest sense of insecurity in public spaces I still live with, several decades after experiencing this in the 1980s and '90s, in Egypt.

To this day, riding a bus, a subway, a train, or even taking a taxi is a source of anxiety, where I feel that for most of the journey I hold my breath. I deliberately seek to calm down, to overcome the sense of dread of any and all forms of travel using public transportation, or where I am alone. Completing the journey and arriving at a destination feels like a huge triumph—a mixture of adrenaline and exhaustion. And this persists no matter which part of the world I am in, or the duration of the journey.

Flashback to a time in the mid-1990s when I see a woman running down the stairs, her face bloodied, with her husband a few steps behind, she screaming for protection, he shouting and pursuing her with a look of near madness on his face, and a cascade of loud curses emanating from his lips. We called the local Imam to help counsel him, for this was not the first time, and we always turn to the religious leaders in times of our deepest need. The Imam, from a small mosque in a small town, maintains it is "the wife's duty not to upset her husband," and "not to push him to be violent…"

At a time when rape is used as a weapon of war, it may seem

almost a luxury to be concerned about riding public transport in time of total peace, or to be furious at an incident of domestic violence, and the role of one Imam in perpetuating it. However, in many parts of the world, appealing for protection from harassment—no matter how severe—from military, political, and even religious institutions, which are supposed to protect and uphold the human rights of all citizens, continues to be seriously challenging. Furthermore, legislation is not sufficient to counter patriarchal norms which are still very much alive and well in these institutions, mirroring near-misogynistic tendencies endemic to some societies.

While centuries of activism for women's rights have effected significant changes in leadership in many institutions around the world, political institutions are only slowly beginning to reflect leadership structures somewhat in line with how the populations themselves are composed. But the military, and especially religious institutions, remain largely male dominated. It is not only male dominance in terms of numbers that can be eschewed. Rather, at the heart of the matter is a seeming persistence to uphold and defend a *culture* which sees women as either too weak to take responsibility, or too strong and thus requiring systematic pushback.

In 2018, the #MeToo movement finally exposed, at least in the West, a long-term complacency about how sexual harassment in diverse public spaces was considered "normal." In many ways, this exposure is an inevitable step toward a sense of shared security; for no woman is safe in any space where she can be sexually harassed and have this be thought of as "normal."

We have yet to hear of the #MeToo movement having a similar resonance and impact outside of the West. And we have yet to live in contexts where gender-based violence—including domestic violence, and sexual *and verbal* harassment of girls and women—is considered to be absolutely beyond the realm of the acceptable.

If the ordinary spaces, including those inside a marriage, can still be "unsafe" for women, in time of peace, and those in power have a prerogative to inflict verbal violence toward women, then is it any wonder that diverse forms of sexual violence take place, among strangers, in times of war?

If no woman is safe, no society can be. In other words, there is no shared security in a space where any woman feels insecure.

In my Islamic faith, an oft noted Hadith (saying of the Prophet, peace be upon him) is one where he says that "*Whosoever of you sees an evil, let him change it with his hand; and if he is not able to do so, then [let him change it] with his tongue; and if he is not able to do so, then with his heart—and that is the weakest of faith*".[1]

The "weakest of faith" means that this is the very least we can do, or the most minimal act of faith required of believers. This is why I work in the field of faith-based engagement. Because I believe that social transformation does not happen *in spite of* the persistence of institutions—especially religious ones—but when some of these very same institutions themselves become complicit in the processes of change. Indeed, when members of these institutions become allies in processes of social transformation, this is the "tipping point" which is catalytic to securing changes in hearts and minds.

Faith-based organizations (FBOs), in their diversity, are not merely the oldest social service providers historically known to humankind, but religious institutions are the oldest organizational structures which continue to function, to serve communities, in times of humanitarian crisis, when state infrastructure may virtually collapse. Moreover, religious leaders, in many parts of the world, are still the most important influencers of behaviors and attitudes.

If violence against girls and women is to be made abnormal, working with religious actors is not a luxury, nor an additional aspect to consider once the "important" sectors are attended to; it is the key to going beyond "the weakest of faith." That is, doing more than the bare minimum.

I started working directly with diverse faith actors, as part of the World Conference of Religions for Peace's Women's Program in 2000. My job was to reach out to women of faith in each faith community around the world, through the male clergy/religious leaders, and to support their own interfaith mobilization for shared objectives. By 2002, Religions for Peace had put together a document reflecting voices of women of faith from diverse religious traditions, reinterpreting their leadership roles within their respective communities.[2]

By the end of 2003, Religions for Peace had compiled a unique Directory and Global Network of Women of Faith, over 350 organizations strong, representing different religions, regions, and areas of work (youth, children, women's empowerment, health, etc.).

But when I started that work in 2000 and right through till 2004, "women's empowerment" was an uncommon word for religious leaders to utter, and few FBOs were renowned for their work in anything to do with gender. In fact, the entire Directory, which was painstakingly built over four years, was removed entirely from the internet in 2004, thus completely deleting a unique and invaluable resource. Why? Because some of the male religious leaders felt that the women of faith organizations which were noted, were not "observant" enough of the religious orthodoxy.

Also, at around the same time, as I joined the United Nations to do this work for the secular multilateral side, none of the UN system entities had recorded their work with FBOs, nor even attempted to develop guidelines on engaging with faith actors, nor could they list whom they worked with in the realm of religious actors.

Nearly two decades later, two important transformations have taken place: On the UN side, the United Nations Interagency Task Force on Religion came into existence and today has a database of faith-based partners with over 500 FBOs from around the world—all UN system partners—and an annual UN Strategic Learning Exchange which convenes UN policy and program advisors with their counterparts in FBOs. On the faith-based side, on April 5, 2018, in a strategic planning meeting for the SDGs between the United Nations Interagency Task Force on Religion (with over 40 faith-based partners representing some of the largest faith-based humanitarian and development providers around the world), "gender justice" was identified as a priority goal by and for all the FBOs.

I believe we are now, by the grace of God, journeying toward shared security. And the journey is also the destination, for it is through partaking of this journey of gender justice that we can change "with our hands" *and* "change with our mouth" to effect shared security.

Notes

1. "When You See a Wrong, Change It with Your Hand …" Stand Up 4 Islam, December 25, 2012. Accessed June 5, 2018. https://standup4islam.wordpress.com/tag/hadith-from-muslim/.

2. Azza Karam, ed., *A Woman's Place: Religious Women as Public Actors* (New York: WCRP, 2004).

Hussein Nabil Murtaja became a spokes-man for victims of wars and armed con-flicts after he was shot in 2006. His youth group, Letters Initiative, empowered marginalized groups within Gaza, many of them in cooperation with the United Nations. In 2012, he joined the first Palestinian Model United Nations, help-ing to spread the concept of constructive dialogue. He is the coordinator for projects at Gaza Group of Culture and Development, a director of the economic empowerment project for poor families in the Gaza Strip, a member of the Youth Advisory Board, UN HABITAT, representing the Arab region, and part of the UN ad-visory group on peace, youth, and security. He has a BA in Engineering and a Higher Diploma in Applications and Entrepreneurship.

The Art of Survival
Peace Our Dream
Hussein Murtaja

The difficult circumstances we are living in drive us to exert more effort and work with a sense of urgency to find quick and effective solutions, especially with regard to achieving security, peace, and justice in our world.

It was not my fault that I was born in a region permeated by conflict and into a fight in which I was one of the victims. Unfortunately, I did not even know who fired the bullet that made my life one filled with silence, suspicion, and fear for nearly two years.

2006: The year in which I was reborn, after a six-month coma caused by a bullet lodged in my head, due to a power struggle at the time between the Palestinian factions (Fateh and Hamas).

I came out of the coma and got a weird feeling as I heard my mother's voice, and as she kept telling me "you are fine." She said: "The sun comes up and shines for you every day, get up and be an engineer just like you promised me."

After a period of time I became an engineer, and I realized that we are created for a certain purpose and to convey a message. I found out that we are created for doing good and for achieving peace and security, and to secure the justice that we all aspire to enjoy.

Since that time, I started working to achieve my goal of living in a society where justice, equality, and freedom to live, to express views and opinions, runs parallel to equal opportunities for all genders; a society in which we respect each other, accept differences of view, and aim for a better world. A society that allows people to live free from violence.

In 2008, I started my work and activities with a project called Letters Initiative, aimed at conveying and communicating the voice of marginalized and vulnerable groups and giving voice to their suffering. The letters were sent to many people abroad in various countries. Our program was discovered by the United Nations, which helped in obtaining financial support for this and many other programs, including psychological support programs for children, Model United Nations, Our City Deserves the Best, and Be the Change initiatives, among others.

As a result of these activities and initiatives, thousands of youth (males and females) joined us and the hope of making change started growing. We focused on civil society institutions as the starting point. We implemented economic empowerment projects for hundreds of poor families and relief and emergency programs, and we started working on a plan for urban development for a better future within Gaza.

Among the thousands of candidates for the Youth Advisory Board of UN-HABITAT (United Nations Human Settlements Program), through electronic elections, I obtained the highest votes and became the representative of the Arab region on the Advisory Board. It was a volunteer position, but contributed greatly to the recognition of the importance of urban civilized cities in achieving security and stability for their citizens. This experience, and the great chance it gave me to add my own voice, have enriched my skills and experience.

Together, we youth leaders from around the globe began to form teams and larger groups and to put more pressure on all to recognize our genuine desire to have a role in building our societies. For my part, I joined with others in the Middle East to carry out several important activities that served this goal. These activities included holding consultative sessions to prepare a study on peace and security, and our role as youth in this matter; holding trainings for young leaders; and workshops and awareness programs to activate the role of youth in society throughout the Middle East. Also, one of the activities carried out was establishing youth councils, especially in marginalized areas including the Al Moghraqa area, Bait Lahia, and the Al Shoka area in Rafah, Palestine, which played a major role in community participation and helped enhance the role of youth in their cities and communities.

The role of the youth councils is to support the villages and cities in which these youth live, and to activate these young people in the process of development, social, and political participation. One of the challenges I remember very well is that many youth hesitated to join, or refused to support and participate in the councils, because they thought their efforts would be in vain. Fortunately, we were able to change their opinion through the impacts and outcomes of the initiatives that we had already begun. As more young people joined the councils, we succeeded in strengthening the role of youth. These situations have encouraged me in my desire to add more activities and initiatives that are centered on youth in Gaza.

In 2016, I was honored to be selected by the Secretary-General of the United Nations to be a member of the Advisory Committee to prepare a progress study on youth, peace, and security within Security Council Resolution 2250. SS2250 is the first of its kind to give young people the opportunity to be integrated into the process of peace-building, in order to achieve security in our societies in light of the apparent inability of governments to control this deterioration. I also got a chance to travel and meet many great people and personalities, and I met and interacted with various communities, noting every step of the way that the desire to live in peace and security is shared universally.

I do believe that it is possible to achieve peace and security, and that it is a result of our activities and our actions. We individuals, institutions, and governments must cooperate in doing everything that brings peace and stability to our societies. And we must exercise our right to make changes for a better future and a beautiful world, by reaching out to each other and reaffirming our common purpose.

 *Lucy Roberts is a Humanities graduate, with an MA in Development Studies from the University of East Anglia, UK. She has been working in Asia, as well as in the Middle East and Africa, for over 15 years, initially in development and later moving into the peace-building field. She has worked with INGOs, the UN, and for the past seven years, the British and American Quakers, currently holding the position of Regional Director, Asia, with American Friends Service Committee, working from Phnom Penh.*

Just Peace
Lucy Roberts

*"I will never attend an anti-war rally; if you have a peace rally, invite
me."* —Mother Teresa

My professional life has meandered from voluntary and direct
development work, to policy work around development issues, to
political peace-building. I am aware of varied forms of oppression
complexly interwoven with the social fabric of many countries, and
my experiences and learning have lead me to believe the solutions
come from within. But I am also conscious of structural forms of oppression beyond the reach of civil society and national governments
in poorer nations, maintaining the status quo between "developed"
and "developing" countries. Many highly committed people come
from the UK and other wealthy countries to work internationally
to address poverty and its varied ramifications, but the structures are
still inherently colonial, generally driven by economic inequalities
between countries, and the power of those with influence over weapons and trade.

What is uncomfortable for me is the repeated focus on the
victim. For gender justice work the focus has traditionally been on
the empowerment of women without engaging men, for work on
economic inequality the focus is on livelihoods and the poor without strategies for capping the rich. And for addressing corruption,
the onus is often on civil society to stand against corrupt practices
without attention to the ingrained corrupt governmental structures
that only the key beneficiaries of the system can address. Likewise,

rich countries help the poor countries to "develop" whilst protecting their own interests, and there are no overarching bodies holding the powerful countries and corporations accountable for their global practices.

Taking my own country as an example, what unsettles me now is the contradiction inherent in its practices. On the one hand, the UK, through the Department for International Development (DFID), provides, amongst other aid, small grants to civil society organizations to address corruption and promote good governance, democracy, and human rights, scrutinizing the capacity of the NGOs to manage the funds well and articulate their intended goals and activities. On the other hand, the UK, a nuclear power with a permanent seat on the Security Council, strategies to promote international business interests, paying no heed to the stringent criteria set for the NGO recipients of funds. When the UK sells arms to Saudi Arabia, is the impact of the engagement on civil society, people's rights, anti-corruption policies, good governance, and democracy considered? According to a report in Middle East Eye, we bomb Syria at a cost of over £500k ($640,000 USD) per airstrike.[1] Have we been through a checklist, as recipients of aid do, and considered such things as the number of direct and indirect "beneficiaries," and whether the intervention is sustainable? Do we identify indicators to show whether UK attacks on Syria are "working"?

The UK and other powerful countries, through the Financial Action Task Force, have also created criteria for aid recipients to prevent money-laundering and keep funds out of the hands of terrorists. The regulations have been the catalyst for new national NGO laws in numerous countries. Autocratic governments with low terrorist threats are using the NGO laws to clamp down on rights organizations and other civil society bodies they consider a threat. The small grants given by donors to promote democratic and open societies are outweighed by the impact of global approaches to anti-terrorism. The unintended, but significant effect of restricting civil society is global and analogous with the rise of neo-liberalism.

In my current work I have a focus on North Korea, and AFSC works to promote a diplomatic relationship between North

Korea and the US. We have worked with North Korea for decades on an agricultural program, in which we take stories to Washington, DC, of normal life in North Korea and put a human face to the people who have been reduced to brainwashed robots or comic figures by the US media for a long time. North Korea has been vilified and victimized by the US, and has, as is clear, become very defensive. The US, until recently, pursued a policy of non-engagement with North Korea unless they agreed to nuclear disarmament. North Korea feels too threatened to do this, and AFSC has been suggesting ways the US administration can engage diplomatically on issues that do not focus immediately on disarmament. For example, talks on the return of the remains of US service people to the States could be a good starting point. Trump, of all people, overrode the US convention of non-engagement with North Korea, or engagement on the condition that they committed to nuclear disarmament, and has included, in his four-point agreement with Kim Jong-un at the Singapore Summit 2018, to receive the service people's remains from North Korea. It is an unpredictable situation, but there is a foothold for further discussion. Further, Trump has canceled some of the provocative joint military exercises with South Korea already. These are key steps for building trust at a macro level, and reflect a shared security approach, which enhances not just the security of North Korean and US citizens, but citizens around the globe.

By shared security I mean security for all, made possible when individuals, groups, societies, or nations are not coerced or oppressed by others. The framework proposes finding shared

solutions to conflicts, and not creating false polemics and traditional zero-sum models. We cannot be truly safe and secure until all communities and countries exist in equilibrium, without coercive military threat and control. The diagram below gives a simple outline of the concept and is one that I use in my work with American Friends Service Committee.

I am in the process of returning to the UK after twenty years of working internationally. I want to be able to express my political views in my country. Working overseas, I am a guest, and though I have opinions on the politics of the countries in which I have lived, it is never "my" country. I am not a legitimate actor, but can bear witness, learn, facilitate, and support strategic developments toward peace and justice.

From what I have seen, there is no doubt that fair and open process and honest, open relationships lead to just peace, whereas oppression and coercion in any negotiation may lead to temporary peace, but not a just and lasting peace. I believe that a shared security approach is the only way to reach personal, national, and international security.

For the UK to rethink its stance in the world, its foreign policy, as well as its approach to building a secure nation for all UK citizens, demands something of a paradigm shift. There are many hopeful signs that this may take place—for the first time, there is greater recognition of. and public acknowledgment by politicians of the correlation between UK actions in Syria and security in the UK. Military action in the Middle East is making citizens more vulnerable to attacks in the UK. Security in the UK cannot be created by military presence on the streets and intelligence investigations alone, but by identifying and addressing root causes of anger, frustration, and discrimination within society.

The public awareness of and opposition to UK arms dealing is growing exponentially. If the leaders in the UK could begin to scrutinize military interventions and international business engagement to the same extent as aid delivery, there would be a marked improvement in global security. If the UK could reduce the amount expended on weapons, we would not be so dependent on the income from arms dealing. This is the case for all countries around the world, including North Korea. I interviewed Mr. O Ryong-il, Presidium Member, Korean National Peace Committee in Pyongyang, North Korea, in May 2017. He said, "We have to be strong enough to protect the national sovereignty and our dignity for ourselves. There are big countries in the neighborhood, they are just concerned with their own interest," and then mentioned that if the pressure was released, North Korea could focus its resources on the well-being of the nation.

If the UK government can act on their recognition that security for all citizens, not just the white population, means developing an inclusive and tolerant society without discrimination, many positive changes would follow. This would be a way of modeling some of the British values we extol. Could the UK government also recognize that poverty leads to insecurity, and investment in comprehensive public services creates security? This is a valid approach to provide secure lives for current and future generations, and national and global threats would diminish. In terms of economics, there are robust plans that show how the UK can exist without the arms trade and unjust international business engagement. Longer term, investing in public services, thus reducing threats and the need for high levels of policing and military presence, is cost effective. Some models are described particularly clearly in Scilla Elworthy's book *A Business Plan for Peace*.

I am moved by the concept within Mother Teresa's quote at the head of this piece. Of course, there is a place for challenging the current status quo, and organizations such as Campaign Against Arms Trade and Stop the War Coalition provide essential and valuable analysis and data to educate both the public and political decision makers. But in addition, we need to build something new from the ground up, as opposed to altering and redesigning what we already have in place. The idea of creating a new model or joining the "pro-peace rally" as Mother Teresa said resonates with me, and I am excited by opportunities to engage in new structures and ways of thinking. I want to commit my energy to envisioning new models and working with them until they gain the momentum, recognition, and support to supersede the oppressive and ineffective structures. Recently I've become more aware of the importance of my personal pleasure in my friendships and relationships with all the people I interact with when the world looks grim politically. There is much joy in the world, emanating from our own special relationships with all the wonderful people we are fortunate enough to know. Our joyfulness overrides our own and others' inclination to abuse and oppress. We are all diminished by insecurity, even if we are insulated by wealth and weapons. With a shared security framework, the only challenge is being open to something new, and once we cross that hurdle, it is a holistic win-win.

Notes

1. Jamie Merrell, "UK Spends $2.5 B Bombing Islamic State in Iraq and Syria," Middle East Eye, February 26, 2018. Accessed September 18, 2018. www.middleeasteye.net/news/ revealed-uk-spends-25m-bombing-islamic-state-iraq-and-syria-134341159

 Brian Ganson heads the Africa Centre for Dispute Settlement at the University of Stellenbosch Business School, a platform for research and dialogue at the nexus of business, conflict, and development. His research, teaching, and consulting focus on socio-political risk mitigation, conflict prevention, and third-party roles in post-conflict and other complex environments. He holds a Master of Arts in Law and Diplomacy from the Fletcher School, Tufts University, and a Juris Doctorate from Harvard University. He tells his mother that his peace-building work is as mundane as plumbing. He continues to work to make that true. He can be reached at Brian@Ganson.org

Plumbing for Peace
Brian Ganson

When people ask about my peace-building work, they seem most engaged by the over-the-top stories: clandestine meetings with criminal gang leaders in Nigeria; navigating the military curfew in Kosovo; coming face to face with the machete-wielding crews contesting gold fields in Ghana; the grandmothers in the Sudan who grimly reminded me that, should the government continue to ignore their demands, they knew where their guns were buried. People's preconceptions and my ego combine to tell a story of peace-building as exotic, dangerous, and exciting.

When I began this work, all that was certainly what I was looking for. Growing up, I had always been the invisible one: the middle child, the transplant to the midwestern high school where the cliques had closed ranks already in kindergarten, the gay kid deeply and fearfully in the closet. UN helicopters made me feel exceptional; jungle treks beyond the boundaries that UN security forces were allowed to accompany me ensured a flow of adrenaline that made me somehow more alive. Larger than life stories of wars and the efforts to end them gave life an operatic quality. The more extreme the situation, the more real I became.

But the peace-building work of which I'm most proud after thirty years, and which I believe has had the most impact, is far from exciting. It takes place in community centers with flip charts as people map what divides them and what connects them. It takes place in boardrooms with PowerPoints whose facts and figures help the powerful confront their role in maintaining negatively reinforcing systems. It takes place writing at a computer, witnessing and sharing the courage of others. Often it simply involves sitting quietly and attentively, letting people tell stories of conflict over and over until somebody ventures to say, maybe we don't want to tell *this* story anymore and begins to construct a new one.

In fact, I've come to think of peace as mundane as plumbing, and myself as a peace-builder—particularly one who often works in other's communities—as a plumber.

When I first headed out to remote assignments, typically to places that had been solemnly declared "post-conflict" at the signing of a peace accord, I thought it was my job to build something new. I was trained in counseling and mediation; I had a degree in diplomacy; I cut my teeth with the international experts at the Harvard Negotiation Project whose stories of intrigue drew me to the field in the first place. The protagonists where I was going had apparently done their degrees in war and conflict; mine were in peace. Egged on by fragility frameworks that emphasized gap analyses and their litany of weak rule of law, weak institutions, and lack of human capacity, I assumed my job was to help these places make fresh starts and plant new seeds in the ashes.

But now I know that my work is never the beginning of a story. On our way to Myanmar under the military regime, a mentor bluntly told me to stop looking for what was missing and start paying attention to what was there. Only then did I start to understand the places where I was working. After all, if things were as broken as the analysts described, how was it that motorcycle taxis in the most remote corners of Sierra Leone had the fuel and spare parts to stay on the road? How was it that a sixteen year old from a poor neighborhood in Mexico had read and taken inspiration from Chinua Achebe? Over generations, the piping of social and economic structures has been laid, the pumps operated, repairs made. Like a plumber, my peace-building contribution starts by understanding the pieces—particularly those that were so strong and resilient that they nurtured and protected people even in the midst of violent conflict and deprivation—that were installed well before I arrived and will endure long after I'm gone. I've learned that my work is more akin to helping to identify and repair a leak than to designing a new water treatment plant.

Despite my high opinion of the insights and capabilities my colleagues and I brought to our work, I was at least aware that we could not, as foreigners intending to get back on the airplane home, accomplish anything like all of what was needed to bring peace to countries in conflict. But we were doing our part, we said: performing analysis, teaching a seminar, or carrying out a "pilot" that some yet-to-be-determined set of actors would embrace and take to scale. We worked opportunistically: if the east of Bosnia and Herzegovina could not be navigated, we went west; if the ears of elites were closed, we talked to grassroots initiatives. We operated under three-week or three-month grants to deliver "our" projects—or, over the course of a year or two, had "local implementing partners" who worked under contract to us. We tacitly assumed that our work in white Land Cruisers would somehow dovetail with the efforts of many others in white Land Cruisers to result in peaceful change. At least, that's what the grant proposals we wrote typically said.

I know better now that such an assumption is a recipe for wasted effort, deep disappointment and, far too often, the subversion of true peace work taking place. It is akin to dumping a truckload of pipes in a poor neighborhood needing clean water and hoping that someone will dig the ditches, someone else will source the connectors, and yet someone else will figure out the valves. After the noise and drama of delivering the material, all that happens is that people fight over what ends up as scrap metal. It certainly doesn't create—or in reality meaningfully contribute to—a functioning municipal water system.

A place experiencing entrenched conflict needs to experience profound shifts in power relationships and institutional arrangements in order to unleash peaceful development. This requires sufficiently broad consensus on the vision for what the new social order might look like and on plans for moving from here to there, taking into account the plethora of forces that may inhibit change. Like a plumbing contractor showing up on the site of a civic center under renovation, we are at best playing a supporting role. Even acknowledging that we bring distinctive skills and experience, we had better let the architect on site direct how our piece fits in with the work of others and understand that we are only helpful insofar as we advance the vision of the proprietors of the building.

Finally, I used to assume that it was the dramatic moves and big ideas that brought peace. Schemes developed in diplomatic missions to bring leaders of warring parties into the same room; plans hatched in UN headquarters in New York or Geneva for post-conflict development that ran to hundreds of millions of dollars—that's where the action seemed to be. Integrated Demobilization, Disarmament and Reintegration. Imagine Coexistence. Business for Peace. These international slogans—whether the frameworks for understanding and action underpinning them were more or less rigorous—exposed our belief that, if we could only get the thinking straight, we could get the action right. The brainstorm and the devising session were our stock in trade; consequently, we held in greatest awe the rock stars of peace-building theory in academia and international institutions.

Today I see the heroism in spade work. For the most part the plumber arrives already knowing what to do. The honor of the work is in showing up as promised, competent skills, careful execution, cleaning up after the job is done, and submitting an honest invoice. In the same way, most helpful peace-building work is routine. We use tried and tested frameworks for mapping conflict systems. We dip into a well-worn tool bag of approaches to collaborative analysis and planning. We host conversations, and more conversations, and even more conversations, until common understandings begin to emerge and solidify. Like plumbing, peace-building happens because people show up and do the work, carefully and deliberately. And I'm pretty sure I had it backward: like a thoughtful plumber who through experience may find better solutions to recurring challenges, only when we get the action right does the thinking become straight.

These reflections lead perhaps to a natural question: what is the system of plumbing on which I am working?

My starting point for an answer is my experience that, across cultures and contexts, people wake up aspiring to the same thing. We might characterize this as a peaceful day: one where the children are fed, they go to school with the prospect for a better future, the sick and lonely are attended to, and none of them experiences violence. And in even the most terrible places, the good and generous people sharing this vision vastly outnumber those who are indifferent to the suffering of others or who would use violence to advance their aims. The critical question for peace-building is not, then, what causes destructive conflict and war; these are the strategies of the few. What we must better understand is that which keeps the many from coming together to insist on and co-create their common vision.

My experience, research, and reflection, together with many others in many places, suggest that certain social mechanisms are required so that coalitions for positive change may coalesce and take action. Where these mechanisms are broken or compromised, communities and societies appear to be far more vulnerable to contentious conflict and destructive deadlock.

I once sat in a room in Kampala in which the topic of conversation was conflict around oil development in Uganda's Albertine Graben. People began to argue over whether gas flaring was happening. Now, one might argue over how destructive gas flaring is. One might argue over who is responsible, or about what should be done about it. But a gas flare is dramatic: an intense tower of flame that can rise hundreds of feet into the sky. One should presumably not be in a heated argument over whether it is happening at all. Yet in Uganda as elsewhere, those in the capital often don't actually know what is happening in the provinces. Even local communities become rumor rich and information poor as people take sides for or against particular actors or forms of development. And of course, some in both places actively manipulate information for cynical aims. People in conflict environments appear to have lost the ability to ask and answer the question of what is happening and why in any comprehensive or mutually credible way.

In Para State in the Amazon region of Brazil, I have spoken over the past months with dozens of community, government, and business leaders about challenges and opportunities for development. Not a single person spontaneously raised the issue of violence—even though murder rates are among the highest in the world, and domestic violence and violence in the schools are daily realities for far too many families. People talk passionately and cogently about land, economic opportunity, and the environment. But they seem to treat the violence and related issues of impunity or security service complicity as unalterable facts of life—like the rain or the heat—or as too big to imagine tackling. People in conflict environments appear to have lost the ability, or even the hope, that they could ask and answer the question of how action can be organized on the critical issues that require all of our efforts working together.

In South Africa where I live, we enter every year into strike season. Employers make offers they fully know will be raised later; workers respond in kind with demands they expect will be compromised. The rituals of increasingly agitated labor protest often follow patterns of the struggle against Apartheid, with even the police union announcing that it will make the country ungovernable if its demands are not met. This is the same country where white mine owners and black union leaders negotiated the creation of the Independent Mediation Service of South Africa to provide for more just settlement of labor disputes even under the old regime. It is the same country whose national system of peace committees created to protect the space for the democratic transition provides inspiration for systemic approaches to violence risk reduction around the world. Yet in South Africa, as in other conflict prone environments, the ability of people to ask and answer the question of what we should do when we profoundly disagree appears to be sorely compromised.

There are any number of reasons these dynamics may have developed in a particular community or society, reinforcing negative interactions over decades or generations. Yet and still, another of my mentors reminds me that even in situations of seemingly entrenched conflict, the system wants to go back to reason; that is to say, as human beings we are not wired to live in states of perpetual agitation or confrontation, and there is, in most all cases, a center that is trying to hold.

Where this is not true, there is perhaps little we as outsiders can do. But given that it is mostly true, we are back to our job as plumbers. We help others map and understand the systems by which their communities and the broader society have historically asked and answered the questions of what is happening, what should be done, and what we will do if we disagree. We diagnose with them why those systems are not working as needed to promote positive change. Is there a particularly contentious issue that acts like a clogged drain to back up the system? Is the social plumbing overwhelmed by issues or circumstances it was never designed to handle? Are there people needing access to the system whose needs were never taken into account?

As journeyman plumbers, we can then share options and ideas to the owners and users of the system: some that look like workarounds, some that represent repairs, and some that are analogous to new extensions that help get the system of asking and answering running more freely. We discuss risks and benefits of different approaches, the scale of effort needed commensurate to the scale of the challenges experienced, and which fit best with their appetite for social renovation. We can provide reasonable assurances through our experience and others' that, with a robust enough social infrastructure for asking and answering simple yet crucial questions, the coalitions for positive social change which they desire can start to flow.

These further reflections bring me to two observations. First, I have perhaps come to the end of the utility of the metaphor of the peace-builder as plumber. Because, after all, I will not to be there to make the repairs or put new social plumbing in place in almost any of the many countries in which I work; I am sometimes a plumbing advisor, but rarely one of the actual plumbers. Second, and perhaps more profoundly, I have come to more fully appreciate that the social plumbing toward which we are working is not only a tool for peace-building—it is itself peace.

I have often discussed with friends and colleagues a paradox of my work: that it is often in the most unsettled places that I feel the most at peace. I used to tend toward pathologizing this: was my witnessing of the aftermath of the Rwandan genocide providing some perverse sense of gratitude or personal well-being?

A woman reflecting on the reasons for her participation in a peace-building organization in the Niger Delta helped me see things in a different light. A number of her colleagues had talked about their pride in what their organization was doing out in the community: peace education, mediation of land disputes, or advocacy for more inclusive public policies, for example, all of which they believed were helping to bring the peace that they so greatly desired to a troubled place. This motivated them, they related, to continue their work under difficult and often dangerous conditions.

She agreed with their assessment of the work but offered that her prime motivation for participation was that it was only in rooms with her fellow peace-builders that she experienced peace. In her daily life, the social fabric was so torn that one hardly got angry when cheated; it was what people had come to expect from each other. Almost no one could depend on anyone else. In stark contrast, within the organization, people from all walks of life came together, willing to do the hard work of understanding each other's social, economic, and political realities, fears, and hopes. They explored ideas for change, their own courage for pursuing them, and their roles in doing so. They didn't always see eye to eye, or always pursue the same agenda. But they could always disagree respectfully and reach collective decisions that seemed to meet the needs of all. Through the compassion and caring exhibited toward each other and the society around them, they were not only planning for peace, or building peace. They were living peace.

This insight, I realized, captures what I have witnessed and experienced time and time again when I engage as fully and authentically in these inquiries as I know how to. It happened in Sierra Leone as I discussed with motorcycle taxi drivers—most all of whom were ex-combatants—the future they wanted for their country and the implications for their own conduct as drivers and as citizens. It happened with the peace-builders in Nigeria as we reflected on the organization's formative years and planned for their next and more ambitious phase of civic engagement. It happened in Oslo as corporate actors began to acknowledge the ways in which their presence and operations had over decades undermined local capacities for peace in conflict-prone areas, and explored how they might instead work in ways that reinforced such capacities. It happened as citizens in Brazil created a new kind of forum in which they could be heard in ways that began to hold their public officials accountable. It happened in my own neighborhood here in Cape Town as neighbors took to the streets—not in angry protest, but in communal dinners in the road that temporarily blocked the endless flow of tour buses and construction vehicles—to reclaim their right to urban development that respected their feeling of community. In these moments, and in many more like them, we are living at peace with ourselves, with each other, and even with the stark imperatives for fundamental change in the world around us.

Plumbing for peace as a noun—the tools and processes and mechanisms and systems and institutions that help us ask and answer important questions about where we are, what we each need to do in order to arrive someplace different, and how we will manage when we inevitably disagree—looks different from place to place. It draws on different histories and imperatives and traditions of those places. It will have different degrees of complexity at group, community, or broader social levels. It confronts different barriers to sustaining these inquiries in the face of broken power relationships and institutional arrangements. It may be dialogical, or it may take different forms of collective action. But in all cases, peace is experienced in plumbing as a verb—the deep and full exploration of who we are and who we might be in relation with each other.

In this we as peace-building plumbers can take great comfort. At any moment in any place, any two or more of us together plumbing the questions of peace can be at peace. And in being so we begin to imagine the repairs to the social plumbing that allow ever more of us—at first often fleetingly, but with thoughtful and careful effort more fluidly and sustainably—to join us.

 *Dr. Maria J. Stephan directs the Program on Nonviolent Action at the US Institute of Peace. Prior to that she has worked at the Atlantic Council, the US State Department's Bureau of Conflict and Stabilization Operations (CSO), and the International Center on Nonviolent Conflict (ICNC). She is the editor of* Civilian Jihad: Nonviolent Struggle, Democratization and Governance in the Middle East, *co-editor of* Is Authoritarianism Staging a Comeback? *and the co-author of the prize-winning book* Why Civil Resistance Works: The Strategic Logic of Nonviolent Conflict. *She writes for the* New York Times, Washington Post, Foreign Policy, Foreign Affairs, *Defense One, and* NPR. *She holds a PhD from the Fletcher School of Law and Diplomacy, and is a lifetime member of the Council on Foreign Relations.*

People Power as Shared Security
Dr. Maria J. Stephan

It is easy to be discouraged about the state of the world. For the fourth straight year, the global level of peace has deteriorated according to the 2018 Global Peace Index.[1] Aggregate freedom scores around the world have declined for twelve straight years based on Freedom House's annual survey, and civic space is shrinking.[2] Civil wars in Syria, Yemen, Afghanistan, and South Sudan continue to rage and destroy countless lives.

These are troubling trends. But amidst the darkness there is even greater light. People are struggling against violence and oppression without arms and winning. Within the past year alone, nonviolent "people power" movements have emerged in unexpected places and achieved surprising results.

- In northwest Pakistan, the Pashtun Tahafuz (Protection) movement has mobilized the civilian population against extra-judicial kidnappings and exclusionary government policies, and won small victories.

- In neighboring Afghanistan, a peaceful march that began in the southern Helmand province following a deadly attack by the Taliban has grown into a national, cross-tribal movement demanding peace.

- A mass popular movement in Armenia that took many by surprise, nonviolently removed a corrupt prime minister from power in just over a week and ushered in a new conversation about the country's democratic future.

- In the Democratic Republic of the Congo, youth activists joined by Catholic Church leaders have put unprecedented pressure on the repressive Kabila government to allow for free and fair elections.

Each of these movements involves ordinary people engaging in collective action, using nonviolent tactics including vigils, marches, strikes, symbolic protests, and social media mobilization to shift power in their societies and challenge injustices.

For me, *shared security* means solidarity. It means standing with and centering the individuals and movements fighting injustices, exclusion, and the tyranny of war in various parts of the world. It means providing national, regional, and international policy platforms to amplify the work of grassroots activists and peace-builders. It means facilitating learning, skills-building, and the sharing of practical experiences related to nonviolent action and its relationship to peace-building practice.

I am hopeful whenever I meet with local activists and peace-builders from South Sudan, DRC, Afghanistan, and other places where the US Institute of Peace (USIP) works. Hearing them describe how they are using creative forms of nonviolent action to push for positive social and political change is inspiring. One such activist is Jacob Bul, a youth leader from the Ana Taban ("I am tired") movement in South Sudan.[3] Jacob is an actor, artist, and the communications leader for the movement. I met Jacob two years ago when he was a Washington Mandela fellow at USIP. He explained how youth in the country were using music festivals, street theater, and other artistic expressions to bring South Sudanese together across tribal, generational, and geographic divisions to demand peace. Jacob is now facilitating trainings in nonviolent action and movement-building to help bring an end to the civil war.

In these troubling times globally, I take inspiration from the heroes of social justice struggles. As a kid growing up in rural Vermont I absorbed the stories of Gandhi, King, and Dorothy Day. I listened to the pro-peace sermons given by the feisty Benedictine monks at the Weston Priory who lived off the land, hosted refugees from Central America, and regularly spoke out against militarism. Meanwhile, my mom, an elementary school teacher, taught her third-graders about the US Civil Rights movement at a time when that wasn't particularly common in mostly white Vermont. My father led classes on decision-making for prisoners in the state jails. Those remembrances stick with you.

I first experienced the power of community organizing while living at the Rutland Dismas House,[4] a transitional home for ex-prisoners and college students, right before starting college. The Dismas House mission is to reconcile prisoners to society and society to prisoners. Volunteers cook the meals, make house repairs, help the ex-offenders find work, and otherwise motor the work of the House. Whenever I find myself down about current events, I remind myself that pockets of organized goodness (like Dismas) exist in all parts of the world.

Years later, after being educated by the wily Jesuits at Boston College, and while pursuing graduate studies, I attended the launch of a new documentary film, called *A Force More Powerful*. It was a film about how unarmed civilians in India, South Africa, Denmark, Chile, Poland, and the US, used strikes, boycotts, demonstrations, and organized non-cooperation to challenge brutal oppression and dictatorship without violence—and won. I decided to deepen my understanding of the phenomenon. With Peter Ackerman (co-author of *A Force More Powerful* and co-founder of the International Center on Nonviolent Conflict) as my dissertation advisor, I honed in on the strategic dimensions of civil resistance.

A few years later I met Erica Chenoweth at a workshop in Colorado. At the time, the prevailing wisdom in our shared field of political science and security studies was that nonviolent resistance couldn't "work" against violent, formidable opponents—or that it couldn't work as well as armed struggle. That adding violence to a nonviolent action strategy would give it a strategic edge and make victory more likely. That certain structural factors like regime type, GDP, or culture would ultimately determine the outcomes of nonviolent campaigns.

Although Erica was self-admittedly skeptical about the overall efficacy of nonviolent resistance, she shared my enthusiasm to systematically test the conventional wisdom, and she is a data guru. We assembled data on close to 330 major violent and nonviolent campaigns from 1900 to 2006 whose political objectives were the removal of an incumbent regime, the withdrawal of a foreign military occupation, and/or territorial independence. The major finding was that civil resistance has been twice as effective as armed struggle—it succeeds about 52 percent of the time compared to 26 percent for violent resistance. These findings have remained constant through 2015.[5] Structural variables like regime type, GDP, and demography were not predictive of the outcomes of these campaigns. We also found that nonviolent campaigns are strongly correlated with democratization (even when they fail), and are significantly less likely than armed struggle to result in civil war after the campaign ends. More recent research by Chenoweth and Perkoski found that mass atrocities are far less likely to occur during nonviolent uprisings than during armed insurgencies.[6]

When I hear activists from difficult environments cite these statistics, making the case that nonviolent resistance is more effective than violence in order to justify their strategic choices, this gives me hope. Human beings have figured out a way to confront formidable opponents without armed force and win. They've done it countless times in the bleakest contexts. Of course, they do not always succeed. But their chances of success are significantly higher if they maintain nonviolent discipline. This makes me hopeful when I think about Syrians, South Sudanese, and Afghans who are fighting nonviolently in the midst of civil war, or Congolese youth who are nonviolently facing down a regime whose soldiers have used live fire on peaceful protestors.

What makes me even more optimistic is the skills-based nature of nonviolent campaigns and movements. Strategies matter and people can learn to be more effective at their nonviolent organizing and activism. They can learn (mostly from each other) about the complementary nature of nonviolent resistance and peace-building—how to use dialogue and active listening to strengthen coalitions, how to sequence nonviolent direct-action tactics to maximize participation and leverage, and how to use negotiation skills to consolidate gains.

Organizations like USIP, AFSC, the International Center on Nonviolent Conflict (ICNC), Beautiful Rising, Rhize, Training for Change, Pace-e-Bene, and others are able to support on and offline trainings, facilitate peer learning, and help forge global networks of individuals skilled in nonviolent action and peace-building. ICNC is equipping activists and organizers around the world with materials on strategic nonviolent action translated into dozens of languages.[7] My organization, USIP, has just produced an action guide on Synergizing Nonviolent Action and Peace-building (SNAP), co-developed by Lisa Schirch and Nadine Bloch, which is already being used by activists in Sudan, South Sudan, and other parts of the world.

A significant new global initiative, the Catholic Nonviolence Initiative (CNI),[8] which is a grassroots effort to encourage the Catholic Church at all levels—diplomatically, educationally, and programmatically—from the Vatican to the community level, to redouble its investment in nonviolent strategies and approaches, gives me further hope. Imagine what would happen if Pope Francis were to issue a papal encyclical on the topic of active nonviolence and just peace. This would provide a 1.2 billion-member global institution that has full diplomatic status the marching orders to double down on nonviolent strategies and work with other religious traditions to advance just peace approaches. It would be a demonstration of solidarity with nonviolent activists and peace-builders, and a boost to shared security globally.

I also hold out hope that militaries in the US and around the world will appreciate the power and effectiveness of civil resistance and other nonviolent strategies—and more strongly advocate for them. Soldiers who have experienced the horrors of war are often the leading voices for greater investment in diplomatic and development strategies. High-ranking officers like Admiral Dennis Blair and Colonel Robert L. Helvey (Ret.) have devised practical manuals focused on nonviolent and non-kinetic approaches to advancing human rights and democracy.[9] Integrating nonviolent strategies in military education programs at West Point, the War Colleges, and the National Defense University would be a tremendous investment in shared security.

In conclusion, let me suggest that putting solidarity into action around a shared security agenda means building bridges between policy, practitioner, and activist communities. It means demonstrating through rigorous research, strengthening through skills-building, and advocating policies that reflect the understanding that people power is a powerful antidote to injustices and exclusion. It means encouraging the donor community to adopt a movement mindset and invest creatively in grassroots activism, organizing, and collective action. It means infusing major global policy initiatives like the UN Sustaining Peace, Sustainable Development Goals, and UN-World Bank Pathways For Peace with an emphasis on those civic actors who are in the best position to build just and inclusive societies.

Solidarity is an expression of hope, and I have great hope that ongoing wars, resurgent authoritarianism, and persecution will be met with even more persistent and creative forms of nonviolent resistance. These strategies have amassed emancipatory victories for centuries and they are capable of challenging the most formidable foes today, both in the United States and around the world. I can imagine a world where ordinary people increasingly know how to disrupt systems of oppression and constructively build societies in which security is shared by all. That's the dream that carries me forward.

Notes

1.   Institute for Economics & Peace Global Peace Index 2018: Measuring Peace in a Complex World (Sydney, 2018). Accessed September 20, 2018. http://visionofhumanity.org/app/uploads/2018/06/Global-Peace-Index-2018-2.pdf.

2.   Michael J. Abramowitz, *Freedom in the World 2018*, "Democracy in Crisis," Freedom House. Accessed September 18, 2018. https://freedomhouse.org/report/freedom-world/freedom-world-2018.

3. Nicholas Zaremba, "In South Sudan, an Artists' Movement for Peace Catches Fire," United States Institution for Peace, January 19, 2018. Accessed September 18, 2018. www.usip.org/publications/2018/01/south-sudan-artists-movement-peace-catches-fire.

4. "Our Mission," Dismas of Vermont. Accessed September 18, 2018. https://dismasofvt.org/about/mission-history-values/.

5. Erica Chenowith and Maria J. Stephan, *Why Civil Resistance Works: The Strategic Logic of Nonviolent Conflict* (Columbia UP, 2011). Accessed September 18, 2018. https://cup.columbia.edu/book/why-civil-resistance-works/9780231156837.

6. Evan Perkoski and Erica Chenoweth, "Special Report: Nonviolent Resistance and Prevention of Mass Killings During Popular Uprisings," International Center on Nonviolent Conflict (Washington, D.C., 2018). Accessed September 18, 2018. www.nonviolent-conflict.org/nonviolent-resistance-and-prevention-of-mass-killings/.

7. ICNC Translations Program. Accessed September 18, 2018. www.nonviolent-conflict.org/for-activists-and-organizers-landing/translations-program/.

8. Catholic Nonviolence Initiative. Accessed September 18, 2018. https://nonviolencejustpeace.net/.

9. www.brookings.edu/book/military-engagement-2/ and www.aeinstein.org/books/on-strategic-nonviolent-conflict-thinking-about-the-fundamentals/

 *Saba Ismail is the Executive Director and co-founder of Aware Girls, a youth- and women-led organization working to empower young women and promote gender equality in Pakistan. She is also co-founder and Vice Chairperson of the Coalition on Rights and Responsibilities (CRY), a member organization of UNOY Peace-builders working to develop young people as agents of change. Saba was listed among the 100 Leading Global Thinkers by* Foreign Policy *and was a Hufford Youth Fellow with the National Endowment for Democracy (NED) in Washington, where she focused on the role of young women in emerging democracies. She also previously served as a member to the International Steering Group of UNOY Peace-builders. Saba has a master's in Biotechnology from the COMSATS Institute of Information Technology, Pakistan. Saba was born in 1987.*

The Art of Offering Options: Empowering Youth in Rural Pakistan
Saba Ismail

While growing up in a fragile country, witnessing bomb blasts, living with the fear of whether I will get back home alive or not every day for years and losing more than 70,000 fellow citizens in the "war on terror," I always had ONE dream: to live in a world where I have freedom from the fear of violence and violent religious extremism, where children do not get killed in schools. I wanted to live in a country where justice prevails, the richness of culture and diversity is celebrated, and an open society is the norm.

I was born in Swabi, a rural village, and raised in Peshawar in the Khyber Pakhtunkhwa Province of Pakistan. To fulfill my dream of a peaceful Pakistan, at the age of fifteen, along with my sister Gulalai Ismail, I co-founded an organization called Aware Girls which works to prevent violent religious extremism and promote peace. Aware Girls, which is led by young women, works to prevent violent religious extremism using a peer-to-peer education model. Our model is one where young people reach out to other young people vulnerable to the violent ideologies and to the recruitment of militant groups, and provide them with alternative narratives based on nonviolence, tolerance, compassion, and pluralism. More than 10,000 young people are actively working all over the North Western Province known as Khyber Pakhtunkhwa Province, Pakistan, and in Afghanistan.

Being a follower of Baacha Khan, the Frontier Gandhi, a Pashtun independence activist against the rule of the British Raj, I believe in the power of nonviolence. We are working to create an environment where there is no space for violent ideologies, and which is more conducive to peace-building, coexistence, and nonviolence. In our model we keep young people at the center of our programs, engaging them as partners in the process of countering violent extremism and building peace. We believe that the millions of young people out there who aren't buying the militant agenda of extremist groups are a huge resource for us, they simply need to be found and engaged.

To counter violent extremism, we—the young women from the platform of Aware Girls—have been working to address the vacuums which provide fertile ground to extremist groups and extremist narratives by promoting active citizen engagement of young people. We promote good governance and democracy, interfaith harmony, and gender equality by working with both boys and girls. When we invest in girls' and women's empowerment and political stability in particular, we take away the oxygen from violent extremist groups.

Working with young people helped me achieve my vision of an open society where people have the freedom to exercise their basic rights including, but not limited to, freedom of expression, freedom of association, celebrating diversity; a society where they feel safe in and outside of their homes, and where religious minorities have the environment to exercise and enjoy their rights. The young people that I am working with are actively promoting interfaith harmony, which is rare in Pakistan.

An open society and shared security are dependent on each other. In my opinion, shared security is an ideological battle that can only be won through trust, mutual understanding, and respect. To be successful in shared security, Pakistanis will have to fight the ideological battle against the supportive mind set of the Taliban, and disarm these militant groups, but most importantly change state policy so that it no longer supports militants even tacitly. This is the only way to a sustainable peace.

As young women working to eradicate violent religious extremism and promoting peace and interfaith harmony, we have been subjected to death threats, attacks on our lives, attacks on our freedom of association, relocation multiple times, and our families being separated for more than a decade. Despite all of these hardships, I believe that it was all worth it because I see young people in Pakistan demonstrating wide support for us, indicating that what they want is peace.

In the name of counter-terrorism and security initiatives, millions of dollars have been actually invested in more weapons, more guns, and more bombs. Every penny spent on a gun, on a missile, on a bomb, is injustice to every kid who wants to go school but cannot pay for it, to every kid who is hungry and not fed, to every girl who is denied her rights, and to every young person who wants to be a leader of their society but is stereotyped as a trouble-maker, as an extremist.

I, and my organization, will continue to work tirelessly to advocate the reallocation of this money toward peace, particularly in the lives of young peace-builders. When it comes down to it, we are the majority, and we have worked hard to be recognized as an integral part of the solution. Without us war is inevitable, and we are here to demonstrate our presence, our active engagement, our strength, and our preference for peace.

Making Society Civil Again

 *Ashutosh Varshney is the Sol Goldman Professor of International Studies and the Social Sciences and Professor of Political Science at Brown University, where he also directs the Center for Contemporary South Asia. Previously, he taught at Harvard (1989–98) and the University of Michigan, Ann Arbor (2001–2008). His research and teaching cover three areas: Ethnicity and Nationalism; Political Economy of Development; and South Asian Politics and Political Economy. He served on the former UN Secretary General Kofi Annan's Millennium Task Force on Poverty (2002–2005). He has also served as an adviser to the World Bank, UNDP, and the Club of Madrid.*

Civil Society: Why, What, and How[1]
Ashutosh Varshney

Civil society is the missing variable in all available traditions of in-quiry. If included, it begins to explain, as essentialism could not, why "long-run" animosities do not embitter relationships between the same ethnic groups everywhere: why, for example, in Northern Ireland, civic interconnections between the Protestants and Catholics make the community of Dunville peaceful, but in Kileen/Banduff, where there is virtually no interaction between them, violence is frequent.[2] Civic links, if they exist between ethnic groups, also resolve the unanswered puzzle of instrumentalism: namely, why, even though political elite may try instrumentally to use ethnicity for political purposes and wish to cleave societies along ethnic lines, they are unable to do so everywhere. In fact, they may not find such efforts sensible at all, and may instead put together winning coalitions in non-ethnic ways. If the electorate is inter-ethnically engaged, the politicians may both be unable and unwilling to polarize. And finally, depending on the nature of civic life, the link between ethnic conflict and institutional designs on the one hand and the connection between ethnic violence and master narratives on the other breaks down. Civic engagement between communities tends to be micro, local or regional, whereas the existing traditions of inquiry are macro, national, or global. Without an investigation of civic life, the power of longstanding hatreds, politi-cal elite, political institutions, and master narratives can be overstated.

If it is so critical to group relations, what kinds of interactions and links between citizens would constitute civic life? And how exactly does civil society contribute to peace or conflict?

Civil Society: Purposes or Forms?

The concept of civil society, though highly popular and much revived in recent years, remains intensely contested. According to the conventional notions prevalent in the social sciences, a civil society refers to that space in a given society a) which exists between the family on the one hand and the state on the other, b) which makes interconnections between individuals or families possible, and c) which is independent of the state. Many, though not all, of the existing definitions also suggest two more requirements: that the civic space be organized in associations that attend to the cultural, social, economic, as well as political needs of the citizens; and that the associations be modern and voluntaristic, not ascriptive. Going by the first requirement, trade unions would be part of civil society, but informal neighborhood associations would not. And following the second requirement, Philately Clubs and Parent Teacher Associations would be civic, but not an Association of Jews in Defense of Israel, or a Black church.[3]

Should we agree with the latter two requirements? Can non-associational space also be called civic, or part of civil society? Must associations, to form part of civil society, be of a "modern" kind—voluntaristic, cross-cutting rather than ascriptive and based on ethnic affiliations? These questions are not simply theoretical. In many societies, group-based, but informal, activities—sports, entertainment, festivals—are often part of the space between the state and family life. And the same is true of ethnic associations, whether they are Black churches in the US, right-wing Jewish groups in Israel, or an exclusively Hindu group like the Vishva Hindu Parishad (VHP), existing both in India and in the Indian diaspora all over the world. All of these groups would meet the first definition of civil society, but none would meet the second or third. Are they part of civil society or not? Why should informal, but group-based activity of citizens be excluded from civil society? Why should ethnic or religious associations not be part of civil society?

A great deal of controversy exists on both points. Both informal and ascriptive activities are considered by many leading civil society theorists to be traditional, whereas civil society is modern. The modernity of civil society is, of course, quickly qualified. Civil society may itself be modern, but not all modern political systems have civil societies. Attacking ascriptive hierarchies and privileges, undermining religion, and instituting a secular order, Communist polities were modern, but the state penetrated all sites of organizational life: hospitals, universities, operas, theater, literary societies. When Tomas, the doctor hero of Milan Kundera's novel *The Unbearable Lightness of Being*, published a short essay criticizing the bureaucratic structures of his Prague hospital, a hospital administrator gave him the choice of quitting surgery altogether, or withdrawing the article and issuing an apology for straying from the ideologically correct, Communist path in 1960s Prague. Kundera's hero, of course, was not entirely fictional. Most observers of Communist societies recognized the realism of the situation. Its civil society humbled and infirm, the state in Communist Czechoslovakia was all-powerful, decimating freedom of expression as well as the institutions that might allow such freedoms. Modernity is a necessary, but not sufficient, precondition for the rise of civil society.

Modernist origins of civil society were originally attributed to Hegel's nineteenth-century theoretical formulations.[4] In recent years, however, the revival of a modernist notion of civil society, it is often suggested, is due to debates in Eastern Europe and the English translation of Habermas's *The Structural Transformation of the Public Sphere: An Inquiry into the Category of Bourgeois Society*.[5] Because the concept of civil society has been so important to the field of political philosophy, it has been explored mostly by political philosophers in recent times.[6] In comparison, though the need for it should be quite clear, analytic work on civil society in the more empirical fields of the social sciences has not been as voluminous.[7] It is only a systematic empirical investigation of the associational and non-associational forms of civic life that can show whether the functions and forms normally attributed to them in the normative literature are also actually observable.

Normative conceptualizations are, of course, not confined to political philosophy. A normative tenor marks scholarship on civil society as a whole. Consider Ernest Gellner, whose writings on civil society have been plentiful as well as influential. "Modularity," argued Gellner, "makes civil society," whereas "segmentalism" defines a traditional society.[8] By modularity, Gellner means the ability to rise beyond traditional or ascriptive occupations and associations. Given a multi-purpose, secular, and modern education, and given also the objective availability of plentiful as well as changing professional opportunities in post-traditional times, modern man can move from one occupation to another, one place to another, one association to another. In contrast is the birth-assigned occupation and place that is traditional in many societies. A carpenter in a traditional society, whether he liked it or not, would always be a carpenter, and all his kinsmen would be carpenters. He would also not generally be involved in associations; and if he were, the association would most likely be an ascriptive guild of carpenters. In such a "segmental" or traditional society, freedom of will with respect to associations, occupations, or places of living, would neither be available nor encouraged, and an ethnic division of labor would exist. An agrarian society, argued Gellner, might be able to avoid the tyranny of the state for, in view of the decentralized nature of production structure, a low level of communication technology, and the relatively self-sufficient character of each segment, the power of the state would not be able to reach all segments of a traditional society. But that does not mean that such a society would be "civil," for instead of a "tyranny of state," it would experience a "tyranny of cousins": "It thrusts on to the individual an ascribed identity, which then may or may not be fulfilled, whereas a modern conception of freedom includes the requirement that identities be chosen rather than ascribed."[9] Civil society, concluded Gellner, is not only modern, but also based on strictly voluntary, not ethnic or religious, associations between the family and the state.[10]

Traditional "Tyranny of Cousins" Versus Modern "civility"?

Both empirically and conceptually, there is an odd modernist bias in the formulations above. Tradition is considered intolerant and incorrigible beyond redemption. And modernity is assumed to promise and deliver such a great deal that much that may be valuable and highly flexible in tradition, including pluralism, is simply defined out of consideration, and much that may be subversive of free will and "civility" in capitalist, if not socialist, modernity is also, by definition, ruled out of court. Even if choral societies in twelfth-century Northern Italy were making it possible for people to connect, their inclusion in civil society *before the rise of modern capitalism*, according to this perspective, is unwarranted.[11]

Each of the central claims in the modernist conception of civil society can be empirically challenged. First, the argument that ethnic or religious associations are ascriptive is only partially correct. A remarkably large number of studies, both in the West and in the developing world, show that ethnic and religious associations combine ascription and choice. Not all Christians have to be members of a church in a given town; not all Black residents in a neighborhood are members of a Black church; not all members of a caste or linguistic group have to participate in a caste or linguistic association. Moreover, it has also been widely documented that ethnic associations can perform many "modern" functions, such as participating in democratic politics, setting up funds to encourage members of the ethnic group to enter newer professions, facilitating migration of ethnic kinsmen into newer places for modern occupation, and modern education.[12]

Many ethnic associations are undoubtedly bigoted with respect to out-groups as well as tyrannical to their own cousins, but that does not exhaust the range of ethnic organizations, nor the variety of ethnic activities. In many multiethnic societies where ethnic groups are arranged hierarchically, where some ethnic groups have historically faced prejudice, the ethnic associations of such groups are known to have been among the most effective organizations to fight for ethnic equality in the workplace, politics, and schools.[13] A large number of Jewish associations in the US, "lower caste" organizations in India, Moroccan, and Algerian groups in France, and Black organizations in contemporary South Africa have performed such roles with considerable distinction, if not always with great success. Similarly, many churches and religious organizations—for example, in Poland and Latin America—are known to have fought the state for democracy and freedom. The forms of association may have been traditional, but the goals pursued were highly modern.

Taking pride in one's ethnic group and working for the group does not, *ipso facto*, make one "uncivil." It matters what the aim of such ascription-based group activity is. That is not a theoretical, but an empirical question. Paradoxically for Gellner, modularity for their group is what many ethnic associations may seek, realizing how important it has become to leave traditional callings and move to modern occupations in contemporary times. Moreover, the ethnic form of association may also be based on a highly modern consideration: low transaction costs. It is less difficult to get people together on grounds of similarity than difference, and once such association is formed, perfectly modern goals may be pursued: making organized but nonviolent demands on the political system; teaming up with organizations of different groups to make a "rainbow coalition" in politics; providing support for entrepreneurship in their community.[14]

In short, the idea that ethnicity and religion are equal to traditionalism and, therefore, they can't perform the functions of civic organizations—allowing people to come together, making public discussion of issues possible, challenging the caprice or misrule of state authorities, promoting modern business activities—has too many exceptions to be considered empirically admissible. Whatever one may think of ethnic associations in general, at least those ethnic associations should be considered part of civil society that meet the functional or purposive criteria specified by normative arguments.

A similar objection can be raised with respect to informal associations or activities. In much of the developing world, especially in the countryside and small towns, formal associations simply do not exist. That, however, does not mean that civic interconnections, or activities, are absent. The sites of civic interactions range from the generally predictable—in that such sites made a public sphere possible in eighteenth- and nineteenth-century Europe as well—to the highly particular and culturally specific. The predictable sites are the neighborhood or village commons, the playground, the halls for entertainment and community functions. However, group interaction is not confined to them, and may also mark some culturally specific sites: the festival venues where people not only participate in a religious activity but also build connections for secular purposes such as politics; the sidewalks where those returning from work habitually walk together and talk, not simply about the weather but also about organizational structures in the workplace, markets, films, festivals, and politics; the village pond where women not only wash clothes and exchange views about families, but discuss school teachers, landlords, and village politics; the milkman's depots where men and women buy milk each morning as well as talk about children, relatives, local government, cultural trends, and national politics; the only TV center of a neighborhood or village where families come together to watch news, stories and films; and in societies where alcohol drinking is not frowned upon, the village or neighborhood pub where people socialize, discuss, make friends, and connect with one another.[15]

In the 1930s, a major civic movement in South India, leading to "reading rooms" in the state of Kerala and turning later into a statewide library movement, was born in the neighborhood tea shops, where people used to come together in the evening, read newspapers jointly, and comment on politics and culture. Watching how many cups of tea were consumed over intense discussions, the tea-shop owners would, of course, be delighted, but the small groups would also find a common public site for discussion as well as fun. Newspapers in the 1930s were expensive: only a few could buy newspapers individually.[16] Sites of this kind may not be associated with formal organizations, immediately or ever, but they allow people to perform many of the activities that formal civic organizations do: connect, talk, share views, formulate strategies for school exams and local politics, and develop a perspective not only on local but also extra-local politics as well.[17] Indeed, popular, as opposed to elite, culture often takes this form in many parts of the developing world.[18]

If what is crucial to the notion of civil society is that families and individuals connect with others beyond their homes and talk about matters of public relevance without the interference, or sponsorship, of the state, then it seems far too rigid to insist that this must take place only in "modern" associations. Empirically speaking, whether such engagement takes place in associations, or in the traditional sites of social get-togethers, depends on the degree of urbanization and economic development, as well as the nature of the political system. Cities tend to have formal associations, but villages make do with informal sites and meetings. Further, political systems may specify which groups have access to formal civic spaces and may form organizations, and which ones may not. Nineteenth-century Europe provided the propertied classes access to a whole range of political and institutional instruments of interest articulation; trade unions for workers, however, were slower to arrive. Some of the spirit of these remarks is conveyed in the commentary generated by Habermas' distinction between the "lifeworld" and "system" in *The Structural Transformation of the Public Sphere*. In its original formulation, the distinction indicated a radical rupture between the significance of everyday interaction, and interaction made possible by institutions and organizations. The latter, according to Habermas, was associated with a modern public sphere. Everyday interaction, as it were, made life, but organized interaction made history.[19] The new history written about the popular struggles of women, peasants, workers, and minorities—those not formally admitted to the public sphere in much of nineteenth-century Europe and America—suggests the limited utility of Habermas' original distinction.[20] Indeed, in his more recent positions, Habermas has all but dropped the radical distinction he drew earlier.[21] Street-corner activity can now be viewed as a serious civic form as well, if more organized and institutional civic sites are not available generally, or to some specific groups.

The point, of course, is not that formal associations do not matter. Compared to everyday forms of engagement, as I argue in this book, associations are undoubtedly a much more robust form of sustained and effective civic interaction between individuals. However, associations do not exist everywhere, for the need for formal associations is not obvious, nor access to them universal. An absence of associations neither stops villages, nor the subaltern, from participating in a public or political discourse. Nor, in the absence of modern associations, do disputes in the villages turn into violence more often. Indeed, rural India, as reported in the previous chapter, was the site of less than 4 percent of all deaths and roughly 10 percent of all Hindu–Muslim riots in India between 1950–95. Peace was maintained not because of associations, but because everyday civic engagement between Hindus and Muslims was enough to keep potential rioters away. In cities, however, such everyday engagement was not enough, and associations were required.

When villages become towns, towns turn into cities, and cities are transformed into metropolises, people begin to travel long distances for work, face-to-face contact is typically not possible beyond neighborhoods, and associations become necessary not only for civil peace but also for many economic, social, and political aims and interactions. We should not look for associations where the need for them is not pressing, or where access to them is difficult for some groups. We should, instead, look at the alternative civic sites that perform the same role as the more standard civic organizations do.

To conclude, at least in the social and cultural settings that are different from Europe and North America, if not more generally, the purposes of activity rather than the forms of organization should be the critical test of civic life. Tradition is not necessarily equal to a tyranny of cousins, and capitalist modernity does not always make civic interaction possible. At best, such dualities are ideal types, or based on normatively preferred visions. Empirically speaking, tradition can often permit challenging the cousins if existing norms of reciprocity and ethics are violated. Similarly, even capitalist modernity may be highly unsocial and atomizing if people in inner-city America stay at home and watch MTV, instead of forming neighborhood watch committees or attending to the abandoned children's homes.[22] Both informal group activities as well as ascriptive associations should be considered part of civil society so long as they connect individuals, build trust, encourage reciprocity, and facilitate exchange of views on matters of public concern economic, political, cultural, and social. While doing all of this, they may well be connected with inter-ethnic violence, though intra-ethnic peace may be maintained. But that is to be established empirically. Theoretically, one should not assume that ethnic associations promote tyranny of cousins or interethnic violence.

Notes

1. Ashutosh Varshney, *Ethnic Conflict and Civic Life: Hindus and Muslims in India* (New Haven, CT: Yale University Press, 2002).

2. John Darby, *Intimidation and Control of Conflict in Northern Ireland* (Dublin: Gill and MacMillan, 1986).

3. For a review of some other definitions, see Axel Hadenius and Fredrik Uggla, "Making Civil Society Work, Promoting Democratic Development," *World Development* 24 (1996): 1621–1639.

4. Kundera, Milan. *The Unbearable Lightness of Being* (New York: Harper & Row, 1984).

5. For an early history of the idea, including Marx's critique of Hegel, see Adam Seligman, *The Idea of Civil Society* (Princeton: Princeton University Press, 1992).

6. Translated by Thomas Burger and Frederic Lawrence (Cambridge: MIT Press, 1989). For a debate built around the publication of the English translation, see Craig Calhoun, ed., *Habermas and the Public Sphere* (Cambridge: MIT Press, 1994).

7. Also see Charles Taylor, "Modes of Civil Society," *Public Culture* 3 (1990): 95–118; Michael Walzer, "The Idea of Civil Society," *Dissent* 20 (1991): 293–304; Jean Cohen and Andrew Arato, *Civil Society and Political Theory* (Cambridge: MIT Press, 1992); and Joshua Cohen and Joel Rogers, eds., *Associations and Democracy* (London: Verso, 1995).

8. The most prominent empirically oriented exception of recent times is Robert Putnam, *Making Democracy Work: Civic Traditions in Italy* (Princeton: Princeton University Press, 1993). The debate generated by Putnam's work is also leading to empirically based scholarship. See Sheri Berman, "Civil Society and the Collapse of the Weimar Republic," *World Politics*, 49 (1997): 401–429, and the special issue on social capital of

American Behavioral Scientist 40 (1997): 575–586. Also see the argument about how civil society can both be related to peace and conflict by Jack Snyder and Karen Ballentine, "Nationalism and the Marketplace for Ideas," *International Security* 21 (1996): 5–40. The latter is among the very few writings that investigate the relationship between democratization, civil society, and war—a subject of great importance.

9. Ernest Gellner, "The Importance of Being Modular," in John Hall, ed., *Civil Society: Theory, History, Comparison* (Cambridge: Blackwell, 1995), 32–55. This article is a good summary of a large number of Gellner's writings on civil society, written both in the reflective and activist mode. Many of these writings, including some polemical essays, have been put together in *Gellner, Conditions of Liberty: Civil Society and Its Rivals* (New York: The Penguin Press, 1994).

10. Gellner, *Conditions of Liberty*, 9.

11. For another argument of a similar genre, see Edward Shils, *The Virtue of Civility* (Indianapolis, Indiana: Liberty Fund, 1997).

12. John Hall on Robert Putnam's *Making Democracy Work* in "In Search of Civil Society" in *Civil Society: Theory, History, Comparison*, 19.

13. For pioneering work on the modernist uses of tradition and ethnicity, see Lloyd Rudolph and Susanne Rudolph, *The Modernity of Tradition* (Chicago: University of Chicago Press, 1967) and Myron Weiner, *Sons of the Soil* (Princeton: Princeton University Press, 1978).

14. See the discussion of a Southern Indian lower-caste movement in Chapter 5 of Varshney, *Ethnic Conflict and Civic Life*.

15. For example, Barbara Wake Carroll and Terrance Carroll, "The State and Ethnicity in Botswana and Mauritius: A Democratic Route to Development?" *Journal of Development Studies* 33 (1997): 464–486.

16. Needless to add, in societies where drinking in public is outlawed or is culturally discouraged, pubs tend to attract the criminally inclined, not the civic-minded. Violence is always possible—and always around the corner.

17. Dilip Menon, *Caste, Nationalism and Communism in South India: Malabar, 1900-1948* (Cambridge: Cambridge University Press, 1994).

18. I have personally had some of the most interesting conversations about politics—local, state, national, and even international—in such neighborhood tea shops in India and have watched modern journalists interview citizens and write stories for their papers there. A rather informal and traditional site has been put to some remarkably modern uses.

19. For the Malaysian countryside, see the discussion of gossip, folk tales, and social revelry in James Scott, *Weapons of the Weak: Everyday Forms of Peasant Resistance* (New Haven: Yale University Press, 1985).

20. See the brief but thoughtful discussion in Harry Boyte, "The Pragmatic Ends of Popular Politics" in Calhoun, *Habermas and the Public Sphere.*

21. Starting with E. P. Thompson's *The Making of the English Working Class* (Harmondsworth: The Penguin Press, 1968), such historical works are by now many. For a quick review of how they relate to Habermas, see Mary Ryan, "Gender and Public Access: Women's Politics in Nineteenth Century America," *Feminism, the Public and the Private* (Oxford: Oxford UP, 1998) and Geoff Elly, "Nations, Publics, and Political Cultures: Placing Habermas in the 19th Century," in *Calhoun, Habermas and the Public Sphere.*

22. Habermas, "Further Reflections on the Public Sphere," in Calhoun, *Habermas and the Public Sphere.*

23. For how civic activity in the U.S. has declined, see Robert Putnam, "The Strange Disappearance of Civic America," *The American Prospect* (1996): 34–48; "Bowling Alone: America's Declining Social Capital," *Journal of Democracy* 6 (1995): 65–78; and *Bowling Alone: The Collapse and Revival of American Community* (New York: Simon and Schuster, 2000).

Dr. Maya Tudor's research investigates the origins of stable, democratic, and effective states across the developing world, with an emphasis on South Asia. She was educated at Stanford and Princeton and holds a PhD in Politics and Public Policy. Her publications include The Promise of Power, *which investigates the origins of India and Pakistan's regime divergence in the aftermath of colonial independence. She has worked as Special Assistant to Chief Economist Joseph Stiglitz at the World Bank, at UNICEF, and in the United States Senate. She is an Associate Professor of Government and Public Policy at Oxford University.*

Why Liberals Should Embrace Inclusive Nationalism
Maya Tudor

These are difficult days to defend nationalism. Open patriotism has become virtually unacceptable in liberal circles. While championing diversity in the form of race, gender, and sexual orientation is welcomed, cosmopolitan elites around the globe decry nationalism as a reactionary force that should be confined to the dustbin of history.

There are good reasons to be wary of nationalism. The history of twentieth-century Europe, whose world wars entangled nearly every corner of the globe, amply demonstrates what some nationalisms can justify: wars, autocratic power grabs, and even genocide. There can be little doubt that strong attachments to national identities have motivated individuals to engage in unspeakable behavior toward those perceived as outsiders.

The combination of horrific nationalist governments in the twentieth century and the distasteful nativist nationalism of the present has led many liberal elites to echo Albert Einstein's view that nationalism is "the measles of mankind." French President Emmanuel Macron recently called for all Europeans to reject nationalism in order to protect democracy.

Despite the very real problems that can accompany nationalist fervor, I want to argue that nationalism should be harnessed by liberal elites to create and protect democracy. Nationalism is a powerful tool. If liberal elites will not use it, they abandon it to those with illiberal sympathies.

Nations Are Enduring Imagined Communities

Nations are imagined communities that meet a human need for a "we." As Benedict Anderson wrote, nations are *imagined* because people will not encounter most of their fellow citizens face to face. Yet nations are still *communities* that fulfill a deep and basic need for human connection in the modern world. Humans connect to others by creating groups through which they develop feelings of self-worth and loyalty. That everyone needs an in-group is one of the most consistent findings of social psychology over the last half-century. Social identity theorists such as Henri Tafjel and John Turner have shown that groups—even fictive groups created for experiments—provide a sense of belonging and status that individuals seek in almost all environments.

A nation is one community that provides this sense of belonging. Cosmopolitan elites themselves readily discount the importance of community belonging because they often have multiple national, religious, or professional communities from which to choose. In the realm of religion for example, Columbia University philosopher Philip Kitcher observes that "authors of contemporary manifestos calling for freedom from religious delusions typically belong to professional communities. Taking that for granted, the lack of similar secular structures for others disappears from their view." There is a strong parallel to nationalism here. As a dual citizen of Germany and the United States who is eligible for Indian citizenship (through birth), and English citizenship (through residence), I may be able to choose more than one national identity. But the same is not true for the vast majority of people around the globe. Even in relatively mobile countries, most individuals are not able to choose their citizenship.

Both because one's national identity is continually socialized and because it is a powerful political resource, it is unlikely to fade quietly away. To the contrary, a nation's founding ideas about who constitutes the national "we" casts a long shadow on contemporary politics because they are mythologized in stories of national leaders, in history books, in plays and poems, in public ceremonies and holidays, and in constitutions that lay down how countries organize, share, and transfer political power. In moments of crisis, be they external wars or internal shocks, political elites harness these narratives to legitimate policies and sacrifices, including the ultimate sacrifice of giving one's life for one's country.

The Janus Face of Nationalism

Cosmopolitan elites rightly worry that embracing nationalism could lead down a path toward fascism. But neither majority antipathy to minorities nor authoritarianism is intrinsic to nationalism. This is because there are two types of nationalism—inclusive and exclusive. My research with University of Michigan political scientist Dan Slater shows that the founding ideas of nations are important in setting out whether nationalisms are fundamentally inclusive or exclusive, and that only *exclusive* nationalisms are detrimental to democracy— defined as representative governments chosen by citizens in regular, competitive elections in the presence of robust civil liberties.

Nationalism is *inclusive* when a country's founding narratives rely on shared ideals or aspirations as the basis of belonging to the nation. Nationalism is *exclusive* when founding narratives of the nation prioritize immutable ethnic and religious groups. Though nationalism is never entirely inclusive or exclusive, countries have exclusive nationalisms when historically fixed identities—race, ethnicity, and religion in much of the world—narratively and symbolically define a nation at its founding. That ethnic heritage centrally defined German nationhood in the latter half of the nineteenth century was one important reason that 1930s Germany accepted the systematic depriving of Jewish Germans' political and civil rights. That Theravada Buddhism, practiced by the ethnically Bamar majority of Myanmar, historically defined the Burmese nation is one reason that few politicians in Burma today stand against efforts to deprive the Rohingya (or myriad other ethnic minorities), of their political and civil rights. When nations are fundamentally defined by a concept of fixed, often ethno-linguistic identity, minorities become a problem to be dealt with—through extermination, expulsion, or assimilation. It is this kind of nationalism that Einstein rightly viewed as undemocratic.

How Nationalism Can Stabilize Democracy

Inclusive forms of nationalism actually can help create and support democracy. Since its inception, nationalism has arguably been a greater force for advancing than undermining democracy. When nationalism emerged in eighteenth-century Europe, it was used by aristocratic elites to wrest away power from monarchs and legitimate a move toward more representative institutions of state that in a limited sense overcame the hereditary distinctions between commoners and nobility. After nationalism first became an accepted idea in England, nationalism was adapted by other elites in new ways to suit their distinct political interests. As Boston University sociologist Liah Greenfeld observes: "the English aristocracy sought to justify [nationalism]; the French and Russian nobility—to protect it, and the German intellectuals—to achieve it." As exemplified in German philosopher Johann Gottfried von Herder's theory of *Volksgeist*, early nationalisms were all thought to have an ethno-linguistic basis.

As the idea of nationalism spread beyond Europe, particularly to colonies where indigenous elites also sought use nationalism to bind together large, diverse populations in anti-colonial struggles for political sovereignty, more inclusive nationalisms emerged. In countries such as India and Indonesia, founding nationalism was defined neither by ethnicity nor by religion, but by a set of principles and goals. India's founding nationalism was predominantly defined by secularism, linguistic plurality, and nonviolent self-determination. As I have argued in my book, *The Promise of Power*, the decades-long commitment to these ideals before independence in 1947 critically explains India's adoption of formal democratic institutions upon independence.

Inclusive nationalisms can help protect democracy in periods of crisis by arming democratic defenders with a historically legitimated set of values that help protect vulnerable groups. Inclusive nationalism was used to protect India's democracy in its most severe political crisis to date—the period known as the Emergency between 1975 and 1977, when Prime Minister Indira Gandhi suspended civil liberties and jailed her political opponents. At that time, the centrality of nonviolent self-determination in India's nationalism helped the political opposition to mobilize against Mrs. Gandhi. Her defeat was perhaps the only time in modern political history where voters stopped a populist autocrat at the polls and brought about a peaceful transition of power.

Though a more exclusive nationalism is ascendant in India today, many Indians are protesting against this national redefinition in part because Indian nationalism has historically been inclusive. This helps explain why a broad range of actors have spoken up to protect democratic institutions, including why the Indian Supreme Court has restrained the Hindu-nationalist agenda in the domains of marriage, mosque destruction, and cow slaughter; why celebrated writers have returned government awards; and why dozens of senior civil servants and civic groups have publicly and consistently protested majoritarian policies and their culmination in communal violence.

A glance at India's regional neighbors gives ample indication of what the country's politics might look like *without* the historical inheritance of an inclusive nationalism. In Pakistan, which adopted a nationalism loosely based upon Islam, violence against religious minorities is virtually unchecked. In Burma and Sri Lanka, an ethno-religious nationalism combining Theravada Buddhism with each country's ethnic majority has laid the ideological foundation for extreme violence and civil war against a broad range of minority groups.

Extending this reasoning to the global level in view of democratic peace theory (the empirically substantiated but contested theory that democracies do not fight wars against one another), inclusive nationalism can be a step toward a more stable and peaceful global co-existence between rooted nationals because such an identity could help to stabilize democracies and delimit wars. However, that inclusive nationalism may have felicitous effects should not blind liberals to the inherent dangers of encompassing ideologies. Like every other -ism, nationalism can become destructive, particularly toward a non-national out-group.

Yet it is worth noting that a strong sense of national identity has not historically impeded generosity toward foreigners or refugees. Just as Brown political scientist Prerna Singh's research shows that strong subnational identities do not preclude a strong national identity, there is no empirical reason to assume that strong national identities preclude a commitment to universal values. Indeed, multiple overlapping identities that are triggered by situationally specific contexts are increasingly the norm in a globalized world in which hundreds of millions of people live outside of their country of birth. New York University philosopher Kwame Anthony Appiah's theory of "rooted cosmopolitanism" goes so far as to argue that a deeply felt commitment to one's local identity is a necessary prerequisite to a genuine obligation to universal identities.

A final reason liberals should celebrate inclusive nationalism is because it creates avenues for national outsiders to eventually become insiders. If membership in the nation is genuinely defined by a set of principles rather than by an ethnolinguistic concept of the *Volk*, then non-nationals can become nationals over the course of a generation or two by moving across borders and subscribing to an adopted nation's principles.

Nationalism is the only political identity capable of uniting millions of strangers together in bonds of solidarity that have motivated the creation of democratic and socially generous states. Declaring all nationalism anti-democratic fails to recognize that nationalism is a needed form of identity in the modern world, one that can peacefully coexist with global cosmopolitanism and liberal democracy. But as Appiah observed in his 2016 Reith lecture, if it is clear that a national "we" must rule ourselves in the modern world, then much hinges on how the "we" gets defined.

 *George Lakey, a Quaker, was one of the authors of the American Friends Service Committee study* In Place of War. *His first arrest was in a civil rights demonstration in 1964 and the most recent was in 2018 in a campaign for economic, racial, and climate justice. He has taught peace studies at Haverford and Swarthmore Colleges and the University of Pennsylvania and led over 1,500 social change workshops on five continents. His most recent book is* Viking Economics: How the Scandinavians Got It Right and How We Can, Too. *Forthcoming from the same publisher is a book on how to conduct nonviolent campaigns for change.*

Envisioning Boldly Enough to Tackle the Threat of Terror
George Lakey

The terror attacks of 9/11 scared Americans badly, and fear gets in the way of vision. The spiritual motion of fear is contraction, while vision is its opposite, the motion of expansion.

For that reason, envisioning shared security in an age of terror might seem next to impossible. However, I learned from the visioning experiments of the late Quaker sociologist and peace researcher Elise Boulding that, when facilitated with enough positivity and structured prompts, people will sometimes surprise themselves by their own creativity.

While teaching at Swarthmore College, I decided to design a vision process for countering terror. My biggest surprise was that even the Pentagon expressed interest in our results.

I surveyed countries that have actually reduced or eliminated the threat of terror they'd faced—the UK with the Irish Republican Army, for example, and Spain with the ETA. Some nations included non-military policies in their approach, like the British choice to prioritize jobs and economic development in Northern Ireland. In that way I collected eight nonviolent tools for a strategy toolbox.

The course I offered on "Nonviolent Response to Terror" filled quickly.

We didn't spend time criticizing military counter-terrorism because criticism, to a visionary, can be a waste of time. To introduce ourselves to the field of counter-terror we read one book by an expert. Then we took up our challenge.

Each student chose a country somewhere in the world that is

presently threatened by terrorism and took the role of a consultant to that country. The student's task was to get to know the strengths and weaknesses of that country and to devise from our nonviolent toolbox a strategy for that country's defense.

It was tough work, and highly stimulating. Most of the students had a ball, and some did brilliant strategizing. Our class work included not only in-depth examination of each of the eight tools, but also periods when students worked in teams to share ideas on how to apply the tools to their various countries.

Students especially liked brainstorming synergistic effects—what happens when technique three interacts with techniques two and five, for example? At the time I wished we had an additional semester to handle the complexity of making all the tools not just additive, but discovering how the whole became more powerful than the sum of the parts.

Some students who assumed that military defense is essential opened to a bigger perspective. They realized that, given the success some countries have had using just two or three of the tools, there is significant untapped potential: What if a country used all of the tools together, with the resulting synergies? In the background hovered the question: Why couldn't populations rely completely on the nonviolent toolbox for their defense against terror?

The Eight Techniques

1. Ally-building and the infrastructure of economic development

Poverty and terrorism are indirectly linked. Economic development can reduce recruits and gain allies, especially if development is done in a democratic way. When Israel used the British tool of economic development for Palestine, for example, there was a reduction of terrorism. (Israelis then undermined their own success by using the tool punitively—withdrawing it in response to a violent attack—contradicting their own good sense).

2. Reducing cultural marginalization

As France, Britain, and other countries have learned, marginalizing a group within your population is not safe or sensible; terrorists grow under those conditions. This is also true on a global level. Much marginalizing is unintentional, but it can be reduced. "Freedom of the press," for example, transforms into "provocation" when it further marginalizes a population that is already one-down, as are Muslims in France. When Anglophone Canada reduced its marginalization, it reduced the threat of terrorism from Quebec.

3. Nonviolent protest/campaigns among the defenders, plus unarmed civilian peacekeeping

Terrorism happens in a larger social context and is therefore influenced by that context. Some terror campaigns have lapsed because they lost popular support. That's because terror's strategic use is often to gain attention, provoke a violent response, and win more support in the broader population.

The rise and fall of support for terrorism is in turn influenced by social movements using people power, or nonviolent struggle. The US civil rights movement brilliantly handled the Ku Klux Klan's threat to activists, most dangerous when there was no effective law enforcement to help. The nonviolent tactics reduced the KKK's appeal among white segregationists. Since the 1980s, pacifists and others have established an additional, promising tool: intentional and planned unarmed civilian peacekeeping. Peace Brigades International (PBI) has for decades mobilized volunteers to protect human rights defenders in situations of terror; in 1989, I participated in PBI's initial team in the Sri Lankan civil war. Nonviolent Peaceforce adds to the field a new access for people who want to become "nonviolent soldiers" but need to be paid for their work so their families can be supported.

4. Pro-conflict education and training

Ironically, terror often happens when a population tries to suppress conflicts instead of supporting their expression. A technique for reducing terror, therefore, is to spread a pro-conflict attitude and the nonviolent skills that support people waging conflict to give full voice to their grievances.

5. Post-terror recovery programs

Not all terror can be prevented, any more than all crime can be prevented. Keep in mind that terrorists often have the goal of increasing polarization. Recovery programs can help prevent that polarization, the cycle of hawks on one side "arming" the hawks on the other side. One place we've seen this cycle of violence is in the Palestine/Israel struggle.

Recovery programs build resilience, so people don't go rigid with fear and create self-fulfilling prophecies. The leap forward in trauma counseling is relevant for this technique, along with innovative rituals such as those the Norwegians used after the 2011 terrorist massacre there.

6. Police as peace officers: the infrastructure of norms and laws

Police work can become far more effective through more community policing and reduction of the social distance between police and the neighborhoods they serve. In some countries this requires re-conceptualization of the police from defenders of the property of the dominant group to genuine peace officers; witness the unarmed Icelandic police. Countries like the United States need to join the growing global infrastructure of human rights law reflected in the Land Mines Treaty and International Criminal Court, and accept accountability for their own officials who are probable war criminals.

7. Policy changes and the concept of reckless behavior

Governments sometimes make choices that invite—almost beg for—a terrorist response. Political scientist and sometime US Air Force consultant Robert A. Pape showed in 2005 that the United States has repeatedly done this, often by putting troops on someone else's land. In his book *Cutting the Fuse,* he and James K. Feldman give concrete examples of governments reducing the terror threat by ending such reckless behavior. To protect themselves from terror, citizens in all countries need to gain control of their own governments and force them to behave.

8. Negotiation

Governments often say "we don't negotiate with terrorists," but when they say that, they may be lying. Governments have often reduced or eliminated terrorism through negotiation, and negotiation skills continue to grow in sophistication.

Combining Tools for a Real World Application

The Pentagon heard about our work at Swarthmore and a policy planning unit invited me to share what we'd learned in applying the tools. The professionals recognized that each of these tools has indeed been used in real-life situations in one place or another, with some degree of success. They also saw no problem, in principle, in devising a comprehensive strategy that would create synergies among the tools. The problem they saw was persuading the US government to take such a bold, innovative leap.

As an American, I see the direct contradiction between, on the one hand, my country's power holders' determination to convince taxpayers that we need a swollen military and, on the other, a new policy that mobilizes a different kind of power for genuine, shared security. I understand that for my country, and for some others as well, a nonviolent revolution to depose the established elite will need to come first.

Success for nonviolent revolutionary movements depends on their ability to project appealing alternatives to the status quo. What I like about proposing an alternative, non-military defense is that it speaks to the real need of my fellow citizens for security in a dangerous world.

Psychologist Abraham Maslow long ago pointed out the fundamental human need for security. Analyzing and criticizing militarism, however brilliantly, doesn't actually enhance anyone's security. Imagining an alternative, as my students did, may give people the psychological space they need to put energy into something more life-giving.

May 2, 2018

 *Jason Tower is a China-based peace-builder and has worked with the American Friends Service Committee since 2008. Over the past decade, Jason has worked on building engagement with business stakeholders on peace and conflict issues, and has developed specific expertise working with Chinese companies in this area. Jason has also built close partnerships with civil society across Southeast Asia and Africa to help address concerns around investments. Jason is fluent in Chinese and has lived and worked in China for nearly twenty years. He was trained as a political scientist and has published numerous articles on peace and security issues.*

The 3.6-Billion-Dollar Lesson:
Beyond the Us vs. Them Business Model
Jason Tower

In early 2011, a report on the website of the then China Power Investment Company (CPI) boasted of the security arrangements that were to be placed around the construction site of the Myistone Dam project, which at that time was set to become the largest hydropower dam in Southeast Asia. The report noted that the site was to "become an island of security" and that no one, especially local armed groups, would be able to "infiltrate" the fortifications placed around the project.

Just two years earlier, Myanmar and China had entered into an agreement regarding the 3.6-billion-dollar project, located at the confluence of the Mali and N'mai Rivers, which also happens to be the source of Myanmar's "mother river," the Ayeyawady River, which is critical for the country's food security and navigation, and also has deep symbolic meaning as a river which unites an otherwise very diverse population.

While CPI emphasized that the Myanmar Army had invited it to construct the dam in this location in the northern highlands of the Southeast Asian country in 2006, public narratives in China spoke of the project as a "gift" to the people of Myanmar, and a solution to the severe energy shortages which plague the country's development today. Yet, the contrast between this story and that being told just a stone's throw away from the dam throughout Kachin State could not be starker. As noted in a letter in May of 2011, the Kachin Independence Organization (KIO), one of Myanmar's largest nationalities groups discussed how the dam could lead to civil war between the KIO and the Myanmar army, pleading for project owners to halt the construction. Sadly, just months later, war broke out, and continues today. Kachin activists point to the dam, and the incursion of Myanmar army troops into Kachin territory that accompanied it as a proximate cause of the war. A wide range of deep-seated historical grievances, including the lack of an inclusive national identify, lack of voice in political processes, and failures of the government to respect the founding principles of the country, continue to fuel the war to the present.

When I first visited the project site in 2010, traveling with a dear friend and colleague, signs of the animosity and frustration being created by the project could not be more obvious. Communities facing immediate displacement spoke of the area as the "birth place" of the country, and a special heritage site; religious leaders emphasized how local groups had not been consulted, and likened the taking of Kachin lands, destruction of churches, and uprooting of livelihoods as "acts of war."

Meanwhile, hundreds of kilometers away in communities along the Ayeyawady River, similar stories of concern could be heard: how would this impact traditional Burmese livelihoods? What would this mean for rice cultivation in the downstream? For fisheries? For people's dreams for the future? Suddenly, communities across the country were linked by a common concern—the pending doom that this project would bring.

For two years from 2010 until 2011, I had the honor of getting to know many activists, artists, scientists, doctors, educators, farmers, and faith leaders who were part of a movement that culminated in the September 2011 announcement by the Myanmar President of the project's suspension in accordance with the "will of the people." Seen locally as a watershed moment, the Myitsone took on great symbolism. For the first time in decades of military rule, the people had stood together, and local voices from across the country had been heard. While the announcement brought excitement to communities throughout the country, at another level, the outcome also generated very serious issues in what is likely Myanmar's most important bilateral relationship: that with China. The gaps in the narratives in two cities seated only 700 kilometers away—Mandalay and Kunming—were just too different. People in China could not understand how a "gift" had been rejected, or why a war had broken out, and how the project's cancellation might have taken on such symbolism.

Over the past several years, I have witnessed many such examples, and heard many similar stories from across the globe of how business results unexpectedly in conflict, damaging relations between companies and communities, communities and government, government and companies, and even between states. At the root of all of these stories are the same mistakes: rather than building relationships, consulting with local people and designing investments with strong popular support, or which may even empower people, investors instead look at communities as threats; they harbor the enduring suspicion that the community may do harm to the investor.

It is unfortunate, but prevailing models of security around investments are "us vs. them" models. According to this way of thinking, security companies are brought in, walls are constructed, fortresses are built around projects, and the community is subject to monitoring. Yet such scenarios are good neither for the companies nor the communities in which they want to invest. As fences get higher, community concerns and distrust of the particular company rise, causing the company to perceive greater levels of risk, leading to greater spending on fences. Who benefits? In the end, probably only the security company, which has a built-in interest in maintaining low-level tensions between businesses and communities, and identifying increasing levels of risks so that it can market ever more sophisticated and expensive security products to corporations.

The "island of security" that CPI aspired to create around the Myitsone Dam was probably the most extreme example; that construction of a dam project might continue with civil war raging just kilometers away is hard to imagine, especially when one of the warring parties pointed to the dam as a proximate cause of the conflict.

So what is the answer? Shared security provides us with an alternative approach: a lens for companies to develop a new model based on consensus building, local buying and empowerment around investments, which, if done right, should lead to dramatic reductions in traditional "hard-security" costs and, if we are lucky, the demilitarization of corporate approaches to security at great savings to all parties. Just imagine if in 2006, CPI had entered Myanmar using such an approach. Could it have found a very different project to invest in that might already have been generating revenue for all parties involved? Would China–Myanmar relations at the government-to-government level, long referred to as a relationship of *bao-po*, or brotherhood, have been damaged in such a way? Would suspicions on both sides have risen to current levels?

The American Friends Service Committee (AFSC) today works globally, among other things, on a shared security initiative referred to as Business and Peace—an effort to build shared security between stakeholders around business projects. Through this work, AFSC builds partnership with companies and communities to try to realize alternative models to business investments.

The notion of shared security, that business interests must find security *in*, and not *from*, the communities that host them is the core of this program. The program dreams of a day when business stakeholders globally see that only by following such an approach can an investment be sustainable for both business and community. It hopes that instead of security departments, businesses establish peace-building departments, which have the function of listening closely to community concerns, and considering all of the different forms of divisions and connections within and around their host communities. If corporate stakeholders worked to become peace-builders and considered carefully the ways in which their activities impact these divisions and connections, they could, at a minimum, avoid "doing harm" or exacerbating tensions within host communities. Taken a step further, this approach could make a major contribution to reducing conflict on a global scale; just imagine if every business group tracked its footprint on peace as carefully as it tracks its profits? What if they developed barometers for understanding levels of tension and conflict within communities, and worked to try to keep these tensions and conflicts from becoming violent?

The story of the Myitsone is one of very mixed emotions: one of war, loss, destruction and anger, but also one of solidarity, empowerment, and standing up in the face of oppression. It also illustrates a very important, and expensive lesson—a 3.6-billion-dollar lesson to be precise—of the failures of traditional, militarized, us vs. them approaches to security. It is my hope that corporate stakeholders everywhere might learn closely from the lessons of the Myitsone, and that business can begin to retool to build new models of security. Shared security offers a clear solution to these problems, and if accepted by business stakeholders globally, business and peace presents one of the most important spaces in which conflict might be reduced on a global scale.

 *Terri-Ann P. Gilbert-Roberts is a Jamaican regionalist with over seventeen years of experience in research and policy development related to Caribbean integration and issues affecting children and youth, including child labor, youth employment, juvenile justice, and youth participation. As a Research Fellow at the University of the West Indies (UWI) Mona, Jamaica, she chairs the SALISES 50/50 Youth Research Cluster which supports evidence-based youth policies and programs. She has been youth empowerment advisor to the Caribbean Community, Caribbean Regional Youth Council, the Commonwealth, and the United Nations.*

In Service of My Fellow Citizens
Nation>Region>World: Layers of Solidarity for Peace
Terri-Ann P. Gilbert-Roberts

Shared Security and Regional Solidarity

I am a committed regionalist. Why? Because, regional solidarity is an imperative for the small, mostly island, Caribbean states that face common existential threats to security and their very survival. Shared insecurity is a feature of the Caribbean experience—emerging from historical bonds of enslavement, exploitation, and colonialism under global capitalism; legacies of structural, physical, and psychological violence now manifest within societies in conflict; and contemporary climate threats from drought, rising sea level, and intensified storms that threaten regional survival.

However, the inherent challenges of that regional experience have provided an opportune context in which Caribbean peoples have learned (and are still learning) to respect our interdependence and shared aspirations for peace, development, and prosperity. Shared security, viewed through a development lens, is therefore the ultimate goal of regional cooperation strategies and institutions. It is through one of those regionalist institutions—the Caribbean Community (CARICOM)—that, as a young volunteer, I first came to appreciate the concept of solidarity and learned to build bridges across a variety of divides—whether across the Caribbean Sea; across individual national identities nested within a Caribbean civilization; across religious, racial, ethnic, and political divides—to connect with the rest of the world.

Although I had traveled all over the world by the time I was in secondary school, I made my first visit to a neighboring Caribbean territory—Suriname—at the age of 18. I went to the city of Paramaribo to represent my country and Jamaican youth as a CARICOM Youth Ambassador charged with a mandate to advocate for the rights of young people to participate in decision-making on regional integration issues. It was in those meetings with other young activists and representatives that I learned, notwithstanding our linguistic and cultural differences, how much young people across the region shared similar aspirations for security of employment (within a shared economic space); for peace from crime and violence; and for opportunities to explore the region and the world (supported by regimes allowing free movement of people for knowledge and cultural exchanges). It was in that regional framework that I recognized the value of sustaining a regional movement among youth from 15 countries, with diverse identities, speaking various creoles alongside Dutch, English, French, and Spanish, but united by a commitment to speak on behalf of young people whose voices were not usually heard, neither at home nor abroad.

My two-year ambassadorial journey also stretched further afield—building bridges with Africa and Asia, through the Commonwealth, so as to appreciate Diasporic connections to my Caribbean home and to form coalitions of advocacy for youth employment opportunities and youth political participation rights. Later, those experiences led to professional pursuits in academic and policy research on youth, including service as a member of the CARICOM Commission on Youth Development mandated to prepare a comprehensive situation analysis of the experiences of youth in the region. When, based on the recommendations of the Commission, Heads of Government signed the *Declaration of Paramaribo on the Future of Youth in the Community*—ten years after the start of my advocacy as a volunteer Youth Ambassador—it was as though my advocacy journey had come full circle. The Declaration was inspired by the authentic voices of young people and formally recognized the imperative of providing space for young people to lead and participate in the construction of our institutional expressions of regional solidarity. These regional experiences have contributed to my perspective of young people as critical partners in development.

Inspirations from an Open Nationalism

On reflection, I have realized that my openness to learning from regional and international experiences also emerged, paradoxically, from my Jamaican nationalist upbringing. From the first day of formal schooling, and countless times since, the Jamaican National Pledge has been a constant reminder of my oath to service in the pursuit of justice, fellowship, and peace at both the national and international levels.

> *"Before God and all [humankind], I pledge the love and loyalty of my heart, the wisdom and courage of my mind, the strength and vigor of my body, in the service of my fellow citizens..."*

Those words inspired my student volunteerism within Jamaica to serve the special needs of older persons, persons with disabilities, and children in the care of the state who had in effect been abandoned. My role was simply to encourage them, provide for their basic needs, and affirm their rights to life, respect and good treatment—the basic rights of citizenship. I learned that even the smallest actions, based on kindness and goodwill, hold potential to grow into more elaborate and powerful forms of activism.

> *"I promise to stand up for Justice, Brotherhood[/Sisterhood] and Peace..."*

These words have guided my advocacy for the adoption of laws and policies to protect children from exploitation through systems of extremely unsafe labor in agricultural, mining, and fishery sectors. They also inspired my service to uplift children in conflict with the law, and under detention in juvenile centers, to remind them of their worth and the potential to make new choices and explore new opportunities after release.

That promise has also been at the heart of my professional work to strengthen regional intergovernmental institutions and regional youth governance networks so that they transform challenging national contexts into shared development outcomes that reflect the identity and aspirations of the diverse peoples in the region. In recognition of the fact that some of the voices of those people would never be known in the formal framework, I focused on creating spaces for excluded voices to be heard, whether in the halls of academia or in national and regional political fora. Young people have been among the most open and gracious partners in those efforts. They have been willing to share their stories and ideas with me, and are always committed to inspiring and encouraging their peers as well as me, even as I seek to offer mentorship and guidance.

> *"...to work diligently and creatively, to think generously and honestly, so that Jamaica may, under God, increase in beauty, fellowship and prosperity...and play her part in advancing the welfare of the whole human race."*

That pledge—which enjoys pride of place among my office wall-hangings, facing me each morning—reflects my small nation's big aspirations for global peace. Its words have encouraged me to use my analytical skills and opportunities for access to high-level academic and political dialogue to represent the voices of young people on the issues that matter most to them; while sensitizing (older) policymakers to the situation of youth across the world. This has been sometimes overwhelming and, at other times, a tedious process of building an "evidence base" for advocacy. However, it has always been worthwhile.

My most recent service on the Advisory Group for the UN Global Progress Study on Youth, Peace and Security has been among the most meaningful of attempts to use research skills to "advance the welfare of the whole human race." The Advisory Group—an extraordinary coalition of twenty-one younger and older leaders from various organizational and other backgrounds, including twenty different nationalities—guided the preparation of a seminal report to the UN Security Council on the diverse ways in which young people are contributing to peace and security around the world. The report makes bold assertions about young people being the "missing peace" at the heart of our aspirations for sustainable development, and recommends innovative strategies for concrete investment in youth networks that effectively promote sustaining peace and security.

Over the seventeen years that I have been working in development, I have been convinced of the necessity of building bridges across national, regional, and international spaces to create multiple layers of solidarity for peace and sustainable development. For me, those bridges and layers are the foundations of shared security; and youth are at the vanguard of achieving it.

The Ongoing Task of Bridging Divides

In addition to crossing geographical divides through regional and international coalitions, we must continue to pay attention to the threats posed by intergenerational divides, as well as vertical and horizontal political divides among groups of people.

I have the privilege to serve in a regional network of Caribbean scholars, practitioners, and youth leaders—the SALISES 50/50 Youth Research Cluster—which is committed to bridging those divides. We operate as a network coordinated at the University of the West Indies which is involved in youth development "Research towards Action through Partnership." In our work to build the evidence base for youth development, we seek to create and maintain positive and encouraging spaces for young people to work with older persons to research and solve development challenges. We also seek to build the leadership capacity of youth organizations and networks, encouraging them to bridge horizontal divides which contribute to undue competition among youth clubs and societies for financial resources and recognition; as well as the vertical divides between, on the one hand, national and transnational youth representatives and, on the other hand, young people organizing at community levels. The 50/50 Youth Cluster further seeks to challenge the false separation of youth organizations from other civil society groups, a practice which dilutes voices of advocacy and weakens hands of activism on important issues, while also marginalizing and excluding young people from effective partnerships.

Conclusion

Throughout, my role has been and will continue to be that of facilitator of young people's ideas and solutions. The unwavering quest of most youth, globally, for peaceful and prosperous futures, as well as their unflagging commitment to authentic expressions of everyday solidarity continue to inspire me. In the visions and aspirations of the Caribbean young leaders which I have been documenting since 2012, some common threads permeate their stories—a clear sense of social justice; eagerness to view the problems of others as shared problems; and willingness to form organizations and networks of solidarity for collective action. Young people think broadly and across levels. Undeterred by inequitable immigration and other policies that prevent them from achieving global citizenship in a real sense, they maintain transnational aspirations. They forge partnerships across geopolitical divides; for example, in the way that the Caribbean Regional Youth Council continues to ensure that Cuban youth and youth from non-independent territories (who are often marginalized within the hemisphere), have rights to participation in the annual celebratory summits for Caribbean Youth Day. As young people forge authentic alliances that use music and culture to fight against injustice and negative influences toward crime and violence, I will stand with them. As they speak collectively and loudly against corruption, organizing themselves to conduct social audits of public service delivery, I will join them. Whether they organize formally in local community youth clubs, national youth networks, regional youth councils and international coalitions; or whether they connect informally for *ad hoc* advocacy and activism, I will continue to invest in their convictions, that we are all most likely to reach our fullest potential, together... indivisible in the pursuit of a peaceful, secure, and prosperous existence.

 Lana Baydas is a senior fellow with the Center for Strategic and International Studies, Human Rights Initiative. Prior to joining CSIS, she worked as an academic and a practitioner in the fields of human rights, gender equality, development, and international humanitarian law, holding posts with the UN, Crisis Action, the ICRC, and the American University in Cairo. She has worked intensively in the Middle East and North Africa (MENA) region, and authored and co-authored publications on human rights in MENA. She holds a PhD and LLM in public international law from the University of Glasgow in Scotland.

Forgotten: A Gender Lens on Closing Civic Space
Lana Baydas

It is often noted that civil society at large should learn from women's groups' successful experiences in establishing their space and advocating for their rights. Women's movements around the world are able to establish coalitions and cross-border solidarity to voice their concerns. The pursuit of a collective voice and message has been underscored in the body of literature. Women's groups, through coalition building, develop local ownership of women's rights and build the needed public legitimacy that makes it harder for oppressive regimes to discredit.

To place the importance of protecting space for the continued operation of women's rights groups, let us consider the context in which they have to operate. The last decade has witnessed a deterioration of respect for human rights and of upholding democratic principles and standards, an alarming trend that has been accelerated in the recent years because of the rise of populism and authoritarianism around the world. The Freedoms in the World report for 2018 indicates a decline of civil liberties and a backslide of democracy, with 25 percent of the world's countries categorized as not free in 2017 as compared with 22 percent not free in 2007.[1] It shows that authoritarian and democratic governments increasingly adopt measures curtailing political and civil rights that in turn close civic space. This trend will unfortunately remain with us for the coming decade at least.

Reasons vary from one country to another, but the common thread is to silence dissenting voices and force citizens to subscribe to a given government's policies and strategies.[2] Governments adopt different tactics and tools to restrict the space needed to ensure active citizen participation and engagement. Reports from the United Nations and international human rights organizations demonstrate that governments have adopted repressive legislation to limit rights to freedom of expression, association, and peaceful assembly. For example, Ghana Police Services have attacked seventeen journalists in the last fifteen months. Furthermore, the Chinese authorities, as noted by the Business and Human Rights Resource Center, have arrested fifty labor activists on the grounds of "gathering crowds to disturb public order," and of "embezzlement." Egypt, Iran, and Turkey continue detaining and intimidating human rights defenders as a means of curtailing their human rights work and activism. Frontline Defenders reported that more than 300 human rights defenders around the world were murdered in 2017 alone. Travel bans have been imposed on activists, human rights defenders, journalists, and representatives of civil society organizations, restricting their participation in international fora.

In spite of the fact that all civil society actors have been adversely impacted by the trend of closing civic space, women activists and human rights defenders as well as organizations working on women's rights find themselves facing not only tactics used by governments to close the space for civil society, but also obstacles imposed by prevailing social norms and discriminatory dynamics.

As a young woman growing up in the Middle East and North African region, I came to the realization that, without having an enabling and open civic space, achieving peace, security, and development in the region would continue to be a dream. This realization came at the time when women's movements from around the world were gathered in Beijing, China, in 1995 to negotiate a capstone document for gender equality in all fields, the Beijing Declaration and Platform for Action. Although I did not attend or participate in the preparatory work leading to Beijing, the energy and persistence for a better future for all women and girls of the world defined my way of thinking and the career path I undertook. The Beijing Declaration clearly establishes the link between achieving gender equality, development, and peace, and securing an enabling civic space. It states that "[w]omen's empowerment and their full participation on the basis of equality in all spheres of society, including participation in the decision-making process and access to power, are fundamental for the achievement of equality, development, and peace[.]"[3]

Despite numerous obstacles, over the last three decades, women's movements around the world have made significant strides because of their continued commitment to activism and civic engagement. Organizations working on women's rights achieved milestones at the international and national level. This is demonstrated by the recognition that women's rights are human rights, and by the adoption of key conventions and resolutions at the United Nations endorsing the notion that sustaining development, peace, and security would not be achieved without eliminating all forms of discrimination against women. The 2030 Agenda for Sustainable Development stipulates, for example, "[r]ealizing gender equality and the empowerment of women and girls will make a crucial contribution to progress across all the Goals and targets. The achievement of full human potential and of sustainable development is not possible if one half of humanity continues to be denied its full human rights and opportunities. Women and girls must enjoy equal access to quality education, economic resources and political participation as well as equal opportunities with men and boys for employment, leadership and decision-making at all levels."[4] Women's rights organizations have scored legislative gains on the protection of their civil, political, economic, and social rights in a number of countries in all regions. Their advocacy and mobilization ensure combatting violence against women becomes a top national and international priority.

I personally witnessed the impressive work of the Lebanese Women's Movement in its efforts to combat domestic violence against women and shift the debate; to assert that it is an issue not governed by the private sphere. Women's groups were collectively able to put the issue high on the national agenda by shedding light on the magnitude of the problem in the country. Offering paralegal and psychological counseling to violence survivors, advancing a draft law on combatting domestic violence against women to the parliament, and creating capacity-building trainings for police officers have been vital to address this human rights violation at the policy and implementation level. There are other successful examples as well. The #MeToo hashtag and the Time's Up campaign that spread through social media put sexual harassment, sexual violence, and the need for effective justice mechanisms under the spotlight. Both movements have demonstrated that these abuses are rooted in systemic inequalities that are global.[5]

Yet, although repressive measures have impacted all civil society sectors, they may have a greater impact on civil society actors working on women rights and gender-related issues. In addition to restrictive legal and quasi-legal measures imposed by the state on civil society at large, women's groups are challenged by discriminatory legal systems, social forces, and dynamics. Societies with restrictive civil society spaces often promote patriarchal values and a dualistic gender framework within a nationalist discourse. Also, according to a Mama Cash report, "increasingly conservative political forces openly frame women's rights... as products of 'western interference.'"[6] This makes women's groups easy targets and the first to be impacted by closing civic space measures.

Strategies to silence female human rights defenders, activists, and female leaders of civil society organizations, often resort to sexualizing them in ways that affect their private lives. Women involved in protests, rights campaigns, social services, legal aid, journalism, and other public action have been targeted for a range of abuses including being subjected to state-sponsored sexual harassment, abuse, and rape. These abuses reflect, or are made worse by, the wider context of gender inequality in societies and the laws that institutionalize it. Ladies in White, a group of female relatives of political prisoners in Cuban prisons, remains a primary target of repression from authorities, with reports of violent arrests spiking in early 2018. Several women were violently arrested by state security agents before their weekly nonviolent and silent demonstration.[7]

Sexual violence is used as "fair punishment" for women on the grounds of their activism. This became a deterrent meant to silence women's and girls' voices—for example, the harassment and abuse of women demonstrating in Tahrir Square in Egypt. These abuses reflect, or are made worse by, the wider context of gender inequality in societies and the laws that institutionalize it. The direct links between state and societal gender-based violence and the decreasing voice and participation of women have been determined by women activists and human rights defenders.

Other methods used include States putting in place legislation that restricts funding sources for civil society organizations. Cambodia, Egypt, Ethiopia, Hungary, India, and Russia enacted draconian laws that restrict non-governmental organizations (NGOs) from receiving foreign funds—a lifeline source for many organizations, labeling them as foreign agents or complicit in the agendas of foreign governments. These measures target the resilience of these organizations and the sustainability of their activities. Once again, the reduction of foreign funding has a greater impact on the survival of women's groups given that they are already operating with limited resources. As a result, many organizations working on women's and gender issues either could not survive and disappeared, or changed their mandate and cause. The failure to allocate sufficient resources for the work of women's groups has been the most serious obstacle to the development, peace, and security agenda.[8]

A number of initiatives have been formed to open a public dialogue on various drivers and factors that lead to closing civic space. I participated in discussions and contributed to the research undertaken.[9] The public debate and the research efforts have ensured that the threats to civil society on the part of governments have been placed in the spotlight. These efforts should continue and provide evidence-based recommendations on how best to address the trend of closing civic space. Yet, what is of utmost importance is to have a gender lens focused on understanding this phenomenon, and to learn from the responses adopted by women's groups to mobilize their local constituents on women's rights and gender issues. Pushing back against restrictive measures and tactics requires an inclusive and comprehensive approach.

Notes

1.   Lana Baydas and Shannon N. Green, eds., "Counter

Terrorism Measures and Civil Society: Changing the Will, Finding the Way," Center for Strategic & International Studies (CSIS), 2018. Accessed September 20, 2018. https://csis-prod.s3.amazonaws.com/s3fs-public/publication/180322_CounterterrorismMeasures.pdf?EeEWbuPwsYh1iE7HpnS2nPyMhev21qpw.

2.   United Nations, "Beijing Declaration and Platform for Action," Fourth World Conference on Women, September 4–15, 1995. Accessed September 18, 2018. www.un.org/womenwatch/daw/beijing/pdf/BDPfA%20E.pdf.

3.   "Transforming Our World: The 2030 Agenda for Sustainable Development," United Nations, 2015. Accessed September 18, 2018. https://sustainabledevelopment.un.org/post2015/transformingourworld.

4.   "The State of Civil Society Report 2018," CIVICUS. Accessed September 18, 2018. www.civicus.org/documents/reports-and-publications/SOCS/2018/socs-2018-overview_top-ten-trends.pdf.

5.   "Women- and Trans-Led Groups Respond to Closing Space for Civil Society," Mama Cash and Urgent Action Fund, 2017. Accessed September 18. 2018. www.mamacash.org/media/publications/mc_closing_space_report_def.pdf.

6.   "La Dama de Blanco Martha Sánchez lleva detenida 16 días," Diario De Cuba, March 28, 2018. Accessed September 18, 2018. www.diariodecuba.com/derechos-humanos/1522194922_38319.html.

7.   *Tightening the Purse Strings: What Countering Terrorism Financing Costs Gender Equality and Security*, Duke Law International Human Rights Clinic and Women Peacemakers Program, March 2017. Accessed 18 September 2018. https://law.duke.edu/sites/default/files/humanrights/tighteningpursestrings.pdf.

8. "The International Consortium on Closing Civic Space (iCon)," Center for Strategic & International Studies (CSIS), 2016. Accessed 18 September 2018. www.csis.org/programs/international-consortium-closing-civic-space-icon.

Jacinda Kate Laurell Ardern is the leader of the New Zealand Labour Party, and the Prime Minister of New Zealand. She joined the NZLP at the age of seventeen, and served on the staff of former Prime Minister Helen Clark and in the cabinet office of British Prime Minister, Tony Blair. She was elected president of the International Union of Socialist Youth (IUSY), and traveled internationally. At age twenty-eight Ardern entered the House of Representatives and championed an end to child poverty and strong responses to climate change, and served as spokesperson for Social Development, Arts, Culture and Heritage, Children, Justice, and Small Business. A charismatic leader, Arden's commitment to poverty alleviation, education, and women's rights fueled her victory.

Honoring the Past and Looking to a Peaceful, Shared, and Sustainable Future
Jacinda Ardern

The Right Honorable Jacinda Ardern has been hailed as one of the brightest stars on the international stage, rising from political activism starting at the age of seventeen to leading her country as its Prime Minister twenty years later. Throughout her life, she has been committed to principles of governance that hold that we are most likely to succeed as a society, a country, or a global community, if we are able to be equitable in the sharing of our resources and recognize the validity of all our many voices.

She has lifted her own voice in support of the arts, stating that "Arts and culture are not a 'nice to have.' They are an essential part of our individual, community and national identity." She has described the Arts Culture and Heritage Portfolio she holds as having three important priorities: "to have an environment where we no longer question the value of the arts, to have young people who consider careers in the arts as viable, and for all communities to have easy access to cultural experiences."

Prime Minister Ardern has a strong sense of history, and what is owed to those who might have come before. In addressing the strong relationship between New Zealand and Australia, in the course of her Address to the Australia–New Zealand Leadership Forum Luncheon in Sydney on March 2, 2018, she pointed out that this bond was not accidental, but rather the result of "deliberate efforts and investments that have been made over the years to get us to where we are." She went on to acknowledge the contributions of a diverse range of communities, including "the business community; academia; sportspeople; Maori and indigenous communities, and of course governments."

With regard to disarmament, the Prime Minister reaffirmed her commitment to "the cause of non-proliferation and disarmament, and to the norms and rules which support those endeavors," and asserted that her government would pursue an early ratification of the Treaty on the Prohibition of Nuclear Weapons. She made these remarks four months into her tenure, during a speech to the New Zealand Institute of International Affairs on February 27, 2018.

At that same event, the Prime Minister described how personal her learning had been, with regard to both the world and the role of New Zealand in that world:

"In my twenties I was elected to the board of an international political youth organization called IUSY. This umbrella organization held consultative status with the UN, and was the largest international political youth movement in the world with 150 member organizations across 100 countries.

The job was intense. I saw the realities of global conflict and foreign policy failures, and witnessed first-hand the distance between the need of many and the ability of the world to help. We were one of few organizations, for instance, that had youth representatives from both Fatah in Palestine and Young Labour from Israel, all sitting at the same table.

I learned about conflict, peace, and change. I visited refugee camps from Algeria to Nepal. I traveled through Israel and Palestine, struggling to move through checkpoints that were patrolled by men who were younger than me, but who looked just as anxious.

On one occasion I visited Lebanon to participate in a seminar on engaging young people in political institutions and campaigns. I remember meeting up with a counterpart of mine—he was a youth leader for a political party and lived in Beirut.

As we walked through the streets he pointed to the locations where various political leaders over the years had been assassinated. It could have been a tour grounded in history had we not passed his own apartment. He stopped me in order to point to the exterior walls near his apartment window. Bullet holes were peppered around the edges. He talked about the night it happened in a matter-of-fact way, with an air of familiarity and the kind of ease with which we might talk about an All Black test match.

It was a profound demonstration to me of just how rare and precious this country is. The freedom to move, vote, speak, associate with others. All of these are underpinned by a set of values and frameworks which we have also promoted internationally, and must continue to do so...

...And so in this uncertain world, where long-accepted positions have been met with fresh challenge—our response lies in the approach that, with rare exceptions, we have always taken. Speaking up for what we believe in, standing up when our values are challenged, and working tirelessly to draw in partners with shared views.

We want an international reputation New Zealanders can be proud of. And while we are navigating a level of global uncertainty not seen for several generations, I remain firmly optimistic about New Zealand's place in the world. Our global standing is high: when we speak, it is with credibility; when we act, it is with decency. Long may that continue."

Still in only her seventh month in office as Prime Minister, and on the eve of the birth of her first child, she has permitted us to share her most strongly held beliefs as articulated in excerpts from two of her landmark speeches.

Address to the Friedrich Ebert Foundation, April 17, 2018, Berlin

Progressive & Inclusive Growth— Sharing the Benefits

Kia ora and thank you for the opportunity to join you here today. I am especially grateful to be hosted by FES.

Some of you may well know that, some years ago, I was the President of the International Union of Socialist Youth. It was a role that gave me an insight into many things—my poor command of other languages was one. In fact if you asked any of my multilingual board members at the time, they would have told you that based on my accent, they weren't entirely convinced I could speak English.

But I also developed a huge appreciation for the many globally focused think tanks within Europe—and I acknowledge FES for the role you play in that regard.

Can I also acknowledge your Chancellor Angela Merkel... In a changing international environment it is imperative that we strengthen ties and relationships with countries who share similar values. I know I am one of many who is grateful for your nation's much needed global leadership at a time when international systems have come under significant strain.

Not only do we share values, though, we share similarities in our political system. Our election was held in September last year, and in the aftermath we faced considerable pressure to speed up our coalition negotiations. In fact, there was a reasonable amount of frustration over the time it took for us to negotiate, produce, and sign our coalition, along with confidence and supply agreements—which was a grand total of fifteen days.

Even if our talks were comparatively short, I have an appreciation for the complexity of such negotiations, whether in your country or mine, not just because of the public pressure that surrounds them, but for the internal party political matters that must also be factored in. It's not easy, because compromise is not easy. Nor is maintaining distinct party identities while also building consensus on issues as a government.

In New Zealand I am focused on demonstrating that coalition governments can champion both consensus, and diverse views, for the national good. Wish me luck.

But for today, my mind is focused squarely on the issues that are dominating the international agenda and have done for some time. Whatever the news headline, the underlying theme in global politics seems to be the same—the rules have changed. Economically, and politically.

For those of us who identify ourselves as part of the progressive movement, there is no question that this unsettled environment has led to challenging questions from the public and voters, and challenging political outcomes in debates, elections, and referenda.

This is not new.

A decade ago, as the President of the International Union of Socialist Youth, I visited the United Nations in New York for a gathering of the Socialist International. Present were leaders like George Papandreou (who at the time was leader of the opposition in Greece), and Joseph Stiglitz. We were there to discuss the emerging financial crisis. At the time we were staring down the barrel of a hugely unsettled period for countries and their citizens, and there was a rallying cry for progressive nations and their governments to respond. Some would argue that response never came. More than a decade later we continue to face the challenges of what I would characterize as a sense of global uncertainty.

Globalization, of course, isn't new. In New Zealand we have grappled with this issue and its impact for decades. But the sense of insecurity seems to have only strengthened over the years. The benefits from globalization have been distributed disproportionately to the few. There is a growing sense that ordinary people are working harder and harder just to stay in the same place.

Add to that rapid technological change where even in a country as small as New Zealand the workforce faces the prospect that more than 45 percent of jobs will no longer exist or will be completely replaced in just two decades. It is little wonder that this sense of insecurity has grown.

As politicians, we have choices in how we respond to this growing but justifiable dissatisfaction. We can offer a message of hope, or we can offer a message of fear.

People need security. They need to hear from their political leaders that we anticipate that change: That we have a plan. That we understand the need for job security.

That we understand the need for housing security. And that we understand the need for hope for the next generation—so that they too can have the future that their parents had, if not a better one. And if we do none of these things, we leave a vacuum for fear and populism.

The challenge for progressive and inclusive movements lies in delivering that sense of security, while also staying true to the notion of open borders, fair trade, international responsibility, and other principles that have guided a country like New Zealand for a number of years.

In New Zealand, I believe we are starting to meet that challenge. The Government I lead is determined to demonstrate that you can be an outward-looking trading nation that also supports and delivers on the basic needs and necessities, including of security, for the people who call our place home.

We want to prove that it's possible for a progressive and inclusive trade agenda.

As a small, island nation, you could say that New Zealanders don't just believe in an open, fair, rules-based international trading system—we are entirely reliant on it.

Without clear, fair, and enforceable rules to trade under, small countries like ours are thrust to the margins, as the large and powerful leverage ever greater privileges for themselves.

New Zealand knows what it means to be exposed to the vagaries of the world marketplace—our key goods exports are agricultural products, which remain the most heavily protected from international competition of all economic sectors in all our key markets.

Unsurprisingly, we've spent the past seventy years investing in the rules now established in the WTO system. Over the past thirty years we have sought to build on that framework through the negotiation of a network of bilateral and regional free trade agreements.

This has enabled us to reduce barriers in our key markets, and give our exporters the legal certainty they need to grow their exports, and our national prosperity.

Our FTA footprint, now covering markets that account for more than half our trade, has given our exporters more choice and flexibility, which in turn has increased the resilience of our economy. So it is deeply concerning to New Zealand to see the rules-based global trading system under such strain.

There are no winners in trade war—only different degrees of losing, with the small and vulnerable inevitably losing the most. That is why we are committed to working with others, like Germany, who share our commitment to the rules-based trading system to ensure the gains of the past decades are not lost.

But we don't just want to maintain the status quo, we want to work to make the rules-based trading system fairer and more responsive to the needs and expectations of our citizens.

Our starting point has been to design our trade policy to address public concerns about the current global economic system—particularly inequality and multinational tax avoidance. It also means applying a progressive and inclusive lens to trade policy objectives in general, and trade negotiating mandates in particular.

As a government, we are in the process of openly seeking the public's view on how trade policy can contribute to addressing our other priority policy goals, such as combating climate change, upholding labor rights, protecting scarce natural resources, and implementing our sustainable development goals.

Some will argue that trade policy is not the right area in which to attempt to advance social and economic goals, but I don't accept that.

To give only one example: agreeing to effective trade disciplines on current subsidies to fossil fuel use and to the over-exploitation of fisheries could make a major contribution toward addressing two of the most urgent environmental priorities of our time—climate change and the decline in global fish stocks.

Progressive and inclusive growth also means ensuring that our trade and economic settings help us meet the greatest challenge faced by our generation: that of climate change.

New Zealand has committed to the goal of a net zero carbon economy by 2050. This is an ambitious target, and one that will require fundamental changes to the New Zealand economy. But this transformation will also throw up new opportunities—especially for those businesses and nations who choose to take the lead. And we can create an ecosystem that encourages that leadership.

But none of this agenda, be it R&D investment, or trade reform, is a means to an end. And none of it on its own tells us much about our success.

When the New Zealand Government was formed five months ago, it was through a consensus that all our pursuits should be driven by an agenda for a better life for all our people, particularly the most vulnerable, a growing and inclusive economy, and the protection of the environment, including action on climate change.

Achieving that means officially redefining economic success.

Next year we will be the first nation in the world to report our annual progress against a range of measures in a living standards framework which tracks the wellbeing of our people and our environment alongside the traditional measure of economic growth.

A broadened definition of progress has been called for by the IMF and the OECD, in response to growing inequality in developed nations, which is not only eroding the social fabric of those countries, but is slowing their economic growth.

For me, it's quite simple. If economic growth is not reflected in the well-being of your people, then we are asking the wrong question.

As Prime Minister, I would find it impossible to tell a child living in a cold, damp home this winter that New Zealand's economy is going well, if her parents have just lost their jobs and they can't afford to turn the heating on.

Our new wellbeing measures will be the reality check to help ensure that when we are designing our trade, social, and economic policy, we're designing it to benefit the many—including the little girl in the cold house—not just a few.

And we've already started that policy redesign. Since the formation of our coalition Government in November last year, we've said we want to see a genuine transformation in the way we create and share New Zealand's prosperity.

We've put child well-being at the heart of what we do, requiring by law the setting of bold targets to reduce the proportion of children living in poverty and hardship. These, if met, would take child poverty and deprivation rates among our children from some of the highest in the OECD, down to the lowest within 10 years.

We also want to build the capability and capacity of our people by rebuilding our core public services, like health and education—the foundation for strong societies.

Education, in particular, is key. Within the 10 years, nearly half of all jobs in New Zealand, as in Germany, could be gone. Our citizens can't afford for us to treat this fact with despair. They need us to plan.

They need us to prepare for the unknown. They're relying on us to plan for just and fair transitions away from twentieth century industries, to modern, clean ones. Without such a plan, towns and communities will wane along with those sunset industries, and anger and disenfranchisement will grow in their place.

Education is crucial to preparing democracies like ours for the technological changes that are dramatically reshaping the nature of work. That is why one of the first changes my Government made was to make the first year of post-secondary education free. Most people who are eligible for what we call "fees free" are first-time adult learners, who are retraining or up-skilling. While research tells us that those who're educated lead happier and more fulfilled lives, it's also true that a small nation like New Zealand simply can't compete on the world stage if our people do not have the skills to do so.

Our eventual goal is for everyone to be earning, learning, caring, or volunteering, so that everyone has an opportunity to contribute in some way, and to reduce social isolation.

But what does all of this add up to? In essence, our own formula to meet the challenges we face by unapologetically putting the wellbeing of people and the wellbeing of our environment at the center of what we do.

Connectedness, inclusion, and the principle of kindness in the way we govern is how we choose to meet the challenge of global uncertainty.

As I stated earlier, New Zealand has greatly appreciated the global leadership that Germany has provided in recent years. In these times of change and challenge, countries that share values and which are prepared to show responsible leadership must stand together.

I look forward to the friendship and partnership which we have with Germany, growing closer still as we each strive to meet the challenges we face as likeminded countries, with a shared vision for a fair society, and a stable and rules-based world.

Change is not only coming, it is here. I truly believe we can make it work for the good of all, and face it with a sense of hope.

Kia ora koutou katoa.

Climate change—challenges and opportunities—a Pacific perspective
Address to the Paris Institute of Political Studies
April 16, 2018, Paris

It may not seem obvious, but in New Zealand the generations before me were shaped by the debate on Vietnam, the politics of sport and apartheid, and the nuclear-free movement. But my generation—my generation will be shaped by climate change.

And when thinking about how this generation will react and how we will collectively respond, I feel hopeful.

On December 12, 2015, it was late in New Zealand when the decision to limit temperature rises was beamed out beyond Paris. It was the cause of much celebration. Seeing the Eiffel Tower lit up with messages supporting this work lifted people's spirits around the world that night. It is truly historic that 196 countries could agree to take this action on climate change. But I am sure every one of the nations present there that day had both their own domestic situations to consider, and their own motivations. My party wasn't the one that signed up to the Paris Agreement, but we have heartily supported it. And I can tell you what is driving us now as a coalition government to fulfill these obligations.

The first is where we are. We are a Pacific nation. We have an extensive coastline and most of our major cities are on the coast. One recent estimate from our Ministry for the Environment suggests that $19 billion of assets are at risk from sea-level rise and flooding events—including five airports, 50 kilometers of rail, 2,000 kilometers of road, and 40,000 homes. Not only that but large portions of our economy are linked to our agricultural, horticultural, and tourism businesses, all of which are particularly sensitive to extreme weather events.

But weather events that have struck us in recent times have struck somewhere else first, and with devastating consequences. I saw this for myself on a recent visit to the island nations of Samoa, Tonga, Niue, and the Cook Islands. Two of these islands had recently endured a cyclone that had affected homes, schools, the electricity network; even the Parliament buildings were destroyed in Tonga. But even before Cyclone Gita, if I was to pick one issue that has been a consistent theme in the Pacific in recent years, it has been climate change.

I know you too have a strong connection with the Pacific with your own territories.

Collectively these islands represent a tiny portion of global emissions. They play almost no role in creating the crisis we now face, but they are already the first to face its devastating impacts. In Tonga, I visited a primary school which had a few weeks earlier been ripped apart by the country's worst storm in decades. The children were taking their classes in tents provided by UNICEF, surrounded by the battered buildings that used to be their classrooms.

The courage and resilience of the children left a mark on me. I was led by officials to see the state of the buildings post-cyclone only to find, after walking across a muddied field, that a child had followed us. She was standing outside one of the buildings that had no roof or internal walls. Through a translator, she told me it was her classroom. She showed me where she used to sit, and pointed to the posters and drawings that were tattered and shredded around the room. It was work that her class had produced, and a shattering reminder of the extreme weather that now rages through these countries on a regular basis.

But it is not only storms that threaten Pacific nations. There is already salt-water intrusion into fresh water supplies. Staple crops like taro have been devastated in some areas near the coast due to salt-water intrusion. And more importantly, some aquifers are at risk of becoming salty.

On top of this, increasing ocean acidification is driven by carbon dioxide absorbed into the oceans, changing the chemistry of the seawater. Warmer and more acidic oceans threaten to deprive communities of the tuna, reef fish, and other marine life which for some represent their main source of protein, and their only reliable natural resource.

All of this could just point to a change in lifestyle or adaptation. Not in low-lying Kiribati and Tuvalu; there the oceans that have sustained local communities for thousands of years could soon rise up to swallow them forever.

Across the Pacific, already eight low-lying islands have been immersed by rising sea levels. While globally the increase is around three millimeters a year, it is more like 12 millimeters per year in the western Pacific Ocean, an effect of the trade winds.

For the Pacific, climate change is not a hypothetical. It is real. And it is happening now.

We know and understand this. New Zealand does not simply sit in the Pacific. We are the Pacific too, and we are doing our best to stand with our family as they face these threats.

All of this tells you a bit about where we are geographically. But it doesn't tell you much about who we are, and that ingredient is just as important in the way we view our global challenges.

There are things of course that you might already know—like the prevalence of certain animals in New Zealand. That goes some way to explaining why agriculture is the single biggest contributor to New Zealand's greenhouse gas emissions.

You probably know we are small, and we make up 0.17 percent of global emissions.

You might also know that we are sports mad—especially rugby league and rugby union, played by both men and women I should add. But none of that tells you about our culture or our character.

New Zealand has a proud record of independence and world-leading reforms. In 1893, our women became the first in the world to win the right to vote. In the decades that followed, we were among the world's first countries to introduce the key foundations of a modern welfare state—universal pensions, healthcare, and education.

We were at the table when the United Nations was born, and we have always stood up for rules-based, multilateral action, whether in the battle against commercial whaling, ensuring fair and consistent trade rules, or standing up against nuclear weapons and testing.

But on the environment, our approach is probably best summed up by one Maori word—kaitiakitanga. It means guardianship, and I would like to think it underpins the motivation for making the decisions we need to for the next generation.

We are a unique government, formed in October last year with the New Zealand Labour Party which I lead, our coalition partner,

New Zealand First, and our confidence and supply partner, the Green Party. We are united on many issues, and climate change is one of them.

Collectively, we have all committed to the goal of becoming a net zero emission economy by 2050. We have committed to making our electricity system 100 percent renewable by 2035. We are preparing to consult with the New Zealand public on legislation to help us reach Zero Carbon that will become law next year. We are setting up an Independent Climate Commission of experts who will develop carbon budgets right through to 2050. That means they'll set the amount of carbon we can afford to put into the atmosphere each year to get us to carbon neutrality, while ensuring we have enough energy available to run our economy and country.

As part of our regional development work and under the leadership of New Zealand First Minister Shane Jones, we have started a program to plant one billion trees in the next 10 years. This will contribute to reducing CO2 emissions, both through C02 absorption and by reducing erosion. To tackle the biggest contributor to our emissions profile, New Zealand has led a Global Research Alliance of forty-nine nations—including France—that is working to identify technologies that can reduce greenhouse gas emissions generated from agriculture. It is our intention to help lead the world to low emission but highly productive agriculture and food production.

But this is not the only industry that is undergoing transformation. Astonishingly, governments currently spend more than $400 billion each year on lowering the price of oil, gas, and coal.

This is an enormous impediment to our efforts. Reducing these subsidies would help cut emissions. That's why, at the Paris climate conference, we launched a communique on fossil fuel subsidy reform that was endorsed by forty governments. France was one of the first to sign on, and has of course taken a leadership role on the role of oil and gas exploration generally.

In New Zealand our sense of responsibility to those whose livelihood is based around the production of fossil fuels means we too have started planning for the future. Several weeks ago, we injected $20 million dollars into one of our oil- and gas-producing regions to explore a range of alternative economic development opportunities. And because of the need to ensure a just transition around fossil fuels, this past week we also announced that we will no longer be granting any new offshore oil and gas exploration permits.

We are making this decision now because we cannot ignore the inevitable. No doubt it would have been politically easier to leave this call to someone else, but I refuse to stand by and watch communities who have economies that rely on these industries try to survive without certainty and a plan for what the next twenty to thirtyyears will look like.

And this brings me to the final point. For all of the fear that surrounds this issue, I come back to that feeling I expressed at the start. And it is one of hope. This is the chance to transform our respective economies, to face our collective future with knowledge. To grow the job opportunities and the health and well-being of our communities as we go. To put people and the need to preserve our environment for the next generation right at the center.

You are already playing a leadership role. And I would like to believe that as a small island nation embedded in the Pacific, we are too. But our action alone will not be enough. Collectively we must call to action not only other governments, but civic society, business, and the public.

Wherever we are, whatever our motivations or our roles, I hope each of us can look back on this period of time and say that we were on the right side of history. That we were humbled in the wake of the science, that we were proud of what others before us made possible, and that we were hopeful in taking on this challenge, and most of all—that we were guardians for the next generation.
Thank you.

 *Hajer Sharief is the co-founder of Together We Build It, which has been working on the democratic transition in Libya since 2011, with an emphasis on youth and women's political participation in the peace-building process. She also co-initiated the Libyan 1325 Network, which advocates for the implementation of UN Security Council Resolution 1325 on women, peace, and security. She also participated, as a researcher and coauthor, in the first civil society report on the implementation of the UNSCR 1325 in Libya. Hajer is the regional contact for the Youth Advocacy Team with UNOY and was recently selected by the Kofi Annan Foundation to act as an advocate for the Extremely Together Initiative, which emphasizes the role of young people in countering violent extremism. She holds a law degree from Tripoli University.*

The Art of Redefining
Born into and Becoming
Hajer Sharief

My journey as a young person to work on promoting peace and human security has been filled with hardship and loss. I bore witness to a peaceful society turning violent. I struggled to complete my education because bloody warfare in the streets forced my university to shut its doors. I woke up one day to the news that my friend had been shot dead while I was sleeping.

The war I lived through in Libya inspired me to devote my life to building peace. I co-founded an organization called Together We Build to encourage local communities to engage in peace-building. In our work we provide both on-ground and online platforms for women and youth to participate in peace and security. Our on-ground activities include capacity-building trainings that we conduct in different cities in Libya, focusing on nonviolent conflict resolution, human security, gender equality, and human rights. Our most recent online platform, "Peace and Security from Libyan Women's Perspective," had more than 1,000 women participating in less than three days, 80 percent of whom were young women between fifteen–thirty years old. This was a clear indication that young women are ready and willing to participate in peace-building when they get the opportunity.

I was appointed by the UN Secretary-General as a member of the Advisory Group of experts for the Progress Study on Youth, Peace and Security, I also work with Mr. Kofi Annan on the role of youth in countering violent extremism. Yet, because of my identity, I am considered a potential extremist in the eyes of many societies. My passport is taken to indicate that I am a probable terrorist to numerous States across the world. My citizenship confines me to all that is associated with the label "immigrant." All of this because some decision makers cannot conceive what else a young person who was forced to live through war might be!

No one can deny the fact that we have all inherited a world where millions of people fail to distinguish between the sound of thunder and the sound of an airstrike. People who live in a world where rain and snow are limited to their seasons while bombs and ammunition fall down year-round on others. This has become a world where young refugees journeying toward a peaceful life start at the shore of the Mediterranean Sea and feel their lives ebb away before reaching the other side.

The UN prides itself on possessing historic worldwide experience on leading the process of peace-building. However, what has been missing for so long is the perspective, experience, and work of the youth who live these wars and must continue struggling in hope that there will be a day to breathe in peace.

Peace-building should be based on the fact that people are not born violent, but born *into* violence. Immigrants are not born poor, but born *into* poverty. That refugees reject violence, and instead seek peaceful lives. And that young people are not idle, but innovative and pioneering change-makers with the capacity and ability to shape the world. I am one of those young people, doing my utmost to create a world where we are defined by our beliefs and our deeds, and not by our age and origins.

Widely known for his pioneering work in conflict transformation and peace-building, John Paul Lederach has engaged in places like Colombia, the Philippines, Nepal, and East and West Africa. He has designed and conducted training and strategy development initiatives in thirty-five countries across five continents. Lederach currently serves as a Senior Fellow at Humanity United, a foundation of the Omidyar Group, and Professor Emeritus with the Kroc Institute at the University of Notre Dame where he continues to advise the Peace Accord Matrix initiative that compares 35 comprehensive accords. Lederach is the author of twenty-two books, including When Blood and Bones Cry Out: Journeys through the Soundscape of Healing and Reconciliation, *and* The Moral Imagination: The Art and Soul of Building Peace.

Indivisible
The Fragility of Boundary-less Belonging
John Paul Lederach

Our security depends on the quality of our relationships, not the size and quantity of our weapons or the strength of our tribe.

When seen from the lens of our galaxy and beyond, we constitute a minuscule and fragile miracle. The miracle is this: We are born an improbable global family.

The most difficult mindset for us to achieve has been the simple notion that ultimately, we are a single indivisible family. As we take our first steps into the inevitable Anthropocene we have ourselves birthed, it no longer is possible to separate survival and global family into boundaried identities. Our survival requires that we cultivate a boundary-less belonging.

This kind of indivisible belonging requires the kind of imagination that I found in the positive deviance of people and communities who have navigated through and out of cycles of trans-generational violence. They hold the seeds of hope, for they have learned that survival started with how they viewed the wider web of relationships that defined their lives.

People who found ways to break out of vicious cycles of violence displayed four kinds of imagination.

They had a grandmother's imagination. The well-being of my grandchildren is intimately tied to the well-being of others' grandchildren, including those who I perceive as a threat and may wish my community harm. I imagine myself in a web of relationships that includes my enemy.

They had a child's imagination. The wonder of looking at the world with insatiable curiosity. A child rarely worries about asking and listening in order to understand. There is a pure wisdom and humility to wonder that slowly erodes toward separation and superiority as we grow toward adulthood. Adult decorum, arrogance in far too many instances, sustains our divisibility. Curiosity requires us to unlearn arrogance, embrace wonder, and seek understanding.

They had artist's eyes and ears. St. Benedict suggested that we must listen—incline was his choice of verb—with the ears of the heart. The artist moves about the world with sensory openness and persistent noticing. Something alive inhabits each moment, place, and experience that seeks an unfolding, a release, an unleashing. The single greatest distinguishing feature of being human has taproots in our capacity for the creative act: the artistic inclination to bring into existence that which does not now exist. Far too often we have let loose our creativity in the service of protection and harm. From the mix of three powders that could "fly and dance" we evolved weaponry capable of destroying our race many times over in the pursuit of safety. Survival requires us to unleash the creative impulse toward re-humanization—the capacity to love beyond boundaries and protect the whole of our global family.

Finally, they had the imagination of intrepid voyagers, the courage to step into the unknown. We can call this the imagination of risk. I have found no evidence that people embroiled in protracted conflict emerged on the other side of great harm without someone taking an unexpected and risky step in the swirl of violence that defined their lives and communities. They were indivisible explorers willing to reach beyond and through the polarization in search of a different, a new quality of relationship. In settings of violence, separation and conflict was known. Peace was the mystery, unmapped with horizons marked only as *where there be dragons*. Risk meant stepping into the unknown without control over what might happen. In spite of fear and against the gravity of warning based in experience, they reached beyond what was known to build a sense of security that no longer depended on narrow walls of tribal safety. They moved toward a sense of that a wider family existed and could be revealed.

In the coming centuries, our security depends on our capacity to embrace the fragile miracle that we are a global family. That embrace requires love, the *real politic* that cultivates boundary-less belonging.

June 2018

Acknowledgements

We would like to thank AFSC and the international directors for their support for the book concept and for recruiting writers including Kennedy Akolo, Marianne Elias, Fabiola Flores Munoz, Alma Jadallah, Lucy Roberts, Andrew Tomlinson, and Jason Tower.

We are grateful to the writers in this book who connected us to their colleagues or made recommendations for other participants who might be included.

A special note of thanks to Cécile Mazzacurati of the Secretariat, Progress Study on Youth, Peace and Security UNFPA / PBSO for her assistance in putting us in touch with many of the global youth leaders included in this anthology.

We would like to thank Saurav Upadhyay for his enthusiastic and timely assistance on a variety of needs, including his constant support with liaising with all the many writers on the administrative aspects of this process.

Kerri Kennedy thanks her ever supportive husband Paul and two wonderful children Maceo and Makaio for enduring her many trips to further global peace and shared security. She would like to also thank her mother, Eileen Kennedy and her in laws, Janice and Paul Wright for their love and support of her family when she travels. Lastly, to her late father, Robert Kennedy, who demonstrated peace every day through this kindness and his strength.

Ru Freeman thanks her late mother, Indrani Seneviratne, and her father, Gamini Seneviratne for their service to their country and to their children near and far.